HISTORY OF LINCOLNSHIRE

Edited by
MAURICE BARLEY

VOLUME VIII

THE AGRICULTURAL REVOLUTION IN LINCOLNSHIRE

by
T. W. BEASTALL

Preface

THIS is Volume VIII in what is projected as a twelve-volumed series on the history of the historic county of Lincolnshire; it is the fifth book to have appeared so far.

Lincolnshire is not one of the favoured regions of England. Unlike many other counties it has never had its own history produced by an industrious eighteenth or nineteenth century antiquary. It is not that there have been few students of history within the county. Rather the size of the county, among other factors, has presented problems in bringing together all this material into a comprehensive historical and topographical account of Lincolnshire, a basis for all future work; and the Victoria County History proceeded no further than one volume.

Conscious of this lack, the Lincolnshire Local History Society (now the Society for Lincolnshire History and Archaeology) took the first steps in 1965 towards a new county history, and in the following year the History of Lincolnshire Committee was born. The aim was to publish a series of volumes which would be at the same time both scholarly and of general interest, written by specialists already engaged in work on particular periods and subjects, and yet in their summaries of recent work aimed at the general reader as well as the scholar.

The Committee has thus planned a series of twelve volumes to provide a more or less comprehensive account of the region from prehistoric times until the middle of the twentieth century. The series benefited immensely from the wisdom and hard work of the first General Editor, Dr Joan Thirsk of St Hilda's College, Oxford, but commitments necessitated that she should relinquish this task. This is then the first volume to appear which has been edited by Maurice Barley, Professor Emeritus of Archaeology in the University of Nottingham. The Committee is deeply indebted to Professor Barley for all his work.

An initial financial basis for the Committee's work was provided by the Pilgrim Trust, the Seven Pillars of Wisdom Trust, the Marc Fitch Fund, the Lincolnshire Association and the Willoughby Memorial Trust. Help in other ways has been given to the project by the Lincolnshire Association, the Lincoln City and County Library and Museum Services, the Society for Lincolnshire History and Archaeology, the Community Council of Lincolnshire and the Department of Adult Education of the University of Nottingham.

Help in the production of this volume has been received from the following: the Marc Fitch Fund; Lord Yarborough and the Marquess of Exeter; the Lincolnshire County Council; and the Midland Bank who generously helped towards the cost of the dust jacket.

Other help must also be acknowledged; of Nigel Mann and Ted Hulatt of Messrs Cox & Wyman who have gone beyond their official duties in helping on the production of this series; of Hugh Robinson who assisted in the revised design of the volume and dust jacket which characterized both the last volume and this one; and Miss M. L. Smith who has supervised the office at 86 Newland since the start of the project. To all these and to many others who have assisted in so many ways, we are very grateful. It is with their help that the Committee presents the eighth volume in

THE HISTORY OF LINCOLNSHIRE

ALAN ROGERS
Chairman, History of Lincolnshire Committee

LINCOLN'S CORN EXCHANGE *built in 1847 by W. A. Nicholson. Lincolnshire has many of these monuments to the agricultural revolution and to the county's place as a leading corn producer in the early nineteenth century.*

HISTORY OF LINCOLNSHIRE
VIII

The Agricultural Revolution in Lincolnshire

BY

T. W. BEASTALL,
M.A.

LINCOLN
HISTORY OF LINCOLNSHIRE COMMITTEE
for the Society of Lincolnshire History & Archaeology
1978

PUBLISHED BY
THE HISTORY OF LINCOLNSHIRE COMMITTEE
86 NEWLAND, LINCOLN

ISBN 0 902668 07 2

SET, PRINTED AND BOUND IN GREAT BRITAIN
BY COX & WYMAN LTD
LONDON, FAKENHAM AND READING

IN MEMORY OF STUART ELKINGTON

Contents

List of Plates

List of Text Figures

Acknowledgements

The author wishes to thank Professor Maurice Barley, Dr Alan Rogers, Professor G. E. Mingay, Dr Joan Thirsk, and Dr Richard Olney for helpful suggestions about source material, comments on the text and assistance with the illustrations in the book. The editor of *Lincolnshire Life*, David Robinson, Alan Readman of the West Sussex Archives and Rex C. Russell made generous contributions from their knowledge of the county and its archives. Mrs C. M. Wilson, Keeper of Lincolnshire History at the Museum of Lincolnshire Life, and Christopher J. Page, Assistant Keeper, were tireless in giving help with source material and illustrations. I thank Michael Lloyd and his staff at the Lincolnshire Archives Office for their help and Laurence Elvin, formerly Librarian at Lincoln Central Library, and his staff for their patient assistance. I am grateful to Philip Wagland, Paul Everson, Miss N. F. Newborn, Miss D. Sheard, W. E. R. Hallgarth and Ruston and Hornsby Ltd for illustrative material and maps, and the Earl of Scarbrough for permission to use his archives at Sandbeck. Routledge and Kegan Paul kindly gave permission for the reproduction of the paragraph on page 14 and I thank Mrs R. E. Barber for the use of her collection of copies of *Lincolnshire Life*, F. and J. Durdy for helpful comments, and Mrs Barbara Bestall for the index.

The plates and figures are published by permission of the following: dust jacket plate, plates 9, 10, 11, 12, 13a, 17, 18, figures 5, 9, 10, 11, 12, Lincolnshire Museums, Museum of Lincolnshire Life (plates 11, 13a, 17 and 18 come from the Hallgarth Collection of early photographs); plate 1 and figures 8, 15 and 16, Lincolnshire Archives Office (figure 8, Lord Monson; figure 16, Mr J. N. Heneage); plate 2, M. Felcey by courtesy of Paul Everson; plates 3, 4, 5 and 6, Lincolnshire Library Services; plate 7a, National Monuments Record; plate 7b, R. E. Hooley and Ruston and Hornsby Ltd; plates 8, 15, 19a and frontispiece, Mrs C. M. Wilson; plate 13b, P. J. Bowser; plate 14, Miss D. Sheard; plate 16, Miss N. F. Newborn; plate 19b, David Lee (by courtesy of Rex Russell). Figure 1 is based on J. Thirsk, *English Peasant Farming* p. 50 by kind permission of the publishers, Routledge and Kegan Paul. Figure 2 is based on a map by Rex Russell. Figure 3 is reproduced by kind permission of the Bodleian Library, Oxford. Figure 17 has been prepared by the staff of the North Lincolnshire Archaeological Unit.

The Geography Department of the University of Nottingham drew figures 1, 7, 13, 14, 15 and 17, and Professor Barley re-drew figure 16 from original drawings in the Lincolnshire Archives Office.

T.W.B.

I

The Agricultural Revolution

THE Agricultural Revolution was a matter of output, scale and timing. Many of its characteristics—increased yields, improvements in livestock, commercial attitudes in farmers—can be seen here and there in medieval Britain even before the Black Death shook the old manorial system and made new methods imperative. The profit motive and changes in land use were evident in Tudor times. The seventeenth century saw an onslaught upon waste land in the great draining operations in the Fens. Yet not until the late eighteenth and early nineteenth centuries were farmers and landowners to realize the great potential of their soil and in large numbers within one or two generations to effect a dramatic increase of output from it. So many were involved in the development at the same time that they became conscious of living at a turning point in farming history. The evidence given before Parliamentary enquiries into the state of agriculture reveals an awareness that at least in certain counties a revolution had taken place. In Lincolnshire many believed it had happened within 20 years of the end of the Napoleonic war in 1815 and though they exaggerated its speed and ignored the long preparation for a major change they were convinced that they had seen an irreversible break with the past.

An account of a revolution in the exploitation of Lincolnshire's soils calls for some analysis and description of them. It can be done by means of a map of farming regions (fig. 1), but to examine a map in the comfort of an armchair is as remote as possible from the experience, now denied to the vast majority of the inhabitants of this island, of growing up and spending a working life in daily contact with soils of one kind or another. To the tourist or the walker especially if he ventures out in winter when most fields are bare of crops, there are subtle variations of colour to be observed: the green or grey-brown of the clays, the red-brown of the limestone heath, the near-black of the peat fen, the fawn of the silt fen

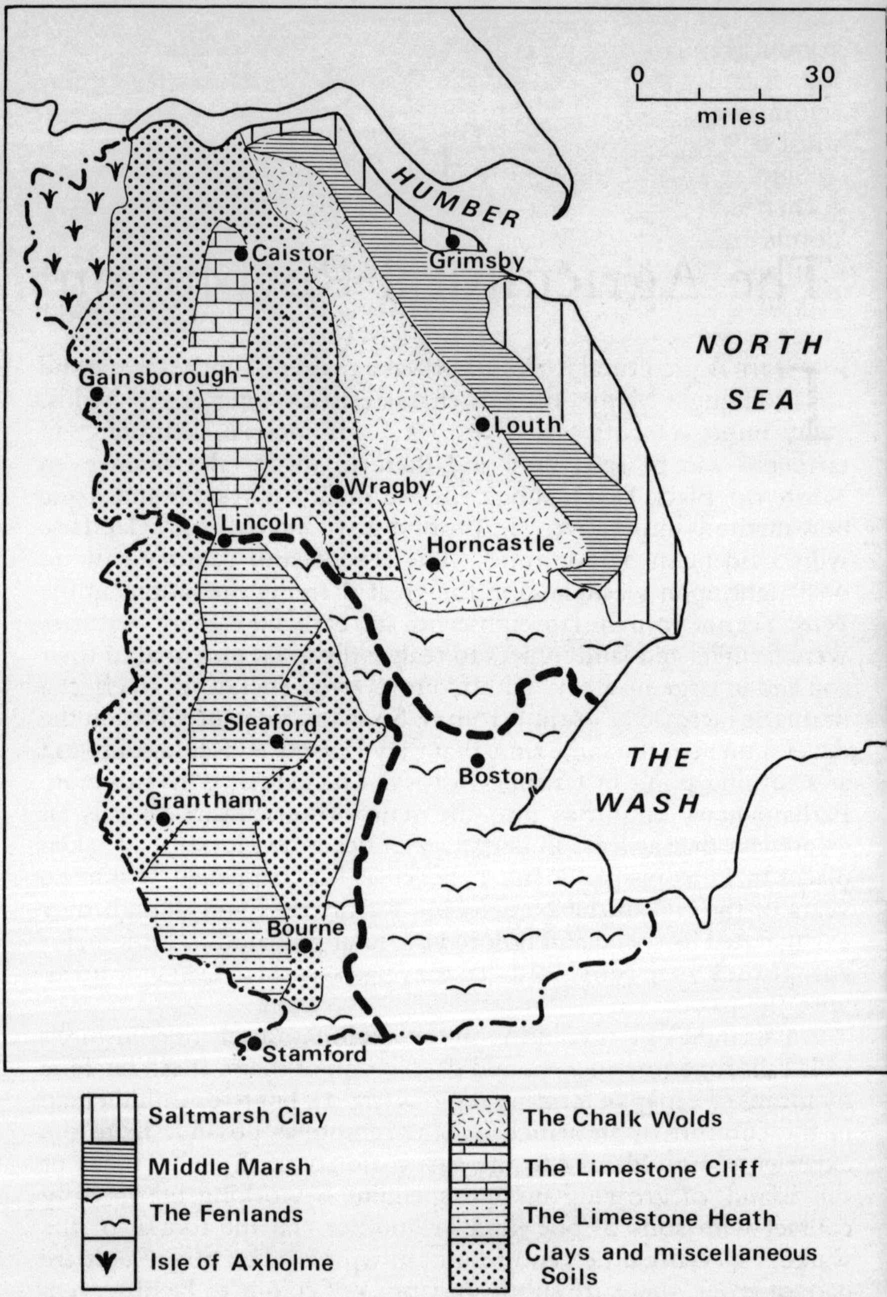

Figure 1. The main farming regions of Lincolnshire. The heavy broken lines indicate the boundaries of the historic divisions of the county.

and the still paler colour of the chalk-flecked wolds. Such a visual comment brings the observer nearer to the physical reality of farming. It still does not convey the variation in the quality of soils within one farm and even from one part of a field to another.[1] We must be content with generalizations.

Since soils reflect the solid geology of the county farming regions form mainly north-south divisions.[2] To the traveller the uplands are dominant, and especially the band of jurassic limestone forming the Cliff and the Heath. The Cliff north of Lincoln has a steep western face and a gentle eastern slope. Narrow as it runs farther north, the ridge is about 200 feet above sea level, with wide views across the clayland to the chalk wolds beyond. As it runs south, the jurassic escarpment broadens, broken only by the Lincoln and Ancaster gaps, to form the Heath.

The chalk wolds dominate north-east Lincolnshire between the clays and the marsh. About 45 miles in length the Wolds vary between 5 and 8 miles in width. There are few rivers in the north where some boulder clay overlies the chalk but farther south the landscape is more varied with sheltered valleys and stretches of woodland. Where they shelve into the fenland in the south, the Wolds have some sandstone and clay surfaces as the chalk there has been eroded. Sheep and barley formed the basis of the farming economy as wheat fared badly on the chalk uplands in the centuries before the agricultural revolution. Sheep were the farmers' great source of income even though the Wolds pasture could not compete with that of the Marsh in richness. Wolds farms were the largest in the county even before 1700 and the occupiers kept many horses for ploughing and like their neighbours on the clays they raised pigs in the more wooded valleys of the south.

Between the Trent and the edge of the Cliff and Heath and again between them and the Wolds lie claylands and miscellaneous soils including peats, sands and gravels. The vale of the Ancholme with carrs liable to flood and stretches of sandy land giving rise to rabbit

[1] The complexity of the pattern of soils may be seen in the form of maps and accompanying monograph in the Soil Survey Record No. 22, *Soils in Lincolnshire I* Sheet TF16 (Woodhall Spa), Harpenden 1977. The area in question; 100 square kilometres centred on Woodhall Spa, includes soils on boulder clay, fen alluvium, sands, gravels and peat. Although in general the Fens contain some of the most fertile soils in the county, most of the land described has 'minor limitations that reduce the choice of crop and interfere with cultivation', and some have 'moderately severe limitations that restrict the choice of crop and/or demand careful management'.

[2] For a map of the solid geology see J. May, *Prehistoric Lincolnshire,* Lincoln, 1976, fig. 2.

warrens, thin woodland, commons and unrewarding peat 'moors' occupied the northern stretches of the county. There is sandy land all the way north from Torksey to the sand dunes near Scunthorpe, Flixborough and Frodingham. In the clays the great need was for sound underdraining and on some of the sand irrigation while the moory peat soil responded to claying and marling. Farmers on the more western clays and mixed soils had, generally, good communications with their customers in Yorkshire and the east Midlands. Wool, corn, leather, skins as well as calves and bullocks were sold across the Trent after being collected in small markets such as the one at Bourne. Even so, the farmers here were probably poorer than those in the other three agricultural regions.

Descriptions of the Fens before the agricultural revolution stressed their unhealthy climate. Not only did the inhabitants suffer from ague, they had to spend a high proportion of their time, energy and treasure defending themselves from sea and river floods. Though there was truth in this view of lives spent in a watery wasteland where only fishing and fowling prospered it overlooks the farmers' success in creating on the Fens some of the best grazing land in the Kingdom. A transformation of the fenland economy had to await the introduction of steam drainage in the 1830s but even in the late seventeenth century the fenlander could list many assets. He had inherited a degree of resistance to the region's climate from the generations which had survived it. He and his neighbours had a wealth of experience in dealing with floods. His arable fields, though small, were fertile. He had fish and fowl to augment his diet and reed and sedge for his thatch and his fuel. Most of all, on both river mud and coastal marsh good grazing land had been established. Cattle, sheep and horses were the small farmers' chief livestock. Meat and dairy produce left the fenlands for London and Midland towns. Dairies were added to farm houses to accommodate the pails, cheese presses and vats which were needed for the trade. Sheep ranked second in the list of animals in the economy, while horses, bred in numbers beyond the needs of this region of small arable acreages, were sold to Nottinghamshire and Derbyshire dealers for use in coal and lead mines or to Yorkshire buyers for breeding.

Whereas some 75 per cent of the cultivated land in a county like Leicestershire would be under the plough in 1700 25 per cent seems to have been arable in the fenlands of Holland. Small farmers who were free from the restraint of leases imposed in upland parishes could interchange arable and pasture land as they thought best. Their husbandry was intensive; their small fields produced barley, probably their chief crop, winter corn, wheat, beans and peas. The fenlands had few parks or gentlemen's seats and the small farmers probably enjoyed traditions of independence tempered by good neighbourliness. In addition, they had good communications by water through Boston and by way of the Witham to Lincoln and the Trent. Boats and fishing tackle were to them what horses and ploughs were to the arable farmer. Market towns—Spalding, Pinchbeck, Swineshead and Kirton in Holland—provided outlets for local produce and a means of breaking down isolation. Even so, his farming prospects and the landscape were more at the mercy of the climate than in any other part of the county. In winter his outlook could become a lake within a few days. In this treeless expanse his livestock had scant shelter from the biting north-easterlies yet in summer his small arable acreages could bake in the shadeless heat as his pasture lands turned brown and brittle until the autumn rains revived them.

In this landscape of wide views the traveller could be forgiven for seeing the Fens as of one piece composed of sky, land and water; not so the fenlander. His ancestors had seen the differences between the three belts of land which ran roughly parallel with the sea. To the west lay the plain flooded by the rivers which wound their way down to the sea from the Midlands. Then lay a belt of higher land on which arable farming could flourish and on which settlement would eventually throw up villages that resembled the market towns of distant Kesteven and Lindsey in their size and closeness. Next and farther east, there stretched the marsh land, that nearest the villages was known as 'high' marsh while nearer the sea, behind the sandy shore in a region still subject to sudden flooding, lay the 'low' marsh. These areas were ribbed by ridges which marked the progress of reclamation by the building of sea walls or banks. The low marsh which was still flooded by the sea did not shrink and fall as did the high marsh which was safe from the sea's attacks. Thus the terms 'high' and 'low' were reversed in geographical terms for the older reclaimed land sank while that 'lower' down was still not dry enough to do so. Here one appreciates the paradox of the fenland economy. As land was rescued from flooding it would sink if its character were peaty so making it more liable to flood. At the same time, land near the river mouths on which the silt was being deposited by the slow moving waters from inland, tended to build up. So one has the fenland phenomena of boats sailing above the level of the fields and a landscape full of the devices using wind and later steam to force the water up to its route towards the sea.

A large part of the fenland lay within the wapentakes of Skirbeck,

Kirton and Elloe in the county division known as Holland but other parts of Lincolnshire consisted of fen country. Eastern Kesteven and south-east Lindsey as well as the Witham valley up to Lincoln and the Isle of Axholme across the Trent in north-west Lincolnshire were fenland areas. Similar to the fenland in appearance and social structure were the marshlands of eastern Lincolnshire. This is a rich agricultural region consisting of a length of boulder clay resting against the eastern slope of the Wolds and overlaid nearer the coast by a zone of reclaimed saltmarsh.

Embanking to claim more and more land from the sea had gone on for centuries. At Tetney there were two sea banks in the early seventeenth century. Between them lay valuable marshland which had first been the Fittes or shore, used first by salt makers and eventually with the building of dikes and banks wrested permanently from the sea to become sheep walk. Near Grimsby it seems from a comparison between a description of its marshes in 1606 and a grant of saltmarsh in the reign of Edward III that about 300 acres were added in 250 years from the sea. The region lent itself as it still does to the raising and fattening of livestock. On the middle marsh where the arable and the grass were both good the breeding of cattle and sheep took place. Farther east the pastures were valuable for fattening while beyond the sea banks on the coast lay the saltmarsh, the domain of the shepherd and his flocks. Horses and pigs were not numerous in the marshland economy. Winter and spring wheat, barley, oats, and for winter fodder, peas and beans were grown by the marshland farmer who had more arable land at his disposal than his fenland counterpart. The farmers here in the early eighteenth century still had a reputation for wealth and a tradition of substantial living behind them. In 1608 the Duchy of Lancaster had considered its marshland farmers at Ingoldmells and its fenland occupiers at Long Sutton to be superior to its other tenants in the county. Their soil was good and they were rich, paying good rents for enclosed land.[3]

Lincolnshire's reputation in farming was to stand high by the mid-nineteenth century but it now seems clear that this was the result of progress made after the end of the Napoleonic wars. The agricultural revolution came late to Lincolnshire and contained elements absent from developments in Norfolk. It should not be assumed, however, that there were no significant changes in the early eighteenth century or that the progress of the first quarter of the nineteenth had no basis in improvements undertaken a century earlier. In the fenland, drainage was essential to any improvement

[3] PRO SP 14/37, No. 107.

and the social disturbances associated with it dominate the seventeenth-century story of agriculture in the lowland regions. By 1700, however, the failures of previous schemes and the opposition of small property owners had been taken to heart by Parliament and discussion of further schemes was cautious. As a result progress was hesitant and real strides had to await the years after 1750. Though the scene in the other farming regions was brighter the fenland picture is one of neglect. The Lindsey Level Undertakers failed to win Parliament's approval, for the objections of the fenlanders carried the day when in 1701 and again in 1711 the House of Lords examined their proposals. Although the Earl of Manchester's scheme for the draining of Deeping Fen, authorized in 1666, effected improvement, there were complaints of decay and flooding during the 1720s and 1730s so that by 1738 it was admitted that profit from the Fens must wait a new initiative in dealing with overflows.[4]

The economy of the fenland parishes appeared still to be based on pastoral husbandry traditionally associated with the region; the rearing of beasts, sheep, horses; the making of butter and cheese; the sale of fish, fowl, hemp and flax.[5] Peas and beans were giving way before an increase in oats by the 1690s and in areas which were safe from flooding wheat and rye were becoming important. With demands for sails and rope in the wars of William III's reign and that of Queen Anne, hemp and flax were profitable. Sheep increased in importance too; many small farmers had 150 in a flock and there are signs that the fenland farmer began to specialize in sheep bred in the uplands, fattened in the fen and sold at Smithfield. Though horses and pigs declined, more cattle were kept in the Fens in the early eighteenth century and geese seem to have replaced wildfowl as a cash source. As wildfowl declined owing to improvements in drainage, geese became more important. Driven on foot to London and Nottingham, they seem to have become a significant source of income by 1700.[6] At Sempringham and Billingborough, however, the Reverend R. Kelham was able to let his duck decoy for £240 a year from 1739, which he had built for £24.5s.10½d, until draining rendered it useless by the end of the century.[7] So wildfowl continued to be valuable until more determined efforts at draining were made.

[4] Joan Thirsk, *English Peasant Farming*, London, 1957, pp. 126–7.

[5] PRO E 134/29 Chas. II, Easter 6.

[6] For a discussion of the stock held by fenland farmers see Thirsk, op. cit. pp. 136–9.

[7] Lincolnshire Library Manuscripts, Lincoln, 4817.

Population levels and buildings afford some indication of a region's agricultural history. When one looks at the population of the three wapentakes of Holland it is clear that the growth of Boston influenced the number of families in Skirbeck where between the mid-sixteenth century and 1723 there was an increase of 300 families. Boston with 471 families in 1563 had some 750 families in 1723 while Skirbeck to the south had increased from 35 to 95. This increase took place within a context of static population levels, however. Kirton wapentake increased its families from 1,443 in 1563 to 1,472 in 1723, a mere 29 in over 150 years. Elloe wapentake which enjoyed an increase of coastal marsh in that period almost doubled its number of families by 1723 to 2,696. Holbeach, Pinchbeck and Spalding increased in population. Spalding as the chief market grew to three times its former size by 1723 while Crowland trebled in population and Market Deeping St. James and Stamford showed increases from 1563 to 1723 which about doubled their populations. An increase in the supply of land, especially of saltmarsh and the earlier successes in draining near Crowland and in Deeping Fen accounted for this expansion. With unstinted commons, opportunities for fishing and fowling, and more land available for ploughing, tenants and landless countrymen were drawn to these regions as they were to the Isle of Axholme where the right to cut turves in the commons was cited as an attraction as early as 1675.[8]

So although the Fens were not distinguished by dramatic improvements in agriculture in the first half of the eighteenth century, they entered upon it with something in hand by way of new acreages, some successful draining, an increased population and some signs of prosperity based upon fen husbandry if town and village building is a guide. At Wyberton, for example, the incumbent was given a faculty in 1687 to rebuild the old mud and stud house in brick and tile with a kitchen, parlour, large staircase rising from the entrance door, 'two chambers, a large study and small closets on the second storey and garrets and a large porch with steps ascending to it at the entrance'.[9] Pinchbeck saw the building of a new vicarage after 1680. In the early eighteenth century more and more parsonages boasted a study, and brick walls and tile roofs replaced the mud and stud thatched dwellings in the Fens. Boston, Spalding and Stamford, on large rivers, were already being marked out by the early eighteenth century for a regional role as commercial centres while Alford, Epworth and Bourne with smaller popula-

[8] Thirsk, op. cit. pp. 140–1.

[9] M. W. Barley, *Lincolnshire and the Fens*, London, 1952, p. 113.

tions were nevertheless acquiring the buildings suitable for the second class of market town in the Fens.[10]

Signs of alternate agriculture, the laying down of tillage to grass and the ploughing up of old and tired pastures, are to be found in the first quarter of the eighteenth century as indeed are leases designed to facilitate tenants' improvements.[11] John Cook of Whaplode was to have from Lady Day 1726 the lease of 80 acres of pasture in Holbeach Marsh for 13 years. He was to build a barn and to divide the land into two equal portions. One part was to be ploughed and was to stay as tillage for four years and then laid to grass. The other part was to be ploughed after five years and to continue in tillage for four after which it was to be laid down in a husbandly manner having been manured. The lessee was to take down the barn if the owner did not want to buy. There was no sign of the award of an away-going crop or compensation by the landlord for any unexhausted improvement but it must be assumed that given the security of a 13-years lease with the landowner paying tithe and land tax, and a rent of £40 a year, the tenant was satisfied with his bargain. If he sowed any land for hemp, woad or flax he was to pay a fine of £5 per acre for land so treated. Some tenants in this region were allowed lower rents in consideration of improvements to farm houses and ditches or for undertaking repairs to farm buildings.[12] These were signs of what land-agents in the last quarter of the eighteenth century would regard as slack estate management.

The picture of the Lincolnshire Marshland about 1725 was one of a static population with a few instances of a decline since 1563. Immingham, Ingoldmells, Sutton-le-Marsh and the settlements between Mablethorpe and Skegness all declined. Grimsby with its silted haven showed a more significant fall. The Marshland farmer was falling behind the rest of Lincolnshire in living standards by 1700. Pressure upon the rich grazing land by the gentry was probably a cause. When the Crown, for example, reclaimed land from the sea it was normally given to the gentry, some of whom did let it to the smaller farmers. Grassland in the Marsh was by 1725 being taken by upland farmers to put with their acreages on the Wolds or the Cliff. Though increased turnip growing on the Wolds was to take off the pressure for pasture land on the Marsh, as the century wore on, demand was to continue. Meanwhile sheep were to remain supreme in the Marsh. There is little evidence in the seventeenth century of conversion of tillage to pasture; engrossing appears to have troubled the Marshland farmer more than either

[10] Barley, op. cit. p. 114. [11] L.A.O. Tyr 4/3, 14.
[12] L.A.O. Tyr 4/1, 3.

enclosure or conversion of arable to pasture. Farmhouses were converted into cottages and farms in the 10 to 40 acres range were falling in number. Those with under 10 acres and those with over 40 acres increased, so producing a wider gap between the large and the small farmer in this region. In the seventeenth century wheat and rye fell back in favour of pulses and although barley held up well as a Marshland crop until the 1690s it too gave way before the pulses as the farmers concentrated upon the production of meat and wool for sale.[13]

At Burgh-le-Marsh tithe income to the Monson family increased for a time in the eighteenth century and then fell off as a greater proportion of the land was held by non-residents or 'foreigners'. Tithe in 1722 was payable on 3,085 acres of which 1,597 acres were held by inhabitants of Burgh-le-Marsh and 1,488 acres by non-resident 'foreigners'. These paid 4d. per acre while the residents paid 1s. an acre. By 1750 the figures were raised to 6d. and 1s. 4d. and by the 1790s they were 7d. and 2s. respectively.[14] This record of tithe payment reveals the taking up of Marshland acres by farmers on the Wold and the Cliff a process which must have been repeated in many other parts of the Marsh. Between 1722 and 1750 the total number of occupiers fell from 159 to 150 but as the number of inhabitants decreased from 87 to 75, the number of non-residents increased. The small resident occupiers of less than 25 acres fell by a quarter. The tendency for upland farmers to rent marshland for fattening stock appears to have accompanied a decline in the small Marshland farmer. This was in a village where enclosure of the greater part of the land had taken place in the seventeenth century with only 268 acres left awaiting parliamentary enclosure in 1839 out of a total of some 4,231 acres. Tithe on the remaining unenclosed land was paid in kind while that on the enclosed acreage had been compounded according to an inventory of 1683–4.

Table 1. *Tithe Composition—Burgh-le-Marsh*

Date	*Inhabitants*	*Foreigners*
	£ s d	£ s d
1722	83.10. 2.	24.15. 0.
1750	101.11. 0.	34. 8.11
1791	156.15. 8.	43.19. 4.
1796	180. 9. 8.	38.17. 2.
1801	165. 7. 8.	42.10. 6.
1806	152. 8. 0.	45. 4. 1.

[13] Thirsk, op. cit. p. 149.

[14] Barley and P. E. Russell, 'Notes on the Agrarian History of Owersby and Burgh-le-Marsh', *LH,* 11, Spring 1953, p. 384.

The tithe lists for 1733 and 1750 reveal another aspect of the changes going on in the eighteenth and early nineteenth centuries, as shown in the following tables with the numbers of inhabitants and foreigners grouped according to the sizes of their holdings.[15]

Table 2. *Occupiers according to holdings*

Date	Less than 10a	10–24a	25–49a	50–75a	75a or more	Totals
(a) Inhabitants						
1722	45	26	10	1	5	87
1750	35	16	12	4	3	70
(b) Foreigners						
1722	26	29	11	4	3	73
1750	31	28	11	4	1	75

In Croft, on the Drake estate, the steward described the effects of increased turnip growing upon the demand for pasture in the Marsh by upland farmers. Once turnip cultivation offered itself as an alternative method of fattening stock then as the Wolds produced fine turnips the richer farmers there were less interested in paying high rents for marshland. Their places appear to have been taken, however, by less substantial or more distant farmers on the Lincoln Edge. Their connections with Marshland parishes continued into the nineteenth century. On the estates of the Earls of Scarbrough, for instance, tenants at Willoughton and Glentworth like the Codds, the Craggs and the Osbornes were renting their landlord's marshland acreages in Tetney, Holton and Skegness from at least 1779 to 1815.[16] In 1726, however, Thomas Lowe was writing about farmers who 'had large estates of theire own up in the would country' and who refused to be 'rack'd' and who were replaced by 'a meaner and more ordinary sett of people, who co'd not afford to use your lands as the former had done, but overstockt 'em, neglected to dress 'em and suffr'd some of the dikes and draines to grow up, and when worse times came on, some of them threw up, others stay'd upon theire farmes but broake, whereas the former sett co'd well beare the hardships of two or three bad yeares, and alwaies paid theire rents punctually, and without trouble, difficulty, or disappointment. This brought a great discredit upon your estate and makes people less inclineable to take those lands which they have seen others succeed but ill with.'[17]

[15] L.A.O. Mon. 8/49/13 and 28/A/19/2.
[16] T. W. Beastall, *A North Country Estate,* Chichester, 1975, pp. 104–5.
[17] L.A.O. Tyr. 2/2/21.

This invaluable comment from an astute estate agent makes all the more understandable the nineteenth-century claim that agricultural improvement depended in a great measure upon maintaining continuity of occupation by tenants 'of capital and skill'. His observations upon the impact of turnip cultivation in the uplands provides a link between these two agricultural regions and their farming economies. 'Till of late yeares, all persons who had estates in the would country made theire rents and profitts of theire estates by breeding of sheep and some cattle, and were under a sort of a necessity of takeing a quantity of marshlands to feed 'em with before they sold 'em (for theire own lands were too poor to fatt 'em). But now of late, since the practice of improveing lands with turnops is set up, they either take that way of so improveing theire own lands and feeding the sheep themselves, or can now sell 'em (tho' leane) into those countrys where they do practice the turnop improvement.'[18]

Another link and a comparison with an upland farming economy is the comparison between Burgh-le-Marsh and Owersby the tithe developments of which have already been noted. It seems that in the early eighteenth century Burgh-le-Marsh had inhabitants with valuable inventories, sixteen with goods worth more than £200 for the period 1551–1743 as against three for Owersby. The yeoman of the Marsh were probably richer than in Owersby and more numerous. Large sheep flocks were usual at Burgh and there the farmers had little use for oxen though some did keep fat oxen as well as draught oxen. Hay was an important crop in the Marsh and so were beans as a fodder crop. Thus 'beast tumbrils' or 'sheep tumbrils' were important possessions indicating the use of a square wooden rack for holding hay for stock-feeding in yards and out in the fields. In the Marsh the production of milk, butter and cheese seems to have been for home consumption whereas in Owersby, between Caistor and Market Rasen, production was for market. While the keeping of pigs seems to have declined, the Burgh farmers were keeping flocks of hundreds of sheep as suggested by the holding of 343 sheep by a Thomas Harrison in 1702. It seems that mutton and wool production were by the early 1700s very important in Burgh-le-Marsh and that arable farming there was a subordinate activity in that it produced the necessary feeding stuffs for sheep and milk and cheese for home use. A comparison of stock held in the two parishes as indicated by inventories throws some light on the differences between Marshland and upland farming in the very early stages of the agricultural revolution.

[18] L.A.O. Tyr 2/2/21.

Table 3. (a) *Farm stock at Burgh-le-Marsh*

	Pigs	Cattle	Horses	Sheep	No. of inventories
1572–1600	41	211	59	959	14
1614–26	26	133	29	964	18
1680–1714	40	198	43	2537*	15

*This total excludes an unspecified number of lambs.

(b) *Farm stock at Owersby*

	Pigs	Cattle	Horses	Sheep	No. of inventories
1551–1600	66	161	39	726	13
1600–50	33	213	46	151	15
1650–1700	11	131	27	152	6
1700–50	8	97	26	529	5

Another link between coastal parishes and those on the edge of the Wolds was the provision of wood for coastal defence imbanking. A farm at Claxby near Alford though considered to be of little value by its owners did at least provide 8–10 acres of woodland which were useful in repairing the sea bank at Anderby. John Teasdale of Cumberworth complained in 1745 to his landlord, the Bethlehem Hospital, that he had lost £60 owing to 'a great and sudden inundation of the sea' at Anderby in 1736 and that frequent inundations had forced him to give up his tenancy. The land agent was in difficulties for he wanted to raise rents to help meet the costs of sea defence. Yet the sea continued its attack. In November 1746 Marwood wrote 'As to the Out End Ground in Anderby I have got the breach repaired, and in fact I had got the banks in such good repairs, I was in hopes of making the tenant that farms the land at £27 per annum for two years last past, to raise it to £40 per annum at Mayday next towards discharging the expense it cost. I am afraid this breach hath put a stop to any raisement at present.' There was pressure on the bank in 1755 and 'a prodigious strong tide' on 15 December 1757 took away some of the earthwork. Repairs estimated at £30 were put in hand but in February 1758 another high tide did much damage at Anderby '... and what to do with it I cannot tell, for it is no sooner repaired but broke down by the violence of the sea'. His successor seems to have been successful in finding tenants who would defend their land from the sea at their own cost and this would have saved the Governors of the Hospital great expense. Much later, in 1807, one of them was confident enough to counter-attack and to attempt land reclamation. Taking a 27-year lease of 80 acres of Out Marsh or Outer Dyke Ground he agreed to embank 40 acres of it from the sea at his own expense within six years. He had to throw up his lease, however, in 1830 when the sea broke in and he could not afford to repair the bank.[19]

Looking back to the enclosure commissioners' report on Lincolnshire in 1607 it is obvious that though their references to 'great depopulations' were exaggerated they did record more than 13,500 acres of enclosed land together with much evidence of reorganization in the shape of decayed farmhouses or cottages made from farmhouses.[20] The Wolds appear to have witnessed more enclosure, amalgamation of holdings and depopulation than the Heath though not of extinction of settlement. Joan Thirsk in her study of enclosure in the uplands between 1600 and 1740 wrote:

'By the mid-eighteenth century only 41 per cent of the wold villages had land waiting to be enclosed, compared with 63 per cent on the cliff north of Lincoln and 55 per cent on the heath to the south.'

The large landowners on the central Wolds pushed ahead with enclosure of some 80 to a 100 acres whereas in the more populated parishes of the southern Wolds smaller acreages involved more disturbance of yeomen, husbandmen and small landowners. Six out of ten Lindsey Cliff villages had some common land after 1750. In Kesteven the 1607 report of the enclosure commissioners pointed to three areas of population disturbance at Welbourn, Honington and Brauncewell, but they survived as settlements. Most enclosure seems to have taken place south of Ancaster while to the north the bleaker limestone ridge awaited the age of Arthur Young before enclosure and associated improvement took place. Celebrated by travellers in the 1720s as fine open country for hunting,[21] the Heath differed from the fertile lands nearer Stamford where parks and ordered estate villages were to be laid out at Corby, Irnham, Belton, Culverthorpe, Holywell, Edenham and Grimsthorpe. Before the age of Parliamentary enclosure this was the most enclosed part of Lincolnshire. It was described by John Cragg of Threckingham in the 1820s.[22] He judged the date of enclosure by the age of the timber in the hedgerows. Population changes in the uplands provide a background to agricultural change in the period 1562–1723.[23] Louth, Spilsby and Horncastle were growing while the villages near by were losing population. Sheep-rearing and

[19] A. E. B. Owen, 'The Barkhams of Wainfleet and their Estates', *LH*, Vol. 2. No. 8, 1961, pp. 7–8.

[20] Thirsk, op. cit., p. 160. [21] HMC, Portland, VI, p. 84.

[22] L.A.O. Cragg, 1/1. [23] Thirsk, op. cit., pp. 167–70.

enclosure designed to promote it together with the growth of market towns accounted for this decline; changes in the Fens probably had some effect for with the ending of unstinted common grazing in East, West and Wildmore Fens when draining was completed, the Wolds villages lost their summer pasturage. From the 1630s stock had now to be kept at home with the completion of the drainage works, so putting pressure on land kept under the plough. Thus stock had to be reduced as it had now to be kept on land hitherto reserved for hay. This jolt to farming fortunes probably caused some migration from the south Wolds parishes. In Kesteven the Heath villages changed little in size between 1563 and 1723 except in a few cases where increases of families can be detected. Perhaps the development of country seats by a number of influential proprietors like the Earls of Ancaster at Grimsthorpe Castle attracted families to help with land improvement, landscaping, building and the provision of rural amenities such as fox-hunting, shooting, fishing and the running of sizeable country households since this part of the county saw the creation of classical country estates and acquired its distinctive man-made scenery of woodland, water, and enclosed, ordered villages.

Evidence of changes in land management techniques in the early eighteenth century is slight. Turnips were being introduced, sainfoin was noted as a crop in 1696 at Oxcombe on the Wolds, and some cony warrens disappeared as the land they occupied was converted to pasture. The fattening of cattle brought into Lincolnshire from less favoured regions had become more regular and had attained the status of a system by the 1720s. Some of the Scots cattle which entered England at the rate of 30,000 a year were taken into Lincolnshire for even the Wolds provided better grazing than the cold pastures they had left. They were useful in helping to meet the rent in a difficult year like 1720.[24] There is no evidence of spectacular change but modest improvement must have been taking place. On the £500 a year estate near Rasen of the absentee Sir Marmaduke Constable of Everingham in Yorkshire the rental was increased by £178 a year by the enclosure of West Rasen in 1728 and even this indifferent landlord defended his woodland from misuse by his tenants, set his face against the cutting of turf on his land held in hand, and insisted through his Lincolnshire agent that tenants must reside on their holdings and not sub-let them to servants. Even so, the complaints of his tenants about the state of their houses in 1731, the fact that his Lincolnshire agent had to strengthen his house with two props and that both he and the Yorkshire agent were

[24] L.A.O. Monson, 2/32.

embarrassed by the cash they were holding when so many improvements were needed, points the way forward to the real changes that many parts of the country were to undergo.[25] That collected rents were quickly sent into Yorkshire by the agent for safety suggests another essential for agricultural growth: namely harmonious landlord-tenant relationships.

An early area of progress was the estate of the Massingberds of South Ormsby between Louth and Horncastle. The estate consisted of some 2,600 acres by 1660 in Ormsby and 1,400 acres purchased by 1714 in Driby. More acres were added at Sutterby between 1714 and 1804.[26] Enclosure at South Ormsby and Calceby had taken place after 1647 and 1672. Drayner Massingberd grassed down the old open fields and took old sheep walks for arable. He began a long, slow, piecemeal process of encroaching upon the upper walks. A memorandum dating from 1670 indicates a pre-enclosure rotation of corn and fallow, sheep and oats and barley for sale. Gradually, breeding and feeding livestock became more important and an 'up and down' convertible husbandry developed in the 1680s. Signs of pressure upon the sheep walk land are found in a letter of 1723 when the conversion of a close of 18 acres of grass to arable was recommended. When, after being well manured for some years, it was ready to 'lay down', then part of the walk was to be taken in for improvements. About the same time the need to send 20 large and 30 small wethers to London for sale on 1 November 1723 was urged as prices there were better than those available locally. In January 1724 the steward lamented that 'I can get no money off the tenants, I have not received one penny from them since I sent you account.'[27] There was no rack-renting, however, and leases were long. Though some ran for two or three years, leases of seven, eleven and fifteen years were granted and they contained limitations designed to keep the land in good heart. Tenants were encouraged to plant trees in stands of timber as windbreaks and as sources of ready cash. Bricks were made on the estate and pantiles were purchased at a time when in neighbouring villages the traditional mud, stud and thatch were almost universal. Rents appear to have been low, considering the landlord's activity as an improver, at 6d. an acre per year for sheep walk land and 1s. to 2s. per acre for arable.

[25] P. Roebuck, 'Absentee Landownership in the Late Seventeenth and Eighteenth Centuries: A Neglected Factor in English Agrarian History', *AHR*, Vol. 21, 1973 pt. 1, pp. 16–17.

[26] B. A. Holderness, 'The Agricultural Activities of the Massingberds of South Ormsby, Lincolnshire, 1638–1750', *Midland History*, Vol. 1. No. 3, pp. 15–25.

[27] L.A.O. MM 7/1A/127 and 132.

Smallholders, cottagers and owners of beast-gates appear to have kept up their numbers in the Massingberd regime. By the early nineteenth century in South Ormsby there were three large farms and 24 cottages. In 1670 before enclosure there had been six farms and 11 cottages. There was some amalgamation of cottages and farms but the labour accounts suggest that work was being found for 150 to 200 or more days in the year for a number of labourers who were cottage smallholders on the estate.[28] Thanks to an early start and a good example by Drayner Massingberd's successors, the estate seems to have enjoyed an enviable reputation for under-draining and well-kept farmsteads in the 1820s, at a time when much rural building in Lincolnshire was still of poor quality. We can see in this estate some of the very early springs of agricultural improvement. Wool was supplied to either West Riding or East Anglian buyers according to price. There was no sign of a regular droving trade to London before the last quarter of the seventeenth century, but the Massingberd estate was quick to occupy Marsh-land for grazing and the Huttoft and Ingoldmells acreages were added before 1660 to this end. Wethers were sold direct from Ormsby for 7s. to 10s. each in the 1660s, but after fattening on the Marsh they sold for 9s. to 14s. each; an early sign of the improving effects of fine marshland grass. The Massingberds made sales in London in 1671 of 90 fat wethers from Ormsby and 52 from Wainfleet and 161 from Ormsby in 1672 at from 7s. to 11s. each. Though jobbing drovers in the 1680s and 1690s appear in the estate accounts buying for local fairs, it is not until the 1740s that Smithfield sales became common in the accounts. Defoe's description of the use made of the roads for sending livestock to London from the Midland counties suggests a well-established practice by his time.[29]

Sainfoin appears to have been grown as a semi-permanent ley in the walks before 1700. Four acres of it were sown in 1672, and by 1674 thirteen fat sheep were raised on it; six were sold for 14s.6d. each. Neighbouring farmers took up the idea, for example, at Oxcombe in 1696 but the wealthier tenants on the estate hired sainfoin land from the Massingberds in the 1690s. The seed was bought in Hertfordshire and sent by sea to Lynn or Boston and thence by inland waterway to Keal Fenside from which it was carted up to Ormsby. By the 1720s, sainfoin was bought in Stamford but it was to be ten years before local suppliers were numerous. In the 1750s and 1760s John Bourne of Dalby was the supplier.

[28] Holderness, op. cit., p. 20.

[29] Daniel Defoe, *A Tour through England and Wales*, I, p. 65.

Whereas in the 1690s 12 to 20 acres of sainfoin were mown annually, in the years after 1710, 150 to 200 acres a year were taken. In the 1720s tenants were clearly encouraged to grow it. By 1714 Burrell Massingberd, Drayner Massingberd's son, had increased the rents by 30 per cent since the 1690s. In 1706 clover was introduced followed by turnips and cole-seed in 1716. Grown for 70 years in the Fens, cole-seed had not been popular on the Wolds. Turnips replaced it at Ormsby in the early 1720s, but the traditions of marsh grazing-husbandry remained strong and turnips seem to have been slow to modify them before 1750.

Burrell Massingberd kept his Hertfordshire servants on his home-farm in Lincolnshire as he claimed that they understood sainfoin best. When he advertised for tenant farmers he made this point, perhaps to impress them with the advanced ideas being implemented on his estate. His agents, however, were local. Though the Massingberd estates were no longer leading after 1728, they appear to have been consistently well-managed. Additions and refinements to leases were made in the 1720s and the system of two or three crops of corn followed by sainfoin was replaced by corn and turnips alternately for six years followed by legumes. In 1754, after Burrell Massingberd's death, the standard Norfolk four-course rotation was applied. The hoeing of turnips, before this was general in Lincolnshire, had been established on this estate, a property which survived the agricultural depression of the 1730s and 1740s. B.A. Holderness observed 'As far as one can judge, the Massingberds were, in nearly every respect, Lincolnshire pioneers of the new techniques for no contemporary estate records reveal any similar developments until well into the eighteenth century.'[30] Perhaps as they are set in context by more research the Ormsby developments will appear less exceptional but it does seem that much of central Lincolnshire remained self-absorbed, backward even, until the great advance of the 1820s and 1830s.[31]

As well as Marsh, Fen and Wold, Lincolnshire has many villages on clays, sands and gravels.[32] In the late seventeenth century changes were occurring here which prepared the way for structural developments after 1750. Care of the land, putting it to the best known use and keeping it in good heart, were the essential characteristics of this region. New crops, implements and management techniques were for later times. A search for acceptable methods of alternative husbandry was made to give more fertility. Agreement between common-right owners did provide for the ploughing up

[30] Holderness, op. cit., p. 23. [31] See Chapters VIII and IX.

[32] Joan Thirsk, *English Peasant Farming*, London, 1957, p. 179.

of old pastures and the laying down to grass of ancient tillage land, but enclosure, especially where population pressures were light, proved to be a surer way. The western and central lowlands of Kesteven, and the sandy, light soils of western Lindsey near Wharton, Risby and Blyton saw much enclosure before the Crown survey of 1607. Effected to increase pasture acreages, there appears to have been little depopulation of the region though the market towns of Winterton, Market Rasen, Brigg, Gainsborough and Wragby increased in size. By the 1690s more livestock was being kept. Fat oxen and beasts were more in evidence on the land taken from tillage and laid to grass and horses were replacing draught oxen. Apart from enclosure the great change of the seventeenth century had been the drainage scheme for the river Ancholme which had disturbed the economy of the Lindsey central lowlands. After the 1640 scheme had made only a limited improvement, the local landowner, Sir John Monson, started again in 1661 with the backing of an Act of Parliament. When the river was examined in 1766 it was again silted and narrow in many parts and effective engineering work had to wait until 1825. It is unlikely that the scheme affected land-use very much before 1700. Some farmers claimed that they could control the in and outflow of water and that the scheme by taking away this control was actually hurtful. Those who supported the drainage believed, as Parliament had done when giving sanction to it, that the land was damaged by flood and that drainage works, if properly maintained, could not fail to be an advantage. Yet judging by an examination of inventories the pattern of barley, pulses, wheat, rye, oats as main crops in that order supplemented by lentils, hemp and flax was unchanged in outline.[33]

The Monson estate at Owersby on the edge of the Ancholme lowlands and the Wolds gives some idea of the changes in villages in central Lindsey and of the growth of a classical estate in the early years of the eighteenth century.[34] A description of the property about 1700 lists

'A Manor and Manor House with right of keeping court all wafes and strays, the perpetual advowson of the Living and all Tythes Impropriate and Vicarial. A windmill with 30 farm houses with other Buildings belonging thereto and 27 cottages containing by estimation be the same more or less 4,835 acres that is to say 3,271 acres of Inclosed meadow or pasture 200 acres of pasture with Furrz 340 acres of arable 545 acres and a half of Ings and Carr meadow 327

[33] Thirsk, op. cit., pp. 187–92.

[34] M. W. Barley and P. E. Russell, 'Notes on the Agrarian History of Owersby and Burgh-le-Marsh', *LH*, 11, Spring 1953, p. 395.

or moor in controversy with etc. yearly rent £1,489.13s.2d.'[35]

Enclosed land for grazing and fodder predominated, but the large acreages of furze point a way forward to the improvements of the middle years of the century, just as the keeping of the manor court looks back to a time when much of the parish was unenclosed. This picture of an estate catches in one short description two of the great changes that parishes like it were to experience; the completion of enclosure and the bringing in for tillage and later perhaps for pasture of the land which ran to furze or to waste for lack of resources to tackle it. Neither of these changes was to be rapid; enclosure was not complete until 1820. Timber for it was purchased in Hull and brought up the Ancholme to Brigg, Kelsey and 'the Hook' at Owersby. A survey of 1744 showed many tenants holding land in severalty in the centre of the parish; indeed some of the practices of the occupiers such as 'overstocking the stubble field and trespassing the corn field' and driving a waggon through another's close to avoid a detour suggest that open field traditions died hard even in the early nineteenth century. They are similar to the offences recorded in the manor court of 1717[36] when fourteen tenants were presented and fined from 4d. to 2s. for overstocking the moor or the carr, or leaving open the gates on the Ings.

The effect of enclosure upon the numbers of farmers in this area, which was favourable to mixed farming and therefore to the survival of the small occupier, seems to have been less than that of financial pressure at times when all farmers were suffering from low prices and uninviting prospects. The Monson rentals indicate a marked drop in the number of tenants between 1724 and 1739. This period was one of good harvests and low prices when small farms even in open field parishes were consolidated. The low grain prices of the thirties and forties caused the engrossing of holdings long before Parliamentary enclosure began. When it did come, enclosure merely accentuated the tendency towards inequality. Landlords, however, were not anxious to disturb the small occupier. Tenants with the means and the skill to manage large holdings were hard to find. Amalgamation of farms took place when occupiers died without heirs or when they failed rather than as a result of a policy of ruthless consolidation by landlords. 1753 was a year of difficulty on the Monson estate with rent arrears at £2,106 whereas they had been £719 in 1727 and £1,148 in 1731. Although there had been rent increases, 1729–32, these had fallen upon the larger occupiers like Thomas Cary who paid over £145 a year in 1723 and over £188 in 1732. Smaller farmers like William

[35] L.A.O. Mon. 9/5/7. [36] L.A.O. Mon. 23/3/2.

Furniss were spared an increase. By 1744 the tenants had fallen in number to 59 from a total of 78 in 1729. By 1791–2 there were 52; by 1805 there were 49.

	1723	1724	1727	1729	1732
Thomas Cary	145. 4.7.	159.14.0.	160 9.7.	160. 8.7.	188.18.0.
Rich. Hewson	22. 7.1.	23.12.1.	23.12.1.	23.12.1.	27.10.0.
Fran. Swallow	11. 0.0.	12. 0.0.	12. 0.0.	12. 0.0.	12. 0.0.
John Settles	44.16.0.	53.10.0.	53.16.0.	55.2.0.	55.2.0.
John Beaumond	14.12.6.	14.12.6.	14.12.6.	14.12.6.	14.12.6.
Wm. Furniss	11. 0.0.	11. 0.0.	11. 0.0.	11. 0.0.	11. 0.0.
Geo. Clark	78.13.0.	85.13.0.	85.18.0.	85.18.0.	85.18.0.
Wm. Clayton	52.10.0.	56.11.8.	56.11.8.	56.11.8.	56.11.8.

It now seems clear that there was from the 1720s to about 1830 a long-term trend towards larger farms and that its causes were varied. Enclosure was only one of them. Land tax payments by owner-occupiers between 1795 and 1825 show that very small owners liable for less than 4s. a year in land tax were increasing rapidly in 37 Lindsey villages whose returns have been examined. Those paying between 4s. and £1 a year increased markedly as well but owners paying £5–10 fell sharply after 1805. In 1790 owner-occupiers of 5–20 acres outnumbered those with fewer than 5 acres by 5 to 1 but by 1830 they did so by only 8 to 7. It seems likely that both tenants and owners in the 20–100 acre category faltered in the period 1795–1825, especially when after about 1810 the high cereal prices of the war years began to fall. The very small farmers who rented or owned acreages of less than 5 acres were increasing but the gap between them and the more substantial ones was growing wider.[37]

[37] G. E. Mingay, 'The Size of Farms in the Eighteenth Century', *EcHR*, 2nd Ser. XIV, No. 3, 1962; J. R. Wordie, 'Social Change on the Leveson-Gower Estates, 1714–1832', *EcHR*, 2nd Ser., 27, 1974; J. D. Chambers, *EcHR*, 1st Ser., 10, 1940; Beastall, op. cit., pp. 100–3.

2

Enclosure

DURING two outbursts of activity in England and Wales in the 1760s and 1770s and from 1793 to 1815 over 6,000,000 acres of open fields, commons, meadows and wastes were enclosed by Acts of Parliament. From 1750 to 1850 about 4,000 Acts were passed but three-quarters of them fell in the two phases specified. While cereal prices were high and interest rates on borrowed capital were generally low, private arrangements for enclosure continued rapidly leaving little documentary evidence but contributing to the dramatic economic, social and visual transformation of the time. Although enclosure had gone on with variations in pace from the Middle Ages, the concentration of activity in two relatively short periods is clear to historians as it must have been to the countrymen of the period 1760–1815.

Probably half of the arable land in the midland and central southern counties was held in open fields in 1700. Kent, Surrey, Sussex, Hertfordshire, Essex and Suffolk had little land left to enclose. To the north and west enclosure had already progressed in an area from Lancashire down to Somerset, while Hampshire and Dorset had few open fields. The enclosure of waste and commons apart from open fields was extensive by then in Wales, Yorkshire, Derbyshire, Lincolnshire and Norfolk. There was much still to do, however, in sub-dividing the enclosed waste into more manageable units and in putting it to productive use. Lincolnshire's agricultural history demonstrates how long the process could take and the variety of influences needed to secure a high return from former waste land.

An Act of Parliament cost more than a private agreement but it had many advantages. The whole of the open fields could be enclosed at once and waste and common land included in a new and more efficient layout. An Act gave legal sanctity and finality to the finished plan and it enabled owners of the greatest acreage to hurry on those who opposed enclosure. Historians have claimed that small freeholders' long-term interests were ignored by their more successful neighbours and that cottagers, denied access to waste land and commons, sank to the level of landless labourers. Whether this was the result of enclosure or the consequence of a trend towards larger farms which Acts to enclose open fields, commons and waste merely accelerated is still debated. Certainly there were forces which encouraged many countrymen of all classes to welcome the prospect of profit and, for some, an invigorating break with ancient restraints.

Usually there were four impulses towards enclosure by whichever means. First it made for more efficient, compact farms enjoying a balance between arable and pasture with better facilities for breeding and rearing livestock. Though these improvements were not inevitable, the belief that enclosure would produce them gave its advocates a confidence which was not confined to the largest owners and the most prosperous farmers. A second aim was to revive old arable land which had been over-cropped by allowing individual farmers the feedom to put it down to permanent grass or long leys. Over-grazed commons and indifferently farmed open-land on the poorer soils of a parish could be ploughed and improved by a rotation of crops after manuring and marling. Third, enclosure increased the total area of land under regular cultivation by dividing wastes and commons. Chalk and limestone downs and wolds, once enclosed, were likely to be brought into regular cultivation piecemeal as farmers' resources and the prospects of profit dictated. Tennyson's Northen Farmer (Old Style) saw in the cultivation of the waste one of his greatest achievements.

'Dubbut looök at the waäste; theer warn't not feeäd for a cow;
Nowt at all but bracken an' fuzz, an' looök at it now—
Warnt worth nowt a haäcre, an' now theer's lots o' feeäd,
Fourscoor yows upon it an' some on it down i' seeäd.'

Finally an enclosure Act opened the way to the commutation or abolition of tithes, the provision of better roads and drains, effective flood control and the replacement, by a workable field pattern, of the old mixture of tiny closes and open fields which was the legacy of a gradual process of enclosure by private agreements.[1]

In Lincolnshire the chalk and limestone uplands were enclosed by Act of Parliament between 1750 and 1780. In the same period the clays and fenlands were undergoing enclosure but the marshland waited until after 1815.[2] The Marsh had less common or waste to

[1] G. E. Mingay, *The Agricultural Revolution 1750–1880*, London, 1966, pp. 77–81, 83, 93, 104.

[2] Joan Thirsk, *English Peasant Farming*, London, 1957, pp. 237–8, 292–3.

break in for cultivation and parishes were heavily populated by small freeholders who lacked the capital and skill for improvement. The upland sheep walks and rabbit warrens of Lindsey, on the other hand, were ideal for improvement. Thinly populated, they invited the enterprising landlord and tenant to enclose and to convert the land to more profitable use as conditions became right for a change to arable farming.

Lincolnshire's reputation for high farming, so celebrated in the middle of the nineteenth century was the result of the combination of many factors. Good landlord-tenant relationships, the development of tenant-right customs, relatively low rents at certain critical periods of progress, improved communications and perhaps the very position of the county in the kingdom itself, given its contacts with the industrial West Riding, the Midlands and the region dominated by London's economic attractions, played their part. Yet the search for the nature of the liberating influences seems to bring one back again and again to enclosure either as an essential cause of progress or as an equally essential expression of a desire for it. It is difficult to imagine that without enclosure the subsequent progress would have taken place, for enclosure surely was the revolution, the irrevocable break with the past on a scale great enough to change the landscape, the habits of thought and even the vocabulary of farming people. Immense though the impact of Parliamentary enclosure was, however, some of the advantages it provided were being actively sought after in the open field parishes of Lincolnshire before the two great waves of legislation from 1760 to 1780 and 1790 to 1820 broke over the county.

The aim of all agricultural progress must be to make the best possible use of the soil available to a group of farmers in individual situations. The work of Rex. C. Russell in Lindsey shows the opportunities farmers had and the problems of land use they solved in ways which are interesting in their logic and their imaginative simplicity.[3] An examination of 47 Lindsey parishes on the eve of Parliamentary enclosure has given certain guidelines. Each common-field system was adapted to the geography and the geology of the parish, which was clearly the essential farming unit. Within the same geographical region two adjacent parishes could devise a system which for them satisfied their needs and yet expressed different social or personal interpretations of how to attain such satisfaction. A balanced relationship between arable, meadow and pasture within the parish unit was usually achieved,

[3] Rex C. Russell, *The Logic of Open Field Systems*, Bedford Press for the Standing Conference for Local History, London, 1974.

though in some places it came about through a three-field system while in others a four or a simple two-field system effected the same judicious use of available land.

When Barton-on-Humber, Waithe, Searby and Bishop Norton are compared, the balance between arable, meadow and pasture acreages is clear. The whole of Waithe parish could have been absorbed in one of Barton's great open fields yet that would not have constituted a viable parish unit for such a field would not have provided for adequate tillage, meadow and pasture land. Hence, 'It was not the number of acres which determined the size of the parochial farming-unit, there had to exist a balance between land suitable for different uses, for arable, meadow and pasture.'[4] A comparison of four more parishes brings out why a four-field system was appropriate in one case.

	Total acreage of the parish	% of parish in arable
Messingham	5,824	24
Kirmington	1,904	64
Yarburgh	1,329	60
Heapham	1,238	54

Messingham, with little of its total area suitable for arable, developed a four-field system to make intensive use of what there was. Not until after enclosure 1798–1804 was its great West Common of poor sandy soil converted to arable after warping from the Trent had been effected.[5]

At Caistor 87 per cent of the parish lay under arable, a very high proportion, for here was ample open common on Caistor Moor. Nettleton farmers, on the other hand, had plenty of permanent rough pasture for their East and West Fields were steep, poor and wet and only parts were kept under the plough. A detailed analysis of parish open fields and areas of old enclosure indicates early settlement patterns. An almost continuous line of ancient enclosures runs through the adjacent parishes of East Halton, North Killingholme and South Killingholme. Keeping to the higher ground between the marsh and the Humber to the east and the Carrs along the Beck which forms the parish boundaries to the west, the line of old enclosure runs roughly north to south. In Habrough parish, however, the old enclosure runs along the higher ground which here runs from west to east. In the villages of East Halton and North and South Killingholme the open fields are either East or West fields while in Habrough they are North and South

[4] Op. cit., notes to figure 1. [5] Op. cit., notes to figure 2.

fields. The names of the pre-Parliamentary enclosure fields then have clues as to the early layouts of these settlements in the salt-marsh clays and the marshland of north-east Lindsey. In Habrough the meadow and pasture needs of the parish were provided for by access to the Marsh which lay beyond the adjacent parish of Immingham. Old enclosures were confined to each parish and rarely connected with ancient enclosure in a neighbouring one. Many estate surveys and valuations testify to the continuing importance of the parish, in that farms are examined not as units but as they fall into different parishes, so qualifying for different poor and church rates, for example. (See Plate 1)

The vocabulary of farmers was affected in that the great fields, with, in some villages a few closes within them, lost their significance and 'field' began to mean the hedged enclosures created by the enclosure commissioners. In the field names of these new enclosures the old outlines of the great fields lingered on but personal, family and even political names were increasingly given to fields as they began to represent the resources of particular farming families or owners of estates. Enclosure represents an effort, on a scale never attempted before, to reach the limits of the area that could be cultivated with a reasonable expectation of a return on outlay. But before the process of eighteenth-century enclosure is examined it ought to be observed that momentous though the results of parliamentary enclosure were, they were only more formal and widely applied changes that Lincolnshire had experienced for a century or more. Enclosed land could be worked side by side with open-field farming including land held 'in ming' or in partnership with another farmer. A rental of the estate of the late Sir John Chaplin dated *c.* 1730 for Tathwell, Maltby, Haugham, Raithby, South Somercotes, Cawthorne, Legbourne, Wrangle, Hullington, Saltfleetby and Grainthorpe shows examples of enclosure, open-field farming and land in ming together with, in Haugham, 'several other parcels of arable land lately divided from the Walk'. These accounted for 52 acres of the estimated 200 acres of the sheep walk. References to the old and the new 'cinque foil' closes suggest enclosures put to the cultivation of artificial grasses.[6] An account and survey of the estates of George Pauncefort on the southern Heath at Witham-on-the-Hill and Braceborough, by Thomas Allen, 1768, shows a mixture of enclosed and unenclosed holdings on a small estate of 570 acres of which 7 acres were waste.[7]

Improvement was possible within a mixture of enclosed and

[6] Lincolnshire Library, Lincoln, 1803.

[7] Lincolnshire Library, Lincoln, 4979.

unenclosed farms, and indeed there was an Act of 1773 to facilitate cropping changes within open field parishes. At Sibsey in November 1782 it was decided to shut off the barley field from stock as it was not sown but fallowed owing to a bad season. It was now to be sown with wheat and not grassed.[8] Flexibility within open field systems was not impossible. Yet when the mixture of unenclosed and enclosed land is looked at from the angle of the surveyor's report the differences in values of land together with the sheer administrative difficulty of accounting for so many pieces suggests that a stage must have been reached in many parishes when an urge to simplify holdings before they were let out became irresistible. A farmer could have several enclosed fields, perhaps known as 'ancient enclosure', some land held in ming, some 'pieces' in the open fields and some enclosures which he was making with his landlord's support out of the sheep walks or 'waste' or warrens. Samuel Malkinson took a farm near Ulceby, Alford, in 1743 for £42.16.8d. a year with half the Landlord's land tax added.[9] The low value of the unenclosed land is clear.

The House and barns	7 acres	£4 rent per annum	
The five acres	5 acres	£3 ,, ,, ,,	
The Hall closes	11 acres	£5.10.0d. per annum	
The Peas crofts	6 acres	£3.13.4d. ,, ,,	
The Butter crofts	10 acres	£5 rent per annum	
Longhags	14 acres	£7 ,, ,, ,,	
The Prince Clover Close	10 acres	£6 ,, ,, ,,	
Field Land in the West	30 acres	£5 ,, ,, ,,	
In the South Field	22 acres	£3.13.4d. rent per annum	
	115	£42.16.8d.	

On the same estate at the same time, Well Farm was let to a tenant with clauses to govern the sowing of sainfoin until 40 acres had been done, the landlord meanwhile to provide wood for the enclosing of the walk. In 1743 another tenant took Ulceby farm for two years with permission to plough up walk land; to seed it down and to enjoy a crop to follow him from the ground that he had not laid down to grass. The landlord was to make a fence to 'enclose the top of the hill' which he was to '... keep repaired making an entire hedge where necessary'. In 1746 when a George Rice was to have the Ulceby farm the landlord was again to enclose land for him with a sod wall and to provide his tenant with materials for repair. 'I shall

[8] *LNQ*, vol. 22 p. 70. The Act for allowing changes of cultivation in the open fields, three-quarters of the occupiers agreeing seems not to have been a dead letter here. 13 Geo. III, 81.

[9] Lincolnshire Library, Lincoln, 2586, James Bateman's estate book *c* 1742–56, pp. 15–18.

inclose the walk belonging to the said farm from the walk that joins to it in the parish of Ulceby with a good sod wall and stake the edge upon it . . . I am to find him wood for the repair of all the dead fences, he leading it during his continuance in the said farm. . . . I am to find St. foin seed sufficient for the laying down the 25 acres now adjoining the present St. foin field and that now has oats growing upon it . . . in case he has a mind to plow any of the aforesaid walk that he shall enclose it with a sod wall and plow it for three years only and then lay it down with St. foin or other seed.' Enclosure of the high 'walk' land could take place through the co-operation of energetic tenants and supportive landlords in the 1740s while open field systems continued on the lower ground of a parish. The time lag between such attacks upon the waste and the enclosure of the rest of the parish could be great but the inconvenience of holding, for example, in the case of Samuel Dashwood in 1775–6, 147 acres in 142 pieces in Alford West Field as well as 110 acres in 117 pieces in the south Field and 310 acres in 52 pieces in 'Little Field' must have impressed itself on those who saw in enclosure a means to more efficient farming.[10] In Claxby parish he owned 707 acres in 233 pieces some enclosed, some open, while at Mawthorpe he had about 60 acres in 64 pieces, some unenclosed, some like his 18 acre holding, arranged in five enclosed pieces.

Waste land was often brought into cultivation after enclosure while the rest of the parish remained open. A landlord who was interested in increasing the cultivatable area of a parish need not necessarily advocate enclosure as the case of Winteringham suggests. Here in May 1724 Sir Thomas Saunderson, later the third Earl of Scarbrough, began to spend about £400 on embanking 70 acres of land from the Humber. Activity seems to have continued until about 1732, yet Winteringham was not to be enclosed until 1762 in the time of the fourth Earl.[11] Morton common near Gainsborough shows that common-right owners could effect improvement without enclosure; indeed they could consider action to make it less necessary, or alternatively to raise the value of a common and therefore their individual interests in it against the day when enclosure seemed inevitable. They could also act to avoid the expense of commissioners who no doubt by 1777 had gained a reputation for being costly. In the minutes of a meeting of the common right owners in August 1777 it was agreed that as seven townships were

[10] Lincolnshire Library, Lincoln, 4272, terrier of an estate in Lincolnshire belonging to Samuel Dashwood by E. G. Fletcher, 1775–6.

[11] Lumley MSS., Enclosure EE/1724, Winteringham, and T. W. Beastall, *A North Country Estate*, Chichester, 1975, p. 89–90.

involved (Morton, Wakerith, Stockwith, Blyton, Wharton, Pilham and Gilby) and 3,000 acres, enclosure might, if the number of commissioners was great, be too expensive to be worth undertaking. So it was suggested that an agreement to stint the unstinted commons and to build one main and cross drains would effect improvements and avoid the expense of enclosure while increasing the value of the commons at a time when talk of enclosure was clearly affecting ideas on land values. They observed, 'Suppose the Proprietors, before an Inclosure takes place should enter into an agreement for a drainage of the Commons, together with a regulation for stinting; it may be seen what effect such drainage has on the good and bad parts of the Common and from which Commissioners may better determine and fix a value on the land when an Inclosure at a further time shall be thought advisable.'[12] Morton was not enclosed until after 1800.

Enclosure by private agreement before the great period of Parliamentary action could have apparently rational and profitable results, as the example of West Torrington in the Wolds indicates.[13] Sanctioned by the Bishop of Lincoln, enclosure was undertaken after private agreement in 1755. The Vicar was given nine acres and another parcel of ten acres as well as £3 towards his stipend in lieu of tithes. A map of 1797 shows the village nucleated, with little evidence of building in what had been the open fields and with large new enclosures arranged in a north-south sequence to obtain three types of land and good access to roads and lanes. Unlike many enclosed villages, such as Barton-on-Humber[14] where the building of farms out of the village began within three years of the award, West Torrington's farms stayed in the village street. The relationship between village layouts, the location of 'new' farms and the date and type of enclosure initiative merits more detailed exploration. By 1797 in West Torrington there were three larger farms of 307 acres, 252 acres and 224 acres as well as one of 165 acres, one of 50 acres and two small holdings of 2 roods, 4 perches and 35 perches respectively. This layout seemed to change very little, for the map of 1797 was used in 1836 unamended when tithe apportionment was undertaken.

Piecemeal enclosure by private agreement had whittled away some of the open fields and wastes. Yet when all possible

[12] Lumley, MSS., EE/16.

[13] Lincolnshire Library, Lincoln, 5204. Survey of West Torrington by Anthony Bower for Sir Robert Ainslie, 1797.

[14] Rex C. Russell, *The Enclosure of Barton-on-Humber, 1793–1796* and Hibaldstow *1796–1803*, Barton-on-Humber, 1962.

reservations have been made about what could be accomplished without enclosure, the importance of the events of 1760–80 and 1790–1820 remains.

'The parliamentary enclosures of the eighteenth and nineteenth centuries were really but the culmination of a process which had been going on without parliamentary sanction for centuries, sometimes rapidly, sometimes slowly ... in Tudor times a process of enclosure to keep sheep *in*, and in Hanoverian times a process of enclosure to keep sheep and cattle *out* of the fields.'[15] Enclosure had come to mean at this time not so much the taking in of land from the Humber, the sea or the heaths, warrens, cliffs and sheep walks as the replacement of a field pattern by another.

On the whole Parliamentary enclosure was undertaken with a care for the rights of property owners both large and small and the commissioners were usually jealous of their reputations for justice and experience. Unfortunately many of them appear to have taken on so much in a short time that some of their deliberations took years to effect. The example of the North Kelsey commissioners may have been exceptional for its snail-like progress, but hardship was caused perhaps in the process of enclosure more by delay than by cost, speed or carelessness for the rights of small owners. The North Kelsey commissioners started work in 1813 as soon as the Act was passed. By 1817 they seemed to be slowing down, from 1822 to 1824 they were meeting only once a year and it was 1840 before the award was executed. Thirty-six out of the original 61 proprietors had died by then. Delay was due to overwork and to participation by commissioners in the numerous improvements that accompanied enclosure. Proprietors were sometimes slow to arrange sales and exchanges of land while their objections and failures to pay their share of expenses held up progress. It was known that in the total change made possible by an award lay the real economic benefits of enclosure; by their own design the commissioners set afoot schemes for improvement while the going was good. Whether they were conscious that in delay there was an element of profit for some of them it is hard to say, but John Burcham, a North Kelsey commissioner, accepted 20 more appointments from 1813 to 1840 as well as being Lord Yarborough's agent. He had his accounts paid, it seems, while others, such as the contractors making ditches and roads, had to wait eight years for theirs to be settled. One owner in this admittedly extreme case of delay was denied access to his new allotment of land for

[15] T. H. Swales, 'The Parliamentary Enclosures of Lindsey', *LAAS*, XLII, pt, ii, pp. 243–4.

years.[16] Land agency coupled with heavy obligations as an enclosure commissioner could help the foundation of a family fortune. John Burcham's bequest of £600,000 to his daughters in 1841 must have owed something to his fees as a commissioner and to his engagement in the general business activity generated in Lindsey during his working life.

Enclosure took ten years at Barton-on-Humber from the award in 1793 and seven years at Hibaldstow from 1796. Even when enclosure was finished, the commissioners or their successors continued to meet to supervise some of the improvements. At Tetney where an award was enrolled in 1779, the commissioners were advertising their activity in the *Stamford Mercury* in February 1832 as they proposed an embankment rate of 1s an acre for Tetney and a 9d drainage rate to be paid to Messrs. Garfitt & Co. bankers of Louth. At Hibaldstow the commissioners met for many years to maintain the bridge over the Ancholme and the new banks against the river. A proposal to enclose the 400 acres of Lissingley Common ten miles south-west of Caistor was announced in the *Stamford Mercury* as early as 5 August 1841, but work on it started in October 1848 and finished in November 1851. To defray the costs of the enclosure, 73 acres were sold to a total of nine purchasers including the Governors of Charterhouse for £1,570.6.3d. The governors paid just over £208 for about nine acres. By the 1790s many enclosure schemes gave an almost conventional, stylized formula for bringing about a change in the pattern of a parish. The Barton-on-Humber award puts it briefly

'... And whereas the Lands and Grounds belonging to the several Proprietors in the ... Open Fields, Ings and Marshes, lie intermixed and dispersed in small Parcels, and the same and also the ... Common Pastures, and other Common and Waste Lands and Grounds in their present State are incapable of much Improvement, and it would be of great Advantage to the Proprietors, if (the parish) ... were divided and inclosed, and specific Parts allotted to the several Persons interested therein, in Proportion to their respective Properties, Rights of Common, and other Interests ...' Improvement was usually measured in terms of rent potential. At Hibaldstow, where turnips and clover were already being grown as open field crops in 1795, John Parkinson and Samuel Turner estimated the probable improvement which the proposed enclosure could effect. The open fields were being cropped once in two years and

[16] Rex C. Russell, *The Enclosures of East Halton, 1801–4 and North Kelsey, 1813–40*, Barton-on-Humber, 1964. See also the review by Joan Thirsk, *AHR*, XIII, 1965, p. 64.

were worth 14s. an acre in the cropped year and only 3s. an acre in the fallow year, or 17s. per two years or 8s.6d. per acre per year. Enclosure would result in a 6s.6d. per acre per year advance. Common land and old leys would increase from 2s.6d. an acre to 10s. an acre and the meadows and carr land would advance from 10s. to 15s. an acre after banking and draining. The costs involved they calculated at five years' purchase on an estate worth 30 years' purchase. The improved value per acre they suggested was about 13s.8d. an acre of which 2s.3d. per acre was the cost of the improvements. Hibaldstow had two great fields, North Field of 800 acres and South Field of 970 acres and common pasture of 1,237 acres broken into nine divisions of old leys, carrs and ings.

Expectation of better times at least for the more substantial tenant farmers made a number of them request to have their new enclosed lands situated away from the village settlement indicating that they looked forward to having new farmsteads built in what had been the open fields. At Barton-on-Humber new farms were going up within three years of the enclosure. At Caistor, enclosed 1796–8, proprietors asked for land for common rights at a distance from their existing homesteads, perhaps suggesting an intention to build, while others wished their awards to lie near their present holdings and their enclosed land. A note of caution was sounded by some, however. The Duke of Ancaster, Arthur Young said, believed that rents should not be increased for three years after an enclosure. Young in calling Barton Field enclosure 'one of the greatest enclosures in England' considered that land could quadruple in value. At Winteringham, Lord Scarbrough's agent observed in 1784, that 'the cause of Winteringham's being before let at a less value, arose from the Inclosure, and the Tenants being under restrictions respecting the Nourishment and Care of the Quicksetts, which was very inefficiently fenced and some parts not fenced at all, so that the tenants could not occupy their farms to the best Advantage'. Enclosed in 1761 and 1762, the farms were let at low rents until 1770 when they rose from £1,395 a year to £1,858. They had shown a rise from £809 in 1765 so this seems to have been a case of a slow return from enclosure, but it also suggests that benefits to a landlord, especially when he was an absentee, could be slow too and that good supervision by an agent was needed to ensure quick success. There is little doubt that values and expectations increased when enclosure took place. Indeed the very mention of it affected decisions and prospects rather as news of the signing of a mining lease could affect land values in industrial parts of neighbouring Yorkshire. The rector of Welbourn wrote in August 1766 about the Hon. G.

Hobart, who was reluctant to sell his land at Dunston '. . . he is so enamour'd with it and expects so many great Improvements soon, that I think you have no chance of success as long as he lives. If the Fens are drained (which is a plan talked of at present) he hopes for his share to have an addition of 200 acres of land, and thinks it in every other respect so improveable that he is determined upon no conditions to part with it'.[17] If there were to be an enclosure of the Heath at Dunston then values would increase, '. . . for the Heath land which Mr Hobart inclosed in this Parish is just let upon a lease of 14 years at 14s. per acre, the land which is not enclosed being let at the same time only 2s. If a plan to enclose the Heath which is talk'd of and probably will be the case . . . you must greatly increase your estate at Dunston'.[18] Here it seems fen drainage and enclosure of the Heath were going together, with the result that owners and occupiers were alerted to the possibilities opening up in their farming region. The district was dominated by Dunston Pillar a land-lighthouse built in 1751 which the enthusiastic incumbent of Welbourn thought was a social symbol as well as a sign of man's determination to tame and make safe a hitherto lonely and even dangerous tract of country. The Pillar was '... the Vaux Hall of this part of the world' for men gathered there and drank Lord le Despencer's health and admired the bowling green and the thriving plantations which '... will be in a few years the paradise of Lincolnshire'. No wonder James Garner, the steward for the le Despencers, would not part with his small property at Welbourn.

The prospects of enclosure could cause acrimony as well as confident expectation. A long and bitter dispute raged between two former friends when Lord le Despencer and the reverend Dr Willis accused each other of at worst bad faith and at best serious misunderstanding over the purchase of freeholds in Dunston lordship. Lord le Despencer had wanted Willis to inform him when freeholds were for sale because he wanted to own all the lordship himself before he undertook enclosure. When he discovered in 1773 that the reverend doctor had during the previous nine years made six purchases for himself, his wrath admitted of little restraint. For his part Dr Willis, made confident perhaps by his acquisitions in a period when values were likely to increase, put up a spirited defence of his conduct. He had spent £3,150, a useful investment to hold against enclosure. In addition to his six new properties he held the mortgage of G. Golding's little farm valued at about £6 a year. Golding was preparing to sell some houses in Lincoln to pay it off '. . . and as

[17] Bodl. Lib., Oxford, MSS., D. D. Dashwood (Bucks.) C5 B11/4.
[18] Ibid.

he expects the Lordship will be enclosed he hopes to be able to live upon his own, tho' I think he will soon want to mortgage again'. So even small proprietors would make plans on the strength of an expected enclosure and there would be others, perhaps mortgagees like Dr Willis, interested in their outcome.[19] By 1776 Lord le Despencer had bought in Dr Willis' purchases.

Expectations of improved rents and land values were, it seems, fulfilled particularly when improvement in the shape of new farm buildings, better drainage and more intelligent management were added in a period of high prices for agricultural produce during the Napoleonic wars. But what of the costs of enclosure and the upheaval that it invariably entailed? Some occupiers and common right owners seem to have sold out before enclosure, so avoiding both cost and disturbance. What use they made of their capital from such sales remains a mystery. Did they invest in businesses like milling or malting or did they or their sons become wheelrights, corn merchants or seed and oil cake merchants of the Lincolnshire towns? Some may have invested their gains in mortgages or the funds. For those who remained the share of the cost of obtaining the Act, having the Award implemented and then fencing their new allotments must have proved a burden. It is important, however, to attempt a definition of the many interests involved and to observe different reactions to enclosure. There were the officials of the open field system, the pinder, the swineherd, the jurymen and the riders who for example in Barton-on-Humber rode round the fields at harvest time night and day to protect the crops of the village community. Most of these functions were swept away by enclosure though at Hibaldstow the pinder's function continued in that the wide verges beside the new roads were let out for grazing to defray the cost of road maintenance and owners could be fined and have their straying stock impounded. Though the village green of 2½ acres was assigned to William Dobson and the Duke of St. Albans, there was still a need for a pinder. Way wardens or surveyors of the highways and dykereeves continued, but now individual owners or the land agent were responsible for many of the activities of the old officials. The common-right owners, some of whom were absentees, had their claims attended to with apparently scrupulous care. In Barton the only common rights disallowed were those for cottages which were mere ruins in the yards or gardens of proprietors. The Vicar, William Appleby, and Robert Bygott had demolished tofts on their premises which had formerly enjoyed common rights. William Morris junior had a property containing 'offices

[19] MSS., D. D. Dashwood (Bucks.) B 19.3/7, 14 and 29.

formerly a cottage' for which no common rights were recognized in the award. The rights to beast-gates and similar claims were allowed at Barton for 808 horses, 695 beasts and 8,213 sheep. Here the proprietors were fortunate as this award was executed speedily. Only three months were needed to decide on new roads and all was completed by the Christmas of one year's work. At the Easter Vestry the three dykereeves were to be elected to attend to banks and drains in the parish. Their expenses and salaries were to be met by the proprietors. In the Easter Vestry and subsequent vestry meetings some of the old communal decision-making continued. The surveyors of the highways with their eight acres for road material and their power to let off verges represented the new officials of the enclosed settlement.

Another group of owners were those with rights to tithe. It would be interesting to know how many tithe-owners sold their rights before enclosure to those who saw in tithe holding a means to landownership when those rights were translated into acreages in an enclosed award. The sweeping away of tithe and its expression, together with that of manorial rights in land, must have simplified and made more harmonious the life of many a parish. In Barton-on-Humber the vicar received 3 acres, 3 roods and 34 perches in lieu of glebe and right of common. In lieu of great tithes George Appleby received four plots totalling 900 acres and the Crown received 35 acres, 2 roods and 34 perches in lieu of manorial rights. The vicar's corn rent was provided for as it replaced his claims to small tithes by the setting aside of three plots of 261 acres and an additional 244 acres as security. Those who were awarded land for tithes had the fencing costs paid for by the other proprietors. At Searby, enclosed under the Act of 1763, the total cost including the fencing and hedging of lands awarded in lieu of tithes was £690 which worked out at 12s. 10½d. per acre or 15s. 5d. per acre when the costs of fencing the land awarded to the Vicar and the Dean and Chapter of Lincoln were allowed. The Lord of the Manor, Edward Weston, bought up some holdings during enclosure from three other proprietors. At Holton-le-Clay, enclosed 1763–6, 23½ per cent of the total area of 1,315 acres was awarded to special allotments, 44 per cent went to the three leading proprietors, Richard Beancliffe, John Pinder and John Ludlam. Six owners with holdings between 45 and 65 acres each shared 23 per cent of the land after the award while 12 smaller owners shared 9 per cent of the land. The vicar for tithes received 94 acres while the Earl of Scarbrough for tithes received two holdings one of 69 acres and the other of 135 acres. For his general allotment in lieu of lands in the open field he was given

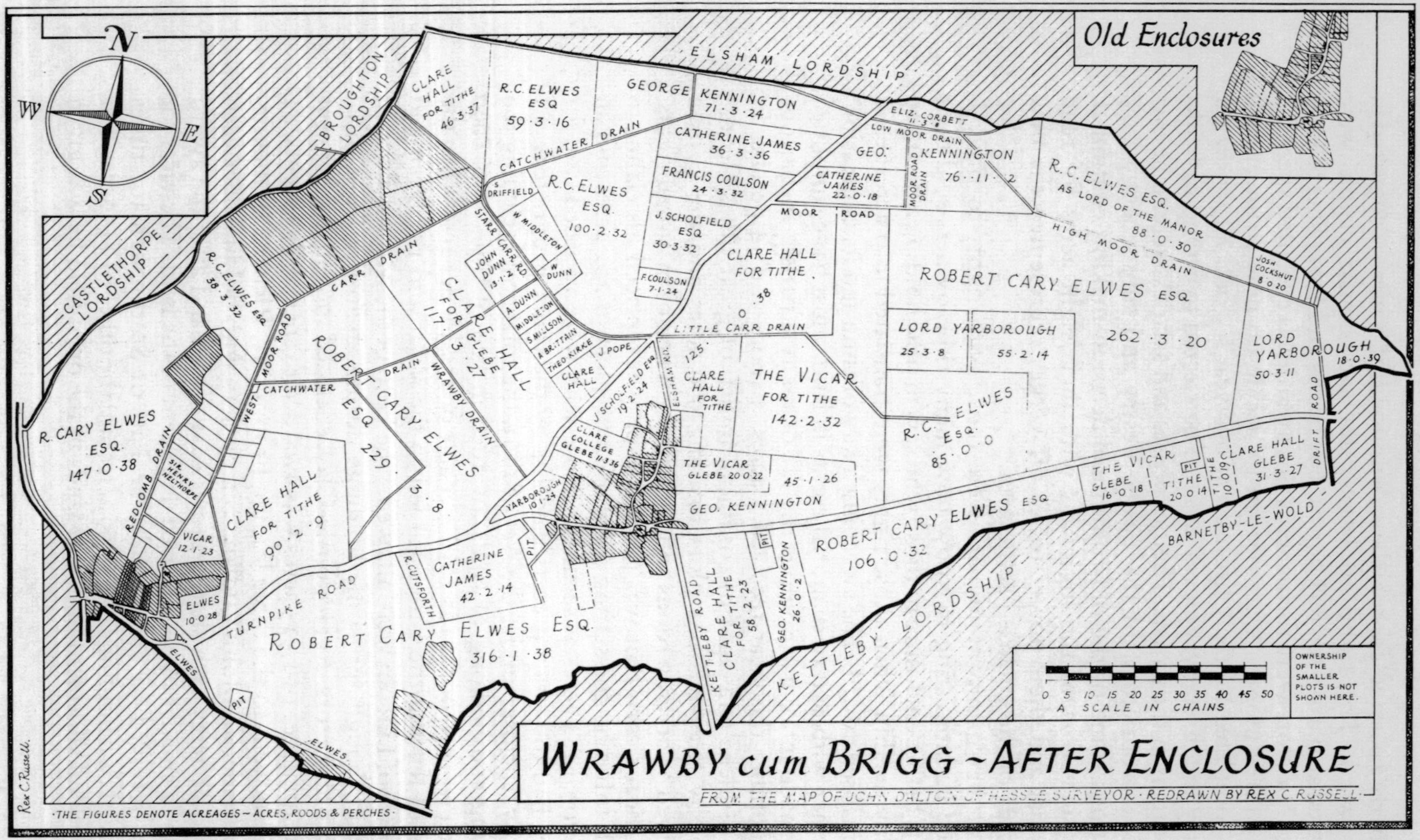

Figure 2. Wrawby parish after enclosure, 1800–5, showing the new allotments and the area of old enclosure. (Rex C. Russell)

51 acres. As these three pieces were together with a road between them, his estate had been much improved by the enclosure. Perhaps the supply of land in Lincolnshire owed something to landowners disposing of scattered acreages which had been augmented by allotments made in lieu of tithes at enclosure.[20] Costs were not apportioned according to acreage alone. For his allotment of 51 acres the Earl of Scarbrough was charged £175.13.6d. for his share, excluding his costs of hedging and fencing. Richard Beancliffe for 254 acres paid only £155.14.8d. As no information in the award throws light on the costing it is to be assumed that quality, value and the situation of the land were taken into account. Elizabeth Lingard with less than a quarter of an acre had to contribute 4s. while Hugh Hamersley for an acre paid 8s.4d. The average cost of the Holton-le-Clay enclosure was 16s.10d. per acre on the area charged. Of course, there were here the usual essential improvements such as four drains with nine brick tunnels to take them beneath the roads, four public roads, three private roads, nine footways as well as stiles and bridges. Tithe owners were treated generously at Hibaldstow, enclosed 1796–1803. Land allotted was to be equal in value to one-fifth of all arable and tillage lands in the open fields, to one-eighth of the enclosed and unenclosed Carr lands, Horse pasture, Ox pasture, Little Carr Common, Middle Dale Common and to one-ninth of the 'ancient' enclosures.

At Wrawby-cum-Brigg, enclosed in 1800–5, Clare Hall, Cambridge, was rector of the Parish and owner of the great tithes. The Master proposed that land be granted in lieu of tithes both great and small on the basis of one-fifth in value of the arable field lands, one-seventh of the common and meadow lands and one-ninth of the old enclosed lands. Even though they desired an enclosure the proprietors disagreed and eventually in September 1794 the advice of Charles Butler of Lincolns Inn was sought. He warned them that the House of Lords would pay great attention to the wishes of a tithe owner and that '. . . the actual weight of the spiritual Lords is very considerable particularly in the passing of inclosure Bills. . . .' A visit by the proprietors' representatives to Clare Hall proved fruitless yet in January 1795 they decided not to go ahead without the consent of the Master. They believed an enclosure would help the long-serving and under-paid vicar and in a letter to Clare Hall they urged his case. The Vicar of Wrawby for his part wrote to the Bishop of Lincoln saying that he agreed to the terms and hoped that the

[20] For a full discussion of the Lincolnshire land market, see B. A. Holderness, 'The English Land Market in the Eighteenth Century: The case of Lincolnshire', *EcHR* 27, 1974, pp. 556–7.

Bishop would too. He went on to press the claims of a family man and to compare landownership with corn rents.

'And I have further to inform your Lordship, that it would be greatly to the benefit of my Family to have lands, instead of corn rents, having a son who holds a small farm in this parish, and I assure you it is the wish of all the proprietors; I well remember your Lordship's recommending corn rents, but in this case it appears to me not so elligible as land, the obtaining of which favor will ever be thankfully acknowledged by

Your Lordship's most obedient and most humble servant
William Hargreave, Vicar of Wrawby.'

It was thought by the proprietors that the Vicar should receive land instead of a corn rent but that unless the Bishop of Lincoln gave his support, then to minimize the danger of opposition to the whole scheme in the Lords and from the Master and Fellows of Clare, a corn rent should be accepted.

Schedules of corn rents were usually based upon the average price of wheat for the previous 21 years as published in the *London Gazette* and then the commissioners calculated what quantity of such wheat was equal in value to one-fifth of the open-field arable, one-fifth of the old enclosed arable, one-eighth of the meadows either open or enclosed and one-ninth of the open or enclosed pasture. The price of this quantity of wheat was apportioned among the proprietors according to the value of the old enclosures and the new allotments. They then had to pay that price or rent to the incumbent, usually quarterly on 1 January, 5 April, 5 July and 10 October. The rent could be altered every 21 years if the average price of wheat had changed by more than threepence a bushel. Three referees appointed by the Justices at Quarter Sessions would then decide on the new corn rent.

Eventually agreement for an enclosure was reached and Clare Hall received in value one-fifth of the arable, one-seventh of the pastures and meadows, whereas the proprietors had wanted to give them one-eighth, and one-eighth of the old enclosures. By July 1800 the commissioners were at work under the Act of that year after 18 meetings, held mostly at the Angel in Brigg, and after the expenditure of heavy sums for travelling to and from Cambridge and to the home of the lord of the manor in Wiltshire. The cost of fencing tithe allotments was £1,153.8.10d. out of a total of £4,950.2.10d., excluding the proprietors' own hedging costs. The vicar received for glebe and common rights just over 36 acres and for tithe 175 acres. Clare Hall received 331 acres for their tithes and the lord of the manor received 88 acres for his manorial rights.[21] Land awarded in lieu of tithe varied from 12·8 per cent in a parish where the tithe burden was light to 32·7 per cent in part of West Rasen. The table below indicates the variations but it shows that the claims of tithe owners were given substantial expression when land allotment was undertaken.[22]

Date of Enclosure	Parish	In lieu of Great Tithes	In lieu of Small Tithes	Total	Acreage Enclosed	Lands awarded In Lieu of Tithes as a percentage of land to be enclosed
		A. R. P.	A. R. P.	A. R. P.		
1800–5	Wrawby	331 2 6	175 3 5	507 1 11	c. 2,976	17·0%
1770–1	Scawby	206 1 2	166 3 17	373 0 19	c. 2,216	16·8%
1796–1803	Hibaldstow	400 2 15	237 3 6	638 1 21	c. 4,233	15·0%
1766–8	Barnetby	300 3 8	204 0 34	505 0 2	c. 2,260	22·3%
1777–8	Kirmington	189 3 4	88 3 12	278 2 16	c. 1643	16·9%
1779–81	Market Rasen		93 3 13	93 3 13	730	12·8%
1772–4	Middle Rasen	245 2 12	143 2 20	389 0 32	c. 2,678	14·5%
1803–6	Kirkby cum Osgodby	236 2 24	115 2 29	352 1 13	c. 1,346	26·1%
1803–4	West Rasen (part)	420 1 27		420 1 27	1,281	32·7%
1790–5	Ludford	199 1 0	Money payment		2,167	
1792–5	Tealby	226 3 7	Corn rent			
1793–1801	Kirton Lindsey	740 0 6	Nil	740 0 6	4,325	

Notes: Scawby: The Acreage awarded to the Vicar includes land for small tithes together with land in lieu of glebe and common rights.

Hibaldstow: Three tithe owners shared the land awarded in lieu of Great Tithes.

Ludford: The annual payment to the Church in lieu of tithes was £122.2s.10d.

Tealby: The yearly Corn Rent to the Vicar was £58.1s.5¾d.

Kirton Lindsey: The Vicar was awarded a Corn Rent of £123.2.1¼d. for his small tithes.

Provision for clerical tithe owners did not escape criticism. Thomas Sandon, steward to Lord le Despencer from 1770 to 1778, wrote that he was opposed to allowing one-seventh in value in lieu of tithes even though it seemed to be general. Tithe owners were free of the costs of the Act and their land was often ring-fenced at the

[21] For a full account of this case see Rex C. Russell, *The Enclosures of Market Rasen, 1779–1781 and of Wrawby cum Brigg 1800–1805*, Market Rasen, 1969.

[22] Ibid.

expense of the proprietors '. . . which gives such Quantity of Lands, from those that ought to have the landed Interest in their Possession that I think it very wrong and possibly, some Time or other may require a Henry the 8th to set to right; I recommend a Yearly Stipend well-secured the best to be given the Clergy, Gentlemen such in my Esteem notwithstanding my Opinion'.[23] This was in 1778, by which time his opinions and language had been moderated. In 1776 he had been asked to have a Mr Bury kept out of Dunston where he wanted to buy the tithes on the strength of a rumour of an enclosure. He would only advance them and so hurt the tenants. Sandon always advised tenants to keep as many beasts as possible as these were less profitable to the 'tithingman' who operated to the 'great Injury of the Inhabitants of Dunston'. In reference to tithes he called clerical owners 'those sons of Plunder, the Church'.[24] Yet for all his complaints he saw the link between successful agriculture and provision for the clergy. The relationship between improved farming, clerical incomes, the restoration of churches and the building of good parsonage houses in Lincolnshire deserves a separate study, for the investment decisions of Lincolnshire clergy must have played a part in the development of country towns and businesses just as their houses and the churches they served enriched the landscape.

Allotments of land were made in most enclosure awards for road surveyors, seven acres, for example, were set aside for them at Wrawby, in which to dig for repair material. Their acreages together with those for tithe and manorial right owners were regarded as special and were often dealt with before the general allotment took place. At Caistor Moor, enclosed 1811–14, the Churchwardens and Overseers of the Poor were given land in and among the general allotments. Special allotments there accounted for 31 per cent of the acreage, the eight largest owners had 41 per cent and the remaining 28 per cent was shared by 40 owners. A special allotment of 72 acres went to Philip Skipwith in lieu of his rights of warren. The acres were deemed capable of improvement so his award marks a step in the long process of replacing warren by grazing land and eventually by arable. At Scawby, enclosed 1770–1, allotment was made to the school which had been founded by Richard Nelthorpe in 1705 for the poor of the parish. Their hedging and fencing were paid for by deducting from the school's share of land an acreage equal in value to the cost of enclosing their allotment.

[23] MSS., D.D. Dashwood (Bucks.) B/19/6/24.

[24] Ibid., B19/6/16, 18, 19.

It was upon the recipients of the general allotments that the real impact of enclosure fell. They bore their own costs, and as we have seen, the costs of others; they or their tenants had to farm during the changeover period. They had to rebuild farms or to decide to work their new allotments from existing farmsteads, so it is to them that one must turn to see a major effect of enclosure.

3

The Cost of Enclosure and its Execution

THOUGH no proportion of acreage was ever laid down, it was generally understood that unless at least four-fifths of the owners of the total acreage of a parish favoured it, an enclosure Bill would be rejected by Parliament. It was thus possible for say five owners to coerce twenty smaller ones and to push through a Bill. In many parishes, however, agreement to enclose took a long time and fear of the reactions of the notoriously independent common-right owners might delay a scheme even when there was general acknowledgement that enclosure was desirable. North Thoresby, at the foot of the Wolds on the Marsh south of Grimsby, enclosed 1836–46, had seen attempts made from 1801; Ulceby, on the south-east Wolds, whose Act was passed in 1824, had seen efforts to enclose from 1801–3. Fulstow, parts of Marsh Chapel, Grainthorpe and South Somercotes, Cleethorpes, Frodingham and Scunthorpe, East Santon, Corringham, Springthorpe and Wrawby all experienced long delays. As early as 1750 Lord Middleton was willing to enclose Dunston heath and the Bishop of Lincoln thought his plan reasonable and '. . . not to the prejudice but advantage of the Poor of the Parishes', yet rumours of an impending enclosure were still affecting owners in the district in 1774 who, on seeing timber being marked in Lord le Despencer's woods, were sure that a new scheme was afoot.[1] At long last in March 1792 calculations were made on the basis of an enclosure of this part of the Heath and in 1793 expenditure began. At Nettleton, on the western edge of the Wolds, Lord Eardley had the parish surveyed at his own expense to save time before the commissioners arrived but the other proprietors were suspicious and the commissioners

[1] MSS., D. D. Dashwood (Bucks.), B/19/8/2, 3, B/19/6/12 and E/2/12.

appointed an independent land surveyor, Maximilian Clifton of Boston, to make a new survey.[2] Some opposition could come from the leading landowner if he considered that his rural amenities were affected or his general influence in a parish. Cary Elwes in 1761 complained that the Wrawby proposal was 'A scheme I never ... will come into, nor recommend to those who come after me.'[3] The owner of Willingham Hall feared that its privacy would be lost unless he could purchase enough land to keep his neighbours at a distance when Tealby parish was enclosed.[4] On the whole, however, the larger owners welcomed enclosure as a way to enhance the value of their holdings and they were in the lead in effecting it. This was reconciled with a concern for the property rights of others. Whether commissioners always began with the largest owners, gave them allotments and then worked down systematically to the lowest it is difficult to say, but at least one commissioner, a Mr Elmhirst recorded his reasons for working the other way round in the late eighteenth century.

'Another observation I, at the first, made and ever after put in practice was this, always begin to line out and allot for the smallest proprieter first (whether rich or poor) in every parish, so as to make such allotments as proper and cõnvenient for the occupation of such, or their tenant (as that might be) to occupy: and so on from the smallest to the greatest; for it is at the advantage of the greatest and most opulent proprieter, that a bill is presented and Act passed ... and therefore there can be no partiality in defending those who cannot help or defend themselves; and a little man may as well have nothing allotted to him, as to have it so far off, or so inconvenient for him, that it is not worth his having, as it would prevent his going to his daily labour; and therefore he must sell his property to his rich and opulent neighbour and that, in some measure, decreases population.'[5]

Small proprietors seem to have been given greater consideration than large or absentee owners when it came to the placing of their allotments. The lord of the manor could lease out his allotment, as indeed could the incumbent, so proximity to land already owned did not matter so much as it did for the small owner for whom travelling time between fields and problems of accessibility could

[2] Rex C. Russell, *The Enclosures of Scarby, 1763–1765, Nettleton, 1791–1795, Caistor, 1796–1798, and Caistor Moors, 1811–1814*, Nettleton, 1968.

[3] Gordon Jackson, 'Cary Elwes—Lord of Brigg', *LH*, Vol. 2, No. 12, 1965.

[4] L.A.O. Tennyson D'Eyncourt LXV/6.

[5] Quoted in T. H. Swales, 'The Parliamentary Enclosures of Lindsey'. *LAAS*, Vol. XLII, pp. 267–8.

materially affect the success of his farming. In his study of Lindsey enclosures, T. H. Swales saw in a number of parishes a degree of success in allocating fields conveniently for the smaller proprietors. At Orby two allotments of six acres and five acres were made next to each other and to an acreage of old enclosure already held by Richard Harrison. Robert Vynor at Baumber was given land to adjoin his land in the neighbouring parish. West Keal had examples of careful sitings of allotments to fit with the old closes. The chief landowner, R. W. Cracroft, received allotments in all six of the old open fields and the allotments for tithe and glebe were not conveniently situated to form a farming unit. At Toyntons Manor the Duke of Ancaster received allotments in all parts of the manor, one as lord of the manor, four for tithes, thirteen in his own right and five in exchange. The rector's glebe and tithe allotments were separated but the small proprietors got one allotment each or two close together.

Enclosure provided an opportunity for owners to exchange holdings and to consolidate their lands. At Dalby-cum-Dexthorpe, where nearly the whole of the parish was owned by John Bourne and the Trustees of Beverley Minster, a complicated series of exchanges took place which successfully extinguished holdings in ming and resulted in the two leading proprietors occupying, and being able to lease out, two compact holdings instead of a confusing scatter of fields. The acreages involved in the deeds of exchange which accompanied enclosure could be extensive as at Welton where the trustees for Miss Massingberd gave up 10 plots consisting of 80 acres with two cottages, barns and a stable for 12 plots of over 94 acres in total. About a third of the Lindsey enclosure awards examined by T. H. Swales included deeds of exchange which the commissioners felt able to sanction and to write into the awards. There were 14 deeds of exchange at Market Rasen and Thimbleby and Edlington and 38 at Hagworthingham. These changes involved giving up old enclosure in exchange for new allotments, ending land held in ming and the exchange of land across parish boundaries. Thus the upheaval of enclosure was used by some to consolidate their property and to make the most of a time when change must have brought with it a feeling of release from past constraints.

Yet did this opportunity for change lead to a reduction in the number of small landowners? Were they, despite the consideration given to their rights of property and the need for convenient allotments, driven to sell their holdings because of the cost of fencing them? Besides paying their own share of the legal and fencing costs of enclosure they had to shoulder them for the tithe and glebe owners as well. An enquiry into the effect of enclosure upon the small owner in 35 Lindsey parishes undertaken in 1947 suggested that the decline in the owner-occupier had taken place before the full pressure of Parliamentary enclosure in the last quarter of the eighteenth century had begun.[6] The number of occupying owners was disproportionately less in the old enclosed villages, 14 in number and enclosed before 1790, than in 20 villages enclosed between 1790 and 1830. In villages that were undergoing enclosure the number of occupying owners actually increased. Taking all levels of occupying owner from the large farmer with perhaps 500 acres of his own land down to the owner of a cottage with a close there was a rise in total numbers in 35 villages examined in 1790, 1800, 1812, 1822, and 1830. The rise was rapid and uniform from 1790 to 1812 but less steep from 1812 to 1830. Those owners who paid less than 4s. an acre in land tax, that is owners of less than four acres each, increased markedly in the period 1790 to 1800. Enclosure did not produce an immediate fall in the numbers of small owner-occupiers and their decline after 1830 must be explained by other factors.

What effect it had upon tenant farmers is difficult to assess. Their landlords were responsible for their fencing costs, and provided that they could survive the period of transition when their parish was being directed by the enclosure commissioners then there seems no reason to believe that enclosure reduced their numbers. Yet as is clear from many awards, enclosure was a time for other major reorganizations such as exchanges of land between owners and it must have been a time when the size of holdings on estates came under review. Given the reluctance of many landlords to evict, enclosure and its attendant charges may not have had much effect upon the numbers of tenant farmers. A study of the effect of Parliamentary enclosure upon the numbers on estate rent rolls or surveys would be useful but it would have to take into account the shake-out of tenants caused by the collapse of farming confidence following the end of the Napoleonic war in 1815. That, rather than reorganization of farms because of enclosure, is probably the real cause of a decline in the number of tenants on estates in the first quarter of the nineteenth century. On the Monson estate at Owersby where seventeenth-century enclosure did not involve the disappearance of the small occupier, rent increases between 1729 and 1734 accounted for a reduction in their number but the

[6] J. D. Chambers, 'Enclosure and the Small Landowner in Lindsey', *LH*, vol. II (1947) pp. 15–20.

significant fall occurred after 1805. The 47 tenants of that year had fallen to 19 by 1833. Old rents had totalled £2,210 in 1803–4 while new rents stood at £3,168. Some of these increases were the result of enclosure making farms more eligible, but not until the fall in cereal prices after 1813 would such increases become burdensome to the larger tenants. Few of the tenants of 1805 became substantial farmers. Given a more careful system of estate management, which was probably little more than 'throwing to' small occupations when they became vacant, then the trend towards larger farms and fewer tenants on the estate's roll would be increased yet enclosure would be only one of a number of reasons for it.[7] Consolidation had had its effect by 1833 as the tabulation shows.

1640	Rental shows	82	tenants (47 cottagers, 35 leaseholders)
1704–5	,, ,,	74	,,
1724–9	,, ,,	78	,,
1734–9	,, ,,	63	,,
1744	Survey shows	59	,,
1791–2	Rental ,,	54	,,
1805	Survey ,,	47	,,
1833*c*	List of farms	19	tenants[8]

The sizes of holdings on the figures available show an increase in the period 1744 to 1805.

Size of holding	*1744*	*1805*
Holdings of less than 10 acres (mainly homesteads)	13	21
10 acres–20 acres	13	3
20 acres–30 acres	6	3
30 acres–40 acres	5	1
40 acres–60 acres	3	5
60 acres–80 acres	4	0
80 acres–100 acres	3	3
100 acres–150 acres	3	7
150 acres–300 acres	6	5
300 acres–500 acres	2	0
500 acres or more	1	2
Median, excluding homesteads	50 acres	94 acres[9]

[7] M. W. Barley and P. E. Russell, 'Notes on the Agrarian History of Owersby and Burgh-le-Marsh', *LH*, 11 Spring 1953, p. 384.
[8] L.A.O. Monson 8/48/4.c.
[9] Barley and Russell op. cit., p. 404.

At Owersby, enclosure was slow and piecemeal but in many other parishes where a major award was implemented the cost per acre of the change was vital to those who qualified for one of the general allotments. The process became more expensive, it seems, as the last phase of Parliamentary action was effected.

	Acreage enclosed	*Cost*	*Cost per acre*
Barnetby, 1766–8	2,260 acres	£1,400.13.1d.	12.4½d.
Kirmington, 1777–8	1,643 acres	£1,285.9.5d.	15.7½d.
Kirton Lindsey, 1793–1801	4,325 acres	£5,267.16.0d.	£1.4.4d.
Hibaldstow, 1796–1803	4,233 acres	£8,243.2.3½d.	£1.18.11d.
Wrawby cum Brigg, 1800–5	2,976 acres	£4,950.2.10d.	£1.13.3d.

The costs of fencing and ditching, of course, were additional to the cost per acre for the Act and its implementation. At Wrawby, for example, the costs of enclosure were £4,950.2s.10d. of which £1,153.8s.10d. went to fence the allotments made in place of tithe. The cost of hedging and fencing the general allotments would be several thousand pounds. Fees made up a proportion of the costs of enclosure and the roads, drains and bridges and fencing the tithe allotments, all of which can be considered improvements, accounted for just under half of the costs.

	£	s.	d.
Fees to the Clerk to the Commissioners, Richard Nicholson of Brigg, including payment for business done previous to the Enclosure (soliciting the Act)	705	6	7
Parliamentary Fees	263	15	6
Surveyor's Fees	566	7	6
Arbitrator's Fees (John Renshaw of Owthorpe, Notts)	27	6	0
Road Making	433	16	0
Drain and Bridges	768	11	0
Incidents and other Solicitor's Fees	161	1	8
Fencing 1. Fencing the Tithe Allotments	1,153	8	10
2. S. side of East Field	53	14	6
Commissioner's Fees: Mr Turner	245	14	0
Mr Leatham	277	11	0
Mr Teal	283	10	0

How the costs were shared between the recipients of general allotments is shown below. Robert Cary Elwes the leading proprietor with 1,372 acres heads the list with a share of £3,061.13s.5d. in costs. Clare Hall, Cambridge, had its 20 acres uncharged with enclosure costs.

The General Allotments	*Share of Enclosure Costs* £.	s.	d.	*Allotments in acres, roods and perches*
1. Robert Carey Elwes, Esq.	3,061	13	5	1,372.1. 9.
2. George Kennington	316	10	3	219.2.14.
3. Lord Yarborough	241	19	0	160.3.16.
4. Catherine James	182	13	8	101.2.28.
5. John Scholfields, Esq.,	110	15	0	50.2.16.
6. Francis Coulson	69	3	3	41.2.35.
7. Clare Hall, Cambridge	—	—	—	20.1.16.
8. William Middleton	28	1	11	15.2. 2.
9. John Dunn	29	8	2	13.1. 2.
10. Elizabeth Corbett	14	18	4	11.3. 8.
11. Samuel Driffield	21	15	4	11.2.28.
12. Ann Dunn	24	10	8	9.3.30.
13. Josias Cockshutt, Esq.,	6	11	8	8.0.20.
14. Robert Cutsforth	24	10	5	8.0. 4.
15. Sir Henry Nelthorpe	30	15	9	7.3.31.
16. Devisees of John Wright	35	10	0	7.1.13.
17. John Pope	14	8	2	6.0.16.
18. William Dunn	14	8	5	6.0.12.
19. John Middleton	18	7	4	5.0.33.
20. Theophilus Kirke	14	7	8	4.3.22.
21. Ann Brittain	14	7	5	4.3.12.
22. Stephen Wilson	14	10	5	4.2.32.
23. John Kelk	14	11	10	4.2.10.
24. Edward Young	14	18	10	3.3.38.
25. William Watson, Esq.,	15	6	8	3.2.25.
26. John Nainby	7	11	1	3.0.13.
27. George Hammond	9	19	1	2.3. 6.
28. The Rev. John Bird	10	0	3	2.2.26.
29. Thomas Ogg	7	12	9	2.2. 5.
30. Jane Cliffe, Widow	11	8	6	2.1.24.
31. William Foster	7	11	6	2.1. 8.
32. Charles Nainby	7	10	5	2.0.16.
33. William Pennythorne	7	12	4	2.0.29.
34. Henry Bentley and Richard Nicholson	7	18	5	1.2.36.
35. Nathaniel Holmes	4	16	8	1.0.20.
36. William Robinson	3	19	0	1.0. 8.
37. Francis Hudson		15	0	1.0. 4.
38. The Rev. John Parkinson		10	0	0.2.32.
39. William Abey		10	0	0.2.32.
40. Christopher Richardson		5	0	0.1.12.

An analysis of the cost of Parliamentary costs of the Wrawby Act shows that at this early stage, fees accounted for about 5 per cent of the total cost.

An Account of Expenses in passing the Wrawby Inclosure Act by G. and T. White, House of Commons (from the Stubbs' Deposit, Lincolnshire Archives Offices. This is a slight abbreviation of the complete account).

	£.	s.	d.
Perusing, settling and altering the Bill	4	4	0
Making Copy of Bill for the House	9	2	0
Brief and Copy for the Speaker	1	4	0
Copies of Committee on the Bill		10	0
Preparing amendments for the Committee	1	11	6
Filling up and altering Bills	1	16	0
Making Copies of Clauses		8	0
Paid House Fees on Petition and Bill	28	15	4
Paid Committee Clerks fees	10	19	8
Paid Housekeepers and Messengers fees	1	10	0
Paid Doorkeepers for delivering bills	1	1	0
Making 2 Bills complete for Ingrossers and press	1	4	0
Paid Ingrossing Fees and Gratuity to Writers	56	8	6
Assistance to examine Ingrossment and proofs	3	15	0
Paid Gratuities to Housekeeper, 4 Messengers and others	2	7	0
Printing Bill and Act	39	3	6
Sending a Bill to the Lord in the Chair and attending him	2	2	0
Paid House fees at Lords	54	0	0
Paid for Orders for Committee	1	1	0
Paid Committee Clerk's Fee and Gratuity	4	4	0
Paid Yeoman Usher and Doorkeepers ditto	5	3	0
Paid for Swearing Witnesses		4	0
Porters, Postage and other small Expenses	3	3	0
Solicitation Fee	21	0	0
(Total)	£254	16	6

Owners could not economize on the standard of fencing and ditching for the commissioners stated in the Wrawby award that definite requirements had to be met. Ditches in the High Field, Mill Field and East Field were to be three feet and a half wide at the top, two feet deep and six inches wide at the bottom. In Brigg Field and North Field they were to be four feet wide at the top, two and a half feet deep and one foot wide at the bottom. On the Commons ditches were deeper at three feet and wider at five feet at the top and one foot at the bottom. Good, thriving quicksetts of white thorns were to be planted fifteen inches from the edge of the ditches supported by posts and rails. Where ditches ran over hills or across ridge and furrow land their depth had to be increased so as to make the flow of water certain. Such instructions gave the countryside a new, ordered appearance, and employment was created for hedgers, ditchers and suppliers of quicksetts; occupiers began to farm within an improved context. They were, while the commissioners held authority, men under orders and although their temporary masters must have been fitful in their supervision if only because they took on so much work in other parishes, the owner-occupiers of the newly enclosed lands emerged as farmers who had survived a revolution. Tenants of the proprietors did not meet the costs of enclosure and though the upheaval of it must have inconvenienced many of them and perhaps caused some to throw up their tenancies, for the most part, where they could work with their landlords to effect improvements, then enclosure was indeed a new beginning in which capability, skill and enterprise were likely to be rewarded. It was a restatement of the relationship which had already been created between the landlord who provided the land, buildings and capital works in return for rent and the tenant who concentrated his capital in seed, equipment, horse power, stock and fertilizer. Given trust between the two, supported by a county system for guaranteeing compensation for unexhausted improvements, then once enclosure had been effected one had the main conditions for success. An example of a landlord's expenses in effecting enclosure once an award had been made is afforded by Sir John Dashwood—King's executors' accounts in 1793 for Dunston.

			£.	s.	d.
By Cash paid for the Expenses of the Inclosure					
Rd. Ellerby Pr. Bill for fencing with Posts and Rails			419	2	0
Jon Robinson	-do-	-do-	205	0	10
Thos. Weatherhogg	-do-	-do-	139	16	7
Jas. Cattin Pr. Bill for stone walling			50	17	7½
Rd. Wooldridge	-do-		44	0	3
W. Showler for banking Pr. Bill			153	16	10
Ditto for Board looking after the Workmen			12	0	0
Expenses delivering the Tickets to the Contractors for fencing			1	7	4½
T. Foster for Sod Walling			61	17	3

A total of nearly £1,088.[10]

On a part of the estate valued at £836 a year in 1792 a calculation was made to allow for the interest of 4½ per cent on the expenditure made on enclosure and to set the interest charge against the annual rent. It shows the heavy costs of draining the Fen and enclosing the higher ground and the costs incurred by a landlord in setting out his farms for the tenants.

[10] MSS., D. D. Dashwood, (Bucks.) E/2/12.

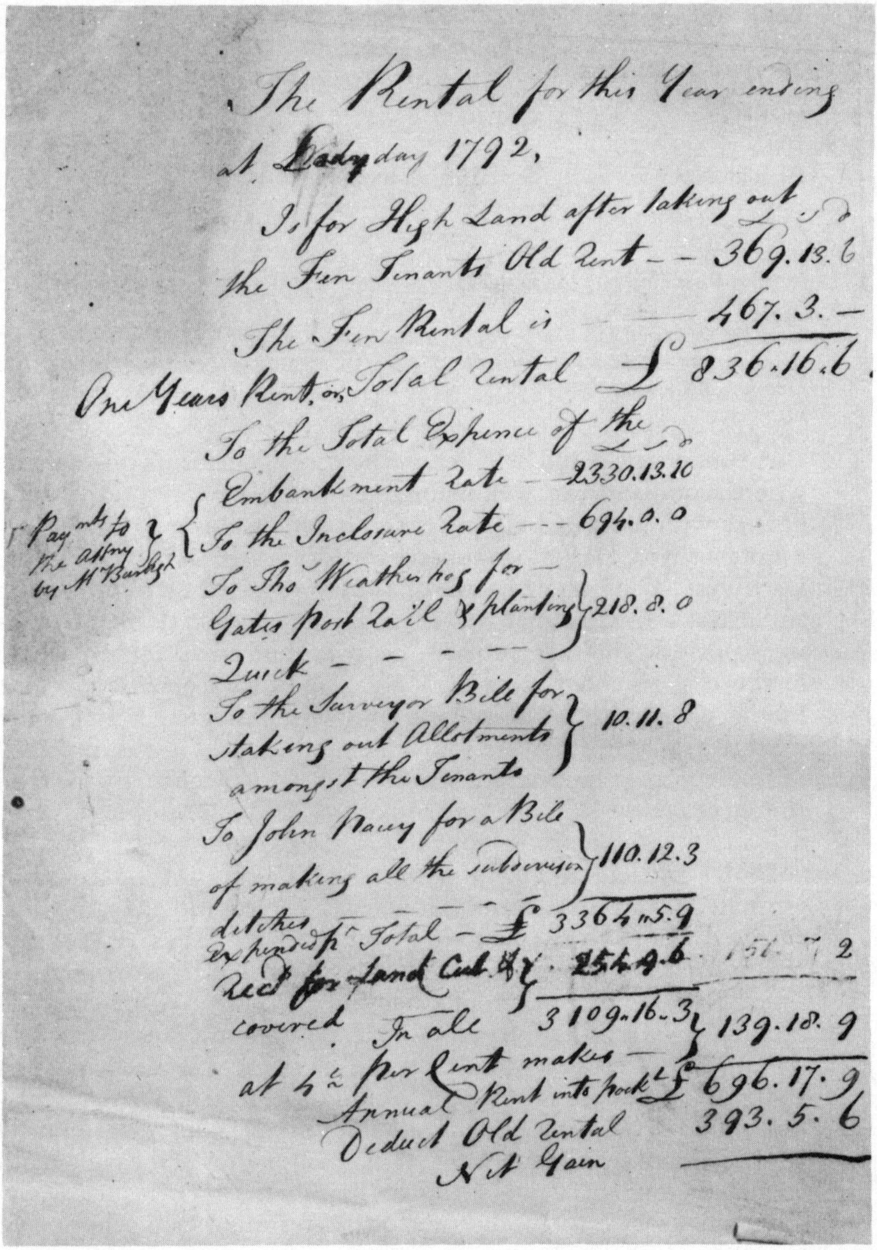

The Rental for this Year ending
at Ladyday 1792,
Is for High Land after taking out £ s d
the Fen Tenants Old Rent -- 369.13.6
The Fen Rental is — 467. 3. –
One Years Rent, or, Total Rental £ 836.16.6
To the Total Expence of the £ s d
Embankment Rate — 2330.13.10
Paym.ts to the attorney by M Bartlett { To the Inclosure Rate --- 694.0.0
To Thos Weatherhog for Gates post Rail & planting Quick — — — } 218.8.0
To the Surveyor Bill for staking out Allotments amongst the Tenants } 10.11.8
To John Nauy for a Bill of making all the subdivision ditches } 110.12.3
Expended Total — £ 3364.5.9
Recd for land Cut &c } 254.9.6 157.7.2
covered In all 3109.16.3 } 139.18.9
at 4½ per Cent makes
Annual Rent into pock.t £ 696.17.9
Deduct Old Rental 393.5.6
Net Gain

Figure 3. Estate records, Dunston (on the Heath) 1793, showing estimated profit arising from the enclosure of the common lands. (Bodleian Library, MSS D. D. Dashwood E2/12)

To the Total Expense of the Embankment Rate	£2,330	13s.	10d.
To the Inclosure Rate	694	0s.	0d.
To Thos. Weatherhogg for Gates, Post, Rail and Planting Quick	218	8s.	0d.
To the Surveyor Bill for staking out Allotments amongst the Tenants	10	11s.	8d.
To John Navy for a Bill for making all the subdivision ditches	110	12s.	3d.
	£3,364	5s.	9d.

Received for land cut and covered	254	9s.	6d.
In all	3,109	16s.	3d.
at 4½ per cent makes	139	18s.	9d.
Annual Rent into pock[t] (£836.16s.6d. less 139.18s.9d.)	696	17s.	9d.
Deduct Old Rental	393	5s.	6d.
Net Gain	303	12s.	3d.

A timber sale could help defray the cost of enclosure on an estate where woodland was well maintained and there was a ready market. As with meeting building costs so with enclosure; timber sales might provide large amounts of ready cash. In 1773 on the Dashwood-King estate a sum of £943 was raised by a timber sale and it was estimated that within the next two years two more sales were possible and that similar sums would be raised at each. Much of the cost of enclosure was likely to be met from them, while leaving all the improving and growing wood standing.[11] Enclosure itself increased the demand for timber and some of it was imported to small ports or havens like Mabelthorpe from Memel, by the Hull suppliers Messrs. Dixon and Moxon who, for example, in 1775 delivered large quantities for the Ormsby estate.[12]

In the calculations made in 1792 for the Dunston estate of the estimated profit on enclosure, it was assumed that the Heath when enclosed would fetch 5s. an acre in rent and 'the Fields' (that is land below the Heath but above the fen land), would be worth 12s. an acre. Expenses of getting an amendment to the Act, fencing and other costs would be 37 years' purchase upon the improved field rental and interest was allowed for at 4½ per cent. It was thought that an increase of some £206 a year would be obtained. These calculations must have been repeated time and time again in the accounts of land agents all over Lincolnshire in the last quarter of the eighteenth century as owners tried to estimate the benefits of enclosure. Many of the agents were themselves enclosure commissioners who appear to have entered the revolutionary period of parliamentary enclosure as land agents or stewards and to have done well in it. Certainly

[11] L.A.O. MCD/489/11/11. [12] L.A.O. MM 7/1A/188.

their influence is hard to over-estimate and some account of them as commissioners is essential for an understanding of enclosure.

The most striking example of wealth and regional influence in Lincolnshire is that of John Burcham of Coningsby, who left on his death in 1841 a fortune which in part at least came from fees and contracts made during his busy life as an enclosure commissioner. When he took on Grimsby as the sole commissioner in 1827 he had 26 years' experience in effecting enclosure awards. His preoccupation with other schemes and with his, by then, varied business activity was a major reason for the slow progress of Grimsby's enclosure. It was not completed until 1840. Yet pressure from an expanding settlement had been increasing since at least 1796 when a new dock for the Haven Company was started. From 1799 building sites, 12 yards by 30 yards, were being set out along the turnpike road and let on 99 year leases. A dispute with Cleethorpes over the boundary came to a head in 1829, when eight men were imprisoned for removing animals from the Cleethorpes pinfold, and in 1830 when the boundary line was settled at Lincoln Assizes. No wonder then that the Grimsby freeholders voted 166 to 30 in January 1827 for the corporation to petition Parliament for a Bill. If they hoped for a speedy settlement they were to be disappointed for John Burcham was made their commissioner.[13] As principal steward to the Earl of Yarborough he had in addition been associated with about 65 enclosures in Lincolnshire, Rutland, Leicestershire, Nottinghamshire and Huntingdonshire. One of his earliest commissions appears to have been at Sotby in 1801 and his fees were something like £2.12s.6d. a day at Alvingham, Binbrook, Hogsthorpe, Swallow and Burton Stather but when implementing later awards he received £3.3s.0d. a day at, for example, Witham-on-the-Hill, Ulceby, Habrough, Grimsby and Trusthorpe. At North Kelsey the Act stated that the commissioners were to receive a total of £500 each, £400 when they had set out the allotments and £100 when the whole Award was executed. North Kelsey was enclosed between 1813 and 1840 and it appears that John Burcham received £800.[14] His last assignment was at North Thoresby in 1836 which was probably the sixty-ninth award with which he was associated.

In addition to this activity he seems to have held many mortgages on a large number of Lincolnshire properties owned by his employer the Earl of Yarborough.[15] He advanced large sums to the

[13] E. E. Gillett, Rex C. Russell, E. K. Trevitt, *The Enclosure of Scartho, 1795–1798 and Grimsby 1827–1840*, Grimsby, 1964.

[14] Ibid., p. 57. [15] L.A.O. Yarb. 3/2/7/1.

Yarborough estate in the 1830s on land in Ketsby, Worlaby, Ruckland, Cawkwell, Wold Newton, Beesby-cum-Hawerby, North Thoresby, Roxton and Immingham and South Killingholme. In 1834 further mortgages were executed on Grimsby, Clee, Weelsby, Scartho, Thornton College, East Halton and Gaxhill. From 1830, when he advanced £140,000 to the estates, his provision of cash rose to £277,000 by 1839. After repayments by Lord Yarborough and his heir, £294,462 was still owing to John Burcham's executors in April 1842. These were surely vast sums for a land agent to command and they serve as a reminder that it is amongst men of his station that one should look for the source of some of the vital working capital that was to make Lincolnshire agriculture so notable in the mid-nineteenth century. After his death John Burcham's executors could hold £303,000 against the estate. They were paid £246,000 and the remainder of £57,000 was paid on behalf of the estate by the Duke of Sutherland and the Hon. Robert Henry Clive of Oakley Park, Salop in 1844.[16] On 10 September 1841 the *Stamford Mercury* said that his two married daughters Mary Hardwicke and Sophia Best had inherited his fortune of over £600,000.

Though powerful, the enclosure commissioner was placed under strict rules by the oath prescribed in the Act. With the Surveyor, the commissioners at Scawby, enclosed 1770–1, swore that they would '... faithfully, impartially, and honestly according to the best of my Skill and Judgement, execute and perform the several Powers and Authorities vested in me as a Commissioner or Surveyor ... and ... make just and fair Allotments of the said Lands and Grounds to the several Persons interested therin; and that without Favour or Affection, Prejudice or Malice, to any person whatsoever'. One of the other commissioners or a Justice of the Peace would witness the oath. The commissioners were now ready to begin their task which can be summarized in 20 major steps though, of course, the sequence below was not always followed exactly.

1. A first meeting of commissioners was held, often in the local inn, after fourteen days' notice had been given on the church door or in a Lincolnshire newspaper.
2. A survey was ordered as there was rarely a satisfactory map already in existence.
3. A surveyor was appointed who took an oath like the one already taken by the commissioners.
4. The surveyor and his assistants measured the parish, including the areas of old enclosure.

[16] L.A.O. Yarb. 3/2/7/15.

5. A map of the entire parish was produced showing the areas of old enclosure in green. The map was signed by the surveyor and accepted by the commissioners.
6. The commissioners, after giving due notice, held meetings to receive in writing or hear the claims for land or rights in the open fields or the commons. Witnesses could be examined on oath and they could be fined or sent to a House of Correction for three months for refusing to attend. Commissioners could not decide titles of land. Appeals might have to go to Quarter Sessions.
7. When all the claims had been recorded, the commissioners published the lists and met to hear objections.
8. The commissioners set aside land to provide material for road repair, usually from one to six acres.
9. The claims of the lord of the manor were translated into land, his fraction of the waste having been laid down in the Act. It was often one-twentieth.
10. The vicar or rector was given land in lieu of glebe land or common right.
11. The claims of tithe owners were expressed in an allotment of land.
12. The commissioners were now free to make allotments of land.
13. New public and private roads were set out, redundant ones having been closed and made over as part of the general allotments.
14. Provision was made by the commissioners to enable the surveyors of the highways, who were responsible for the upkeep of the public roads under the Act, to maintain them by letting off the pasturage at the sides (after it had been allowed to grow for seven years) or by selling the hay from road sides and around their stone or gravel pits. Footpaths six feet wide were provided and marked on the map.
15. Drains were provided and bridged and rules were made about the size and depth of connecting ditches.
16. The commissioners directed farming during the period while the Act was being effected. They could levy fines and award compensation for distress.
17. The commissioners sometimes held an enquiry to decide a disputed parish boundary.
18. A permanent legal record, the Award, was made.
19. A meeting was called to read, date, stamp, sign and seal the Award. One copy was given to the Church; one was given to

the Clerk of the Peace in Lincoln or to a Court of Record at Westminster. A fee for inspecting and copying parts of the Award was published. If Duchy of Lancaster land was the subject of the Award then the Duchy received a copy.

20. The commissioners then saw that the allotments were fenced, usually within six months, and arrangements were published for receiving payment of the expenses of enclosure by nominating perhaps the lord of the manor as receiver.

When it is remembered that this procedure or one much like it had to be followed each time an award was made, it is not surprising that some commissioners were slow and that distress could result from their delays when they took on too many awards. Their responsibilities could continue long after an award was carried into effect. At Orby, for example, where a tenant farmer was growing turnips in ten acres of the open fields in 1790, it was promised that he should enjoy a rent reduction on his 173-acre farm and then his new rent was to be judged by the commissioners. At Hogsthorpe a similar provision was made for a rent to be fixed by them.

The meetings of the commissioners must have depended upon services from innkeepers and their staff, stationers, instrument-makers, newspaper-publishers, carpenters, printers and those who would hire out horses and gigs. Though few came near John Burcham's record, some dealt with over 20 awards during a working life in which they were active farmers or stewards. It was not unusual for commissioners in Lindsey to be engaged on three or four awards at the same time. Samuel Turner of Cammeringham was involved with five or six enclosures when in 1793 he began work on Kirton Lindsey and before he was finished there he had committed himself to 14 further enclosures. Described in the *Stamford Mercury* on 4 July 1817 as '... a man very generally esteemed and respected' he had been involved in 27 enclosures, only two of which were out of Lincolnshire; Caunton and East Stoke in Nottinghamshire. His first was at Ludford in 1791–5 and the last to be finished was Hogsthorpe and Mumby-cum-Chapel in 1811. Another of the Kirton Lindsey commissioners, John Parkinson of Asgarby had undertaken at least 15 parishes and took on nine more before he had finished at Kirton Lindsey. In all he appears to have tackled 30 enclosures from Welton le Wold in 1770 to Burton Stather, Thealby and Coleby in 1806. He was agent for Sir Joseph Banks of Revesby Abbey. John Grantham of Stallingborough was engaged in seven enclosures from Keelby in 1765–6 to Winterton in 1770–2. Mathew Maw of Bigby acted as a commissioner in eleven

Linsey enclosures from Barnetby-le-Wold 1766–8 to Amcotts in 1779. Benjamin Codd, a tenant of 900 acres under the Earl of Scarbrough at Glentworth, was a commissioner for nearby Kirton Lindsey and for 14 other enclosures between 1794, when he first appeared at Faldingworth, to Caistor Moor between 1811 and 1814. In that time he had assisted at Gainsborough 1795–1804, Isle of Axholme Commons 1795 and Morton in 1796. Sir John Nelthorpe's steward and agent, John Wilbur of Barton-on-Humber was a commissioner at Hibaldstow, Caistor, Barrow-on-Humber and South Ferriby, all between 1796 and 1804. He had served too as a surveyor at Barton. A notable Nottinghamshire commissioner, John Renshaw of Owthorpe with 16 enclosures to his record in his own county engaged in 12 Lincolnshire enclosures from Gainsborough in 1795 to Wildmore Fen and Ashby in Bottesford, both started in 1801. [17]

Not all the Lincolnshire commissioners were from the county. Nottinghamshire was joined by Yorkshire in providing some of them. Isaac Leatham from Barton-le-Street had written the *General Report on the Agriculture of the East Riding* in 1794 for the Old Board of Agriculture. After acting for East Riding enclosures he undertook Wrawby, Louth, Sotby, Belchford, Burton Stather and Coleby and Swallow. Jonathan Teal of Leeds worked as a surveyor or commissioner for some 24 parishes in Yorkshire and came to Wrawby as a commissioner. John Lund of Bootham, York, assisted at Market Rasen. John Dalton of Hessle who did surveying at Barton-on-Humber, Barrow-on-Humber, South Ferriby and Burton and at Thealby and Coleby appears like some of the commissioners to have taken on too much for at a meeting at the Angel Hotel Brigg, 18–20 February 1802, he was reprimanded and threatened with replacement for failing to supply the essential details for the drawing up of the Wrawby Award. Starting in 1774, William Fillingham of Syerston Hall was a commissioner for 23 Nottinghamshire, 12 Lincolnshire and 7 Leicestershire awards as well as one in Derbyshire and another in Rutland. He was also a successful farmer with investments in canals.[18]

Anthony Bower of Lincoln advertised for assistants in the *Stamford Mercury* in 1802. He required four 'perfect masters of surveying' to help him keep up with the demands of the commissioners he was

[17] Peter Eden, *Dictionary of Land Surveyors and Local Cartographers of Great Britain and Ireland, 1559–1850*, Folkestone, 1975, has biographical details of many Lincolnshire enclosure commissioners.

[18] K. S. S. Train, 'The Fillinghams of Syerston Hall', *Trans. Thoroton Society*, Vol. 74, 1970, pp. 22–30.

serving. Pressure of business often appears to have affected their choice of inns for their meetings. Unless members of the public had to be invited, and this was not always the case, they met where their many engagements allowed. Commissioners were allowed £2.2s. a day and surveyors from 2s. a day with 1s.6d. for assistants. In the case of the Hibaldstow enclosure 1796–1803, John Parkinson and John Wilber appear to have collected more than their fellow commissioner John Renshaw. He was given £178 while Parkinson received £256 and Wilber a little over £278. He seems to have spent 133 days on the work for Hibaldstow spread over eight years as follows, 17 days in 1796, 51 in 1797, 16 in 1798, 17 in 1799, 16 in 1800, 6 in 1801, 6 in 1802 and 4 days only in 1803. No doubt 1800 saw the main task of the commissioners completed. They had met at the Inn of Mrs Rebecca Good at Spital-in-the-Street, at the Angel, Brigg, at the Reindeer, Lincoln, twice at the Saracen's Head, Lincoln, at the White Lion, Brigg, and at the Angel, Sleaford, to suit the agent of the lord of the manor. They twice repaired to the Inn at Redbourn in 1800, once for three days in February and secondly for a day in May. Their expenses for the visits reminds us of the effects of such activity on the social as well as the business life of the towns and larger villages.

	£.	s.	d.
10 dinners	1	0	0
Ale and Porter		6	0
2 bottles of sherry		9	0
9 bottles of Red port	1	11	6
Oranges, Apples and Biscuits		6	8
Tobacco, etc.		1	0
10 Teas		10	0
	4	4	2

Waiter 10s.6d., Ostler 7s, Chamber Maid 7s, Boots 2s.6d.

They were to discuss the enclosure still further at the White Hart, Gainsborough, at Redbourn again in 1802 and finally at the White Hart, Lincoln in January 1803. The hotel trade can only have been affected temporarily by the many meetings of commissioners in various parts of the county but the expectations raised by enclosure must have had a stimulating effect upon apparently unlikely aspects of business life. More obviously, it made work in the parishes for others besides the innkeeper who in the autumn and winter mornings had to pack luncheon baskets for the commissioners as they saw the restaking and actual allotment going on, when farmers had harvest safely behind them and they could give time to the great rearrangement of their familiar surroundings. For the labourer John

Middleton at Hibaldstow it meant work when he was given the task of fencing the tithe allotments for the commissioners at £2.4s. for every 28 yards. For the cabinet-maker William Johnson from Barton-on-Humber it meant work too in supervising this part of the enclosure. New drains demanded cutters and new roads had to be surfaced so at Scotter the commissioners met at the Sun Inn to receive tenders for forming and stoning the Gainsborough and Kirton roads in June 1810. In April 1811 they appealed in the *Stamford Mercury* for offers to the specification for roads thirteen feet wide and ten inches thick, covered to eleven feet wide and four inches thick with 'medium-sized Spurn gravel'. The gravel would come along the Humber and the Trent to be landed at Susworth. Tetney's new facings for the sea banks which were constructed during enclosure came down the Humber from Hessle. They required 2,600 tons of stone. The cleaning of ash pollards and 'firewood' growing in Helpstone fields made work in 1811 when as part of the enclosure felling had to start. That enclosure gave to the landscape a denuded look at first is likely, especially as the need for timber was great and local as well as foreign or regional supplies were taken. Once the hedgerows developed and the planting of trees for sale or to provide fox and game cover became established, then it must have recovered its wooded appearance in a different pattern. The *Stamford Mercury* in October 1811 advertised a sale at Helpstone of 1,450 willow trees in 60 lots, 'the most part fit to saw into boards and rails, and the greatest part with very fine tops which will split into rails, the remainder fit for hurdles....'[19]

Enclosure increased the demand for labour to keep up the new works. The roads, fences, drains, bridges, gates, sea walls, jetties and new farm buildings meant more activity for a host of rural tradesmen. Nurserymen like Benjamin Bull of Wyberton near Boston must have enjoyed good business. He offered 'ten hundred thousand of exceeding good and strong thorn quick' for sale in 1796.[20] Hull and Newark felt the demand in Lincolnshire for quickthorns. In 1805 Messrs Ordoyno and Gaunt of Newark were offering two-year old white thorn quicksetts. '... clean and well-rooted. They are well worth the notice of those Gentlemen engaged in planting new Inclosures, and will be sold low....'[21] An advertisement in the *Stamford Mercury* for 29 October 1824, indicates a demand at Ulceby for both labour and hedging.

'A number of Workmen wanted to complete the Works upon the

[19] See L.A.O. RA 2/A/1/1–4 for evidence of wood sales at Revesby Abbey.
[20] *SM.*, 4 November 1796.
[21] *SM.*, 25 February 1805.

... Inclosure; Application to be made to the Agent upon the work. Also wanted, 300,000 good 3 feet Ash Plants, and 500,000 good strong Quick, a level sample of both sorts, with the lowest price, prompt payment, post and carriage paid, to Rev. Joseph Corbett, Mareham le Fen near Horncastle ... No inferior samples need be sent.' This demand, when added to the demands upon labour and materials for draining, must have increased the general economic activity of the Lincolnshire towns which was in turn reflected in new public buildings, inns, warehouses and shops.

4

The battle against water

As the area fit for cultivation was increased by the bringing into tillage of the old sheep walks, warrens, heaths and the cliff lands north of Lincoln, so in the fenlands of Lincolnshire a process was being painfully worked out to the same end. This process was much older and more steeped in political and personal controversy than the work of increasing cultivatable acreage elsewhere.[1] By the beginning of the eighteenth century much of the fenland had already been drained, especially in the south of the county. A pattern of new channels and dykes now rested upon the older one of meandering streams and slow-moving rivers. Yet dissatisfaction with fenland drainage remained. To some extent the frustration felt by those whose interests demanded good drainage lay in their very success. A mark of progress in removing waterlogged stretches of land was that the land itself began to sink and so it became more vulnerable to flooding. Watercourses were now riding high across sinking acreages of peat and more and more effort was needed to raise the water to them, to embank it there and to convey it safely to the sea. The problems included making sure that the river outfalls to the Wash were adequate, that sand banks were not allowed to form, that sluices were correctly located and well maintained, that silting was reduced and that the nature of tidal scours was well understood. The falling of the land level was, perhaps, the greatest single problem and upon its solution rested the hope for a better use of fenland acreages. Yet natural obstacles were made higher by the addition of human opposition to change and by the conflict of many interests other than those of agriculturists.

At the beginning of the eighteenth century it has been estimated that some 363,000 acres crossed by the rivers Welland, Glen and Witham needed a determined attack by drainers as there were signs of deterioration from the standards of the 1640s.[2] There were,

[1] Joan Thirsk, *English Peasant Farming*, London, 1957, Chapters 1, 2, 5 and 6.
[2] H. C. Darby, *The Draining of the Fens*, Cambridge, 1956, p. 144.

however, those who still opposed draining because of its adverse effect upon dairy farming. They agreed that it caused shortages of fodder, thatch and fish and they voiced their fears in a petition of 1784.[3] Fish, fowl, milk, butter and cheese were essential to the farming economy of many fenmen. Peat for fuel, reeds for roofing and bread from spring corn grown in patches completed a pattern of requirements which their familiar environment satisfied. For them a dry summer was to be feared for it could upset their trade in fish for the London market and reduce the numbers of duck, mallard, teal and widgeon to be caught in their Dutch decoys from Sleaford to Crowland and Wainfleet to Boston. (See Plates 3–6)

Deterioration in the Fen drainage was partly the result of complacency after a period of exertion but more tidal silting may have caused a clogging of outfalls and over that even the most energetic scourer of dikes several miles from the sea had no control. Losses through sheep rot and disease amongst cattle in the 1730s owed something to the bad fen drainage while distemper in cattle in East, West and Wildmore Fens in 1747 may have convinced many farmers that damage on this scale demanded radical remedies.[4] The knowledge that enclosure in the uplands was beginning and that the arrangements for sharing commons were coming under strain through over-stocking and over-grazing probably pushed opinion in favour of draining and enclosure by about 1760. Furthermore the arrangements for effecting the work did not include, as they had done in the seventeenth century, shares of land for the Crown or the engineers and the payment for the drainage by a graduated tax based on expected benefits seemed reasonable and acceptable. Economic conditions about 1760 for the expenditure of large capital sums were favourable. The windmills introduced in the 1720s had drained some areas at the expense of drowning others and they had drawn great quantities of mud into the channels. These were the mills with twelve sails or wings which had impressed Defoe as the more powerful ones threw up 12,000 tons of water in half an hour.[5] In the early nineteenth century it was thought that improved drainage as part of the enclosure of the uplands had increased flooding on the Fens. Formerly water had remained on the land until it evaporated but Arthur Young saw the sudden rises in water levels on the Fens as a function of the enclosed state of the Wolds. Floods were '... caused by the great number of inclosures which have been made

[3] W. H. Wheeler, *South Lincolnshire*, Boston, 1896, p. 211.

[4] Thirsk, op. cit., pp. 206–7.

[5] Daniel Defoe, *A Tour through the Whole Island of Great Britain*, 1724, 1725, and 1727, ed. G. D. H. Cole, 1927.

in the upland counties, whose waters are now carried rapidly to the rivers that flow through the fens'.[6]

The pressures for a new effort against flooding were increasing but as with enclosure the prospect of improved rents and higher values for land on the market exerted its attraction. Meetings of landowners to hear the reports of engineers like John Grundy of Spalding in November 1774 took place in London, and in Lincolnshire towns like Spilsby.[7] Sir Joseph Banks was observed by John Cragg of Threckingham chairing a meeting attended by 70 people in the autumn of 1799 about the draining of Wildmore Fen. It was no easy matter but he conducted business in a 'masterly manner'. Sir Joseph thought that as the Church had done well out of the allotment of land in lieu of tithes it should pay for chapels to be built for the worshippers in the developing settlements.[8] Action against the sea as well as flood water had its financial, even its patriotic, attractions. James Creasy gave an opinion about the embankment of salt marshes at Moulton, Whaplode, Holbeach and Gedney at a meeting of interested parties in London in April 1791. In correspondence with the steward of the Drake estate he observed

'Mr. Drake on the most moderate computation will get as much land as will sell for ten or twelve thousand pounds by the proposed embankment.'

His correspondence stressed that there will be 'no injury to the poor' and that the scheme will give the merit of 'making the Kingdom larger'. There were five landowners interested and their success depended upon the drawing up of a mutually agreeable scheme.[9] It was reckoned that 4,600 acres were involved, of which 4,370 admitted of profit. The cost of £17,765 would not include some £2,234 for costs of getting an Act of Parliament but the salt marshes now worth 2s.6d. an acre would, after four years of protection by an embankment, be worth 14s. an acre or £14.7s.6d. an acre on 25 years' purchase. The cost per acre to each landowner would be £4.11s.6d. and the profit £9.16s.0d. an acre. If £9 an acre clear profit were assumed to allow for loss of interest on money and waiting time it was still '... a very sufficient inducement'.[10]

Local landowners, seeing that the Sewer Commissioners could not deal with the problem of the low, wet lands beside the Witham

[6] Arthur Young, *Annals of Agriculture*, xliii pp. 131 and 551–2.
[7] L.A.O. Tyr 4/3/20.
[8] *LNQ*., vol. II p. 134.
[9] L.A.O. Tyr 4/3/26, 30, 32, 38.
[10] L.A.O. Tyr 4/3/40, Report on South Holland or Holbeach embankment by Peart, Boulton and Kent, for William Drake.

from Lincoln to Boston, secured an Act of Parliament in 1762, which gave them powers over a wide area to Heckington in the south and to Wildmore and West Fens in the east. Six divisions within this were created, each responsible for its own area but with an obligation to relate to the scheme as a whole. The Witham, which had a fall of only 16 feet in 20 miles was widened, deepened and straightened. A quarter of a mile up river from Old Boston Bridge, the Grand Sluice was opened in 1766 to exclude the silt of the tidal waters. Coasting vessels had now access to Lincoln and by Fossdyke to the Trent. The hopes of the Promoters were justified in the short term. Many of the troubles of the Witham fens reported in the 1730s seemed to be at an end. The river had suffered from tributaries which were stronger than itself and the attempts by private effort to put in mills, drains and embankments had not prevented the flooding of thousands of acres of good pasture land for three or four months in the year. The building of the North Forty-foot drain through to Holland Fen was not a success. After 1762, however, the district committees elected by parishes with power to levy rates and to manage pumping stations produced a significant change. Local enclosure Acts followed in individual parishes, and land now protected from flooding by new embankments was letting at from 11s. to 17s. an acre, whereas in its former state it had fetched but 1s. and 6d. an acre.[11] Sir Joseph Banks of Revesby celebrated the opening of the Grand Sluice in 1766 with a great display of hospitality including the serving of strong ale from buckets with the aid of a horn.[12]

Unfortunately the Grand Sluice obstructed the scouring of the tide and the haven silted up again, so causing water to back up and to overflow the river banks miles inland. Reliance on improved gravitation seemed to have been misplaced. The help of windmills was sought to lift water into the Witham, but in wet seasons the lack of wind rendered them ineffective. Steam pumping after 1825 successfully raised water to the level of the river when there was greatest need. Meanwhile, as a result of the Witham Navigation Act of 1812, some work had been completed on the outfall from the Grand Sluice and upon a new channel from Lincoln to Bardney. Even so there were to be disappointments ahead, but contemporaries were optimistic and even self-congratulatory on the success they achieved. Arthur Young quoted the figures of one estimate.[13]

Mr Parkinson's Table of the Improvements in Drainage by Acts in which he was a Commissioner.

[11] H. C. Darby, *The Draining of the Fens*, Cambridge, 1956.

[12] *Lincolnshire Life*, June 1967, p. 51.

[13] Arthur Young, *Gen. View*, 1813, p. 280.

	Acres	Improved Value £	Old Value £	Improvement £
Tattersall embankment	892	838	387	450
Alnwick Fen	1,097	703	54	648
The nine embanked fens to Lincoln	19,418	15,534	1,941	13,592
Holland Fen, eleven towns	22,000	25,300	3,600	21,700
	48,407	42,375	5,982	36,390

In West, East and Wildmore Fens as much as 40,000 acres could turn into a morass in a wet year. They remained unenclosed until 1801 and virtually undrained, for Arthur Young rowed across part of them in 1799. Parishes in Skirbeck Hundred together with some in Lindsey had rights of common there. Arthur Young claimed that one sheep per acre 'rotted' on the three fens and that there was much cattle rustling.[14] Work began on these fens in 1801 and by 1807 most of it was finished, with excellent results. New sluices, weirs and dykes together with widened drains made it possible to push the water into the Witham below the Grand Sluice near Boston. Until the land sank so far as to create the danger of more flooding in the 1860s, it enjoyed a high reputation for its fine crops of oats and cole-seed. In the fenland of Kesteven and in Holland Fen, improvements began under an Act of 1765 and further work on rivers and dykes produced a drier landscape and the inevitable sinking that went with it. Here again, as with the Witham, expensive alterations were contemplated at the end of the Napoleonic Wars, but real progress had to await the adoption of steam engines under the new Acts of 1848 and 1849. By 1868 W. H. Wheeler thought that the level drainage was as near perfect as engineering could make it.[15] J. A. Clarke estimated in 1852 that there had been about 700 windmills at work between Lincoln and Cambridge but that the Lincolnshire Fens were served by 17 steam engines ranging from 10 to 80 horse power, each lifting water from 6 feet to 20 feet and improving something like 222,000 acres.

Since 1765, parishes in Kesteven and Holland had agreed to enclose and drain their fenlands which was some advance at least though Bourne and Morton fens flooded three years out of four and in Great Hale and Heckington the fen flooded every winter from 1795 to 1801.[16] Between the Welland and the Glen lay some 15,000

[14] Arthur Young, *Gen. View*, 1799, p. 223.

[15] W. H. Wheeler, *History of the Fens of South Lincolnshire*, Boston, 1896, p. 108.

[16] David Grigg, *The Agricultural Revolution in South Lincolnshire*, Cambridge, 1966, p. 29.

acres drained in the seventeenth century by the Adventurers, but north of this lay undrained and unenclosed fen held in common by the parishes of Spalding and Pinchbeck. To the south-west some Kesteven parishes held common rights on the fen, led by the most populated one, Market Deeping. The value of their fenland common depended upon the state of the Welland outfall and when, under an Act of 1794, improvements were made to it and an embankment of the waterway to Wyberton Roads was planned, prospects brightened. Although only part of the plan for embanking was effected to Fosdyke Bridge, the commons of Deeping Fen were enclosed in 1801 and real improvement was seen before the familiar story of sinking levels and recourse to windmills began. About 50 mills were too few to make certain the carriage of water out of the ten to Vernatt's Sluice from Pode Hole, where the interior drains joined. Near the border with Cambridgeshire between the Welland and the lowest part of the Nene, drainage depended on local cuts to the sea, as this area had seen no major schemes. An area along the Old Shire Drain was well served and, unlike most of this district, was relatively dry in the 1790s when the rest of it was in a lamentable condition. Under an Act of 1792 the South Holland Main drain was cut from west to east to join the Nene outfall at Peter's Point. John Rennie who drew up a plan in 1813 for a through drainage system wrote of the flooding of thousands of acres in the winter and spring. The decay of the Nene outfall, improved as long ago as 1753 by the making of Kinderley's cut, was the cause.[17]

Although the Fens had to await the arrival of steam pumping before drainage problems came near to solution, attempts to keep water off the land were accompanied by other changes. The most important of these was enclosure. It was not inevitable that newly drained fens would be enclosed but although in some parishes there was a long time lag between draining and division into severalty, in most parishes one improvement led to the other. Over 80 per cent of the fen parishes of Holland and Kesteven were affected by Parliamentary enclosure, a higher proportion than anywhere else in the county.[18] The complications were greater too where for example in East, West and Wildmore Fens 50 parishes had rights of

[17] For a fuller discussion of the disappointing results of late eighteenth century drainage schemes see Grigg's, *Agricultural Revolution in South Lincolnshire*, pp. 23–32; J. Rennie, *A Plan for Completely Draining South Holland*, London, 1813; *Report and Plan for the Improvement of the Outfall to the Sea . . . and for the Drainage of the North Level and South Holland*, London, 1814; J. Carter, *Observations on the Proposed Improvement of the Nene Outfall in reference to the Drainage of South Holland*, Spalding, 1822.

[18] Joan Thirsk, *English Peasant Farming*, London, 1957, p. 213.

common. Overstocking, disease, injury, flooding and the drying up of pastures in droughts made even the most conservative consider new ways. A realization that better sheep and cattle were now being produced elsewhere added weight to the arguments of the enclosers. From 1766 to 1806 enclosure went on steadily in Kirton Wapentake but in Elloe and Skirbeck it took longer. As late as 1844 the awards for East, West and Wildmore Fens had not been finally executed, owing to disputes about payment, though the owners were in full possession of their allotments. In Holland Fen, 1768–73, serious disturbances over enclosure involved the invasion of a Boston attorney's office and the destruction of papers by angry fenlanders. Rick-burning, sheep-maiming and the demolition of gates greeted the completion of enclosure. There had been popular opposition to the Commissioners here as early as 1757. Six Boston magistrates had written to William Burrell Massingberd at Ormsby about the activities of 200 people who attacked the dams in West Fen and of the need to have a ready company of dragoons and two companies of foot to restrain them.[19] Yet small farmers survived the enclosure and small farms in the Fens continue to prosper in this century. Arthur Young observed 'In the parish of Frieston, containing about 3,000 acres, there is not one plot of more than 48 acres together, belonging to one person; some late purchasers have raised it to 60 acres.'[20]

Across the Trent in north-west Lindsey, the Isle of Axholme farmers, though troubled by flooding, had by careful management, turned the inundations of the tidal river to good account by warping their land. Silt was deposited on fields which had been banked off from the rest when water from the river was allowed on to them. Like their fenland counterparts, the islanders were occupiers of a mere four or five acres but they were hard-working, independent and happy according to Arthur Young's description of them. They relied on family labour, neighbourliness, barter, hire and frugal living. Their soil was fertile. They grew corn, potatoes, hemp, flax and beans. Their aim in life was to buy another piece of land. To this end they would '... work like negroes' and put up with a standard of living lower than that in the poor house. An owner of 20 acres, however, could support a family in some comfort. Though these observations hardly applied to the fenland farmers of south Lincolnshire their wish to own land was equally strong. The importance of the small owner was not upset by the carving out of some

[19] Op. cit., p. 214; L.A.O. MM. 7/1A/162.

[20] Arthur Young, *Gen. View*, 1813, pp. 22, 19; Revd W. B. Stonehouse, *The History and Topography of the Isle of Axholme*, London, 1839, p. 33.

large farms in the newly drained and enclosed parishes. Deeping St. Nicholas, created in 1846 out of Deeping Fen, had 53 of its 73 holdings with more than 100 acres each. That was 72 per cent as against an 11 per cent proportion for the Fens as a whole. Kesteven had most farms of a large size—100 acres and over—Axholme had the smallest farms of five acres and under. Holland, Kesteven and Axholme had roughly the same proportion of, for these regions, 'middling' farms of 5–20, 20–50 acres and 5–100 acres in the 1870 national returns for farm sizes.

Another change which better drainage facilitated was the paring and burning of peat soils in preparation for crops which were followed by pasture. The surface of peat by the 1870s was probably only 3–4 feet from a former depth of 5–8 feet in parts of the Fens. From the 1820s the digging up of the clay which lay beneath it had become widely practised. When clay was mixed with peat evaporation was reduced and the soil became more solid. Siliceous matter was thus available for the wheat stem and the peat still present in the soil gave carbon for the green leaf and stalk of cole. The result was a highly fertile, productive soil for wheat, oats, cole-seed and turnips worth in the 1850s, James Caird believed, 35s. an acre.

How the newly-won land was held for cultivation and how the victory of the drainers over flooding was made secure is the story of steam-pumping. Though difficulties lay ahead the land had been won for cultivation. It now remained to make good the farmers' hold over it. In the Napoleonic wars optimism in this campaign was high. Sir Joseph Banks wrote in 1801 to Lord Liverpool that arrangements for the enclosure of 40,000 acres involving 50 parishes were complete and that cultivation of 20,000 acres of private land could begin. In 1805 he thought these changes were more significant than Napoleon's victory at Austerlitz. Land was fetching, he claimed, £30 to £50 an acre with the purchasers paying the costs of enclosure. He continued 'The quality of land which is to be won to the public from thistles in summer and wild ducks in winter as you have seen, and which did not, I am confident, on any average of years bring to the occupier 5s. an acre or indeed 1s. to the landlord, is 40,000 acres at £50 an acre, that is, £2,000,000 of money ...'[21] About the same time Lord Monson was the principal owner in the Lincoln West Drainage, which released some 4,000 acres in a scheme of 1804 devised by John Rennie. He had seen before his death that more than wind power was needed to hold the hardly-won gains of the drainers. His suggestion for a steam-engine system

[21] National Library of Wales, MSS., 12415, E34; Banks Letters, p. 466, quoted by Sir Francis Hill, *Georgian Lincoln*, Cambridge, 1966, p. 175.

at Pode Hole was not taken up when Thomas Pear reported on the unhappy state of the Deeping Fen in 1815. Some 30,000 acres were depending upon 50 windmills for their safety. Rennie's suggestion in 1818 of an expensive new cut of 8½ miles to Hobhole which would cost £123,000 and improve 13,000 acres without the application of steam-power was, not surprisingly, rejected on the grounds of cost. Suspicion of steam, conservatism, the fall in agricultural prices after about 1813, fears of running costs and reluctantly-surrendered faith in the efficacy of gravitational drainage combined to hold up the recourse to steam-power. Then in 1823 Thomas Pear advised steam-power for Deeping Fen and Parliament gave authority to the Trustees to apply it and to call for a rate of 15s. per acre with a further 5s. on the consent of three-fifths of the owners.[22] Management was made easier by a consolidation of the trusts in 1856.[23]

Two steam engines named appropriately 'Kesteven' of 60 horsepower and 'Holland' of 80 horsepower were erected in 1825.[24] Both ran until 1925. Together they cost £17,000 and they drained 30,000 acres. A windmill cost £1,000 to build in 1800. By 1830 the Pode Hole engines were costing £100 per horsepower, which was expensive. In October 1829 a test was staged and it was decided that running costs could be reduced by improving the state of the drains and by allowing more water into the drains near the engines. More water meant fewer dips to raise the same amount, so by keeping the drains high, costs could be contained. Steam clearly did not reduce the need and therefore the demand for labour to attend to the drains; indeed its application made cleaner drains essential. Lord Carrington suggested calling in an expert, R. Mylve, to give an opinion; the resulting scheme cost £7,000 and involved the removal of a privately owned windmill. It was found that Yorkshire coal had to be used at the rate of 10½ lbs. per horsepower per hour, whereas only 8 or 9 lbs. of Newcastle coal were needed for the same result. Steam then, used for so long in mine drainage in the Durham and other coalfields, had at last come to fen drainage. James Watt had shown an interest in its application to land drainage in 1769, but the firm of Boulton and Watt did not supply complete engines and the need to deal with more than one supplier may have inhibited the drainers

[22] W. D. Miles, *A History of Deeping Fen and Pode Hole Pumping Station*, Spalding, 1965; 4 Geo. IV *c.* 76, 1823.

[23] 19 and 20 Vict. *c.* 65, 1856.

[24] Richard L. Hills, *Machines, Mills and Uncountable Costly Necessities*, Cambridge, 1967, p. 157. Much of the following description is based on his book, especially pp. 48–53, 120–8.

from using steam, especially when they had a well-tried alternative in wind-power which was free. The fenlands were distant from the coalfields and before the coming of the railways fuel supplies were expensive. The use of steam to augment wind was, however, considered in 1803 when Rennie suggested a steam engine to help a windmill raise more water to Fossdyke and the Witham. He used steam portables to pump out water from his drainage works and some of these small engines he mounted in boats. Once the application of steam was made at Pode Hole other engines were erected in a period when admittedly the worst of the post-war farming depression was lifting but when prospects for agriculture were still uncertain. An engine for South Fen at Pinchbeck costing £3,000 for 20 horsepower for 3,000 acres appeared in 1829 while in 1833 a 20 horsepower engine to tackle 4,000 acres was built for Spalding Marsh. Nocton, Potterhanworth and Branston acquired a 40 horsepower engine for some 5,600 acres in 1834–5 and others in Blankney, 1834–5, Timberland, 1839, and the Bardney-Stixwould engine of 30 horsepower to tackle 2,610 acres of 1846, were among the early applications of steam to the Witham fens. The Deeping Fen cost worked out at from 1s to 1s.4d. an acre, per annum with 8d. allowed for 5½ per cent interest on an outlay of £20,000. Rennie in a period of inflated wartime prices had estimated 3s. and 8d. per acre per annum for a similar scheme at Waterbeach in 1814. A large windmill in the late 1820s cost about 1s.6d. per acre per annum so steam was a little cheaper but its main attraction lay in its reliability and greater effectiveness. (See Plate 7)

Increased security from flooding together with claying and marling helped to produce the conditions of agricultural revolution on the Fens. Claying could be effected in the 1830s for about 50s. per acre. The peat, now thinner with more effective draining, could be cut through and the clays brought out, mixed with peat and spread. Some fenmen thereafter grew little but wheat and oats. With no tenancy restrictions, owner-occupiers could continue this cropping or experiment with vegetables, red mustard, chicory, hemp and woad. Enclosure and draining seemed to release the energies of many farmers.[25] Joseph Cook Arnall, a corn inspector of Boston, and George Calthrop, a corn merchant of Spalding, both emphasized the importance of widespread corn growing in 1836. Boston market in 1829 had seen 72,964 quarters of wheat sold, but by 1831 the figure was 131,370 quarters, and this at a time of doubtful prospects in farming. George Calthrop could remember Deeping Fen as nearly waste but rents were now 35s. to 40s. an acre and land

[25] Thirsk, op. cit., p. 228.

changed hands at £50 to £70 an acre. Though the acreage under oats had fallen the demand in the stables of town-houses remained high and the Fens could meet it. Wheat was sent to Yorkshire and London and occasionally to the west coast of the country, to Newcastle and Scotland.[26] The dramatic rise in wheat production around Spalding in the 1830s was related by contemporaries to the effective steam draining of the period. In two generations the region had become an exporter of wheat, when in the life of George Calthrop's father there had been talk of a small inflow. In 1835 Calthrop told the Select Committee he had exported 30,000 quarters of wheat. During the past five years he believed the secure drainage of the Fens had made wheat growing on a big scale an attractive proposition.[27] Wheat was the principal crop in Kesteven and Holland fenlands by 1870, though potatoes and pulses had become more widely grown in Holland. In the Wildmore Fen in the mid-nineteenth century a rotation began with a root fallow, followed by wheat, beans and then wheat. A five course rotation was cole-seed, oats, wheat, seeds and wheat around Bourne Fen, while in Kesteven beside the Witham it was cole-seed, wheat, seeds, wheat, oats and wheat. As in the upland regions, the heavy emphasis on wheat was accompanied by generous application of artificial manures and by intensive use of labour to remove couch grass and to keep the drainage channels clear.[28]

There was in this picture of colourful change a more subdued side. In the old arable areas of Holland, crop selection was not immediately affected by the draining and enclosing of the Fens. In parishes such as Leverton and Bicker, where old cultivated lands had been held by livestock farmers whose tillage land came second in their list of priorities, old rotations continued and root crops and artificial grasses were slow to appear to vary the traditional fallow, wheat, pulses, wheat or barley of Arthur Young's day. As the Fens went under the plough the older arable areas began to benefit from the attention of farmers who were now predominantly arable in outlook and practice.

In the Isle of Axholme, the practice of warping improved the quality of the soil. It did not increase the area for arable, but as it involved the use of the Trent it has something in common with the activities discussed so far, in that the farmers were using the water resources of their parishes to increase output from the land. Arthur

[26] BPP 1836 vol. VIII. Minutes of Evidence before the SC on Agricultural distress, March 1836, Q. 9602/3, Q. 7830.

[27] Ibid., Q. 3115–19, Q. 7991–2.

[28] Thirsk, op. cit., pp. 224–5, and table 37, Crops in the Fen 1801 and 1870.

Young discussed the practice at length. The islanders had never been stock-raisers like their fenland counterparts in Holland but after about 1770 they intensified their arable farming on improved soil and led the way to a farming economy based on wheat, potatoes, hemp, flax, beans and ultimately market-gardening. By 1852 less than one-seventh of the Isle was given to grazing.[29] The silt which choked up river outlets was drawn into canals, from whence by tidal force of the Trent, it was poured into carefully prepared enclosures made from timber or banks of sods and limestone. These temporary structures were about six feet high and served to turn the fields into pools or lakes which gradually drained away and evaporated to leave behind a layer of from six to sixteen inches of highly fertile soil. Evidence of warping is still to be found from the Warp Farm at Morton near Gainsborough, northwards on the east side of the Trent to Burringham Warping Drain on Brumby Common. To the west of the Trent from the Warpings near Crowle Common down through Bilton, Epworth and Haxey parishes to Owston Ferry an extensive area was thus improved.[30] (See Plate 2)

The nature of the land to be warped did not much matter as the depth of the deposit, if the warping was expertly done, was so deep. Arthur Young saw 400 acres being warped at Morton in one piece which when finished would be sold to pay for the rest of the warping in the parish. A rent of 30s. an acre was offered for it. A Trent sluice had cost £1,200 and the scheme for 2,600 acres would, in 1796, cost £4,846. He observed warping at Althorpe, Amcotts and Gainsborough. Warp could be carted and spread on sandy soil for turnips. It was claimed that it equalled dung in its effect.[31] A temptation was to over-crop, with successive years of wheat and beans without manure and with only the occasional bare fallow, for 13 or 14 years together. A more rational, and by 1850 the more general course on warped land, was wheat and potatoes alternately, plentifully assisted with cow and horse dung brought from Hull and even London to produce yields of ten tons of potatoes per acre. On the second class warp land, more distant from the main source of the silt, the cropping was wheat and beans varied with an intermediate crop from barley, oats, clover, flax, turnip seed or onions. The most distant land or third grade warping had four courses of a fallow, of part rape or turnips, part potatoes and part bare fallow succeeded by wheat or oats, then clover, eaten on or seeded, or

[29] Op. cit., p. 230.

[30] Arthur Young, *Gen. View*, 1813, pp. 314–26.

[31] Paul Everson, 'Cropmark evidence and the reclamation of Blyton Common', unpublished article, Lincoln, 1977.

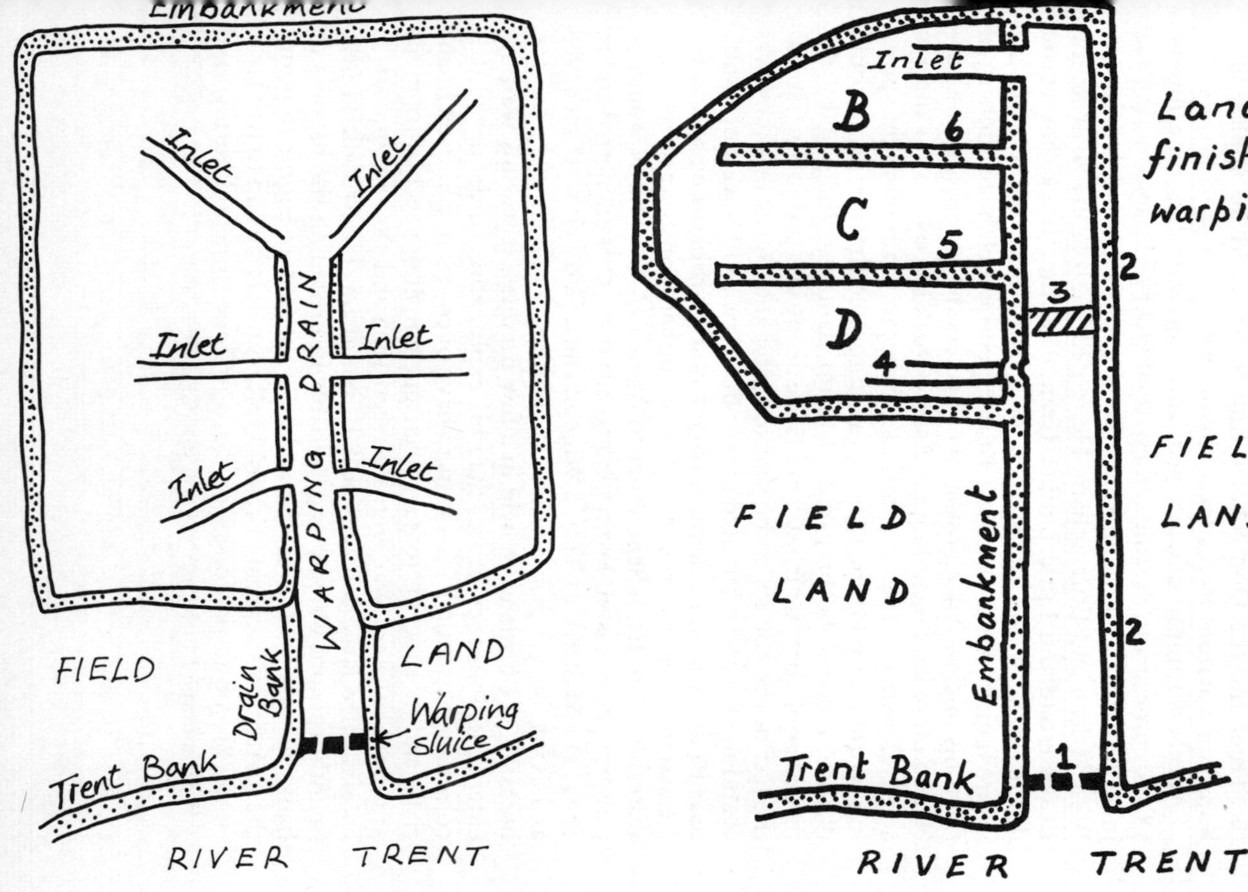

Figure 4. Plans of warping in the Trent Valley, near Morton and Blyton

KEY:
1. Warping sluice.
2. Bank to prevent the water overflowing the land finished.
3. Dam to be put into the Drain when warping D.
4. Tunnel to take off the water.
5. Bank to regulate the flow of water whilst warping C.
6. Bank to regulate the flow of water whilst warping B.

beans, and in the fourth year wheat or oats. On the sandy lands which had been warped successfully the first sign of market gardening appeared with onions, carrots, turnips for seed and for pulling. One of the larger Axholme farmers, Peter Cranidge of Crowle, whose diary 1780–1817 covers the period when market garden produce could expect to find a ready sale in Doncaster, Thorne and Hull, grew barley, oats, wheat, beans, potatoes, flax, hemp, apples and hops on his 150-acre farm. He sent cheese to London while his wheat, butter, wool and lambs went to local markets. The Humber, the Trent and the Don enabled him to transport his apples, flax, hops and potatoes to his local customers.[32]

Another glimpse of a warped land economy, this time for the 1840s, comes from the unusual estate of Henry Healey who in 1824 inherited land at Frodingham, Crosby, Scunthorpe, Gunhouse, West Halton and Burringham. He rented High Risby farm on the Elwes estate and Little Limber Grange on the Brocklesby estate during part of the time when he turned his resources to the improvement of the land near Burringham which he had inherited from his uncles. After raising over £30,000 by mortgages, he purchased more land including the Ashby Duck Decoy in 1834 and 350 acres. Constructed in 1812, this Decoy became famous in the sporting world and when in 1845 it was suggested that a railway could disturb a decoy he prepared to claim damages. Judging by the record book for it which still exists the decoy was productive. It was the last in the county to be worked after the one at Friskney was abandoned in 1878. Situated in woodland two miles west of Ashby near to the lias escarpment, its shape is still visible. The season for attracting birds into the canopies or tunnels constructed over the waterways ran from September to April and 2,800 birds would be caught in one season. From 1834 to 1835, 6,357 were netted and in 1864, 211 Mallard, 27 Teal, 2 Wigeon and a Gadwell were recorded as having been taken within 20 minutes while in 1875 on one occasion 155 birds were held in a few minutes. It was his warping enterprise, however, rather than his exploitation of the decoy that commands attention. He seems to have over-reached himself financially and there seems to have been an element of speculation in his grand schemes for warping. Between 1828 and 1837 he appears to have tackled large acreages near Burringham. His woodland near Scunthorpe and Crosby was valuable in providing the barriers or banks necessary for warping and he employed an engine to pump the water to his warping drains. Unfortunately he had to pay large sums, £1,700 in one case, for damage done to neighbouring land

[32] Scunthorpe Museum Archive × 501, Cranidge Papers.

when his banks broke. He spent £31,760 on warping in the late 1820s and 1830s at Burringham and Ashby but it was to these lands of some 1,000 acres that he turned in the 1850s when, having sold off land at Frodingham and Crosby to Charles Winn and Sir Robert Sheffield, he concentrated on farming to raise valuable crops of wheat, beans, potatoes and seed. He appears to have sold crops of wheat and potatoes in the fields by auction and to have cut poles and sold them in Leeds, Huddersfield and Halifax. On 18 August 1843, for example, he sold at Burringham 200 acres of wheat, 60 acres of beans and 50 acres of potatoes. The next year he offered 240 acres of wheat, 42 acres of beans and 90 acres of potatoes. The wheat included Tommy Towle's Red Wheat, Pure Wellington, Chitham White Wheats and Fison's celebrated Norfolk, from 'the warp soils'. He sold four varieties of potatoes and two of beans; Golden Podded and Fullard's Prolific.

By 1844 the warp expert to whom Healey had paid so much in the 1830s, Thomas Lockwood, was in charge of showing prospective buyers the lots before the sale. Morley and Sons, auctioneers, advised those who were interested to apply to Thomas Lockwood the Warper. Their sale publicity for 1843 even allowing for the exaggeration natural to auctioneers, does preserve some of the enthusiasm generated by the success of warping.

'By the subdivision into small Lots (a plan which has been previously adopted with considerable advantage to the purchaser), the Auctioneers hope to be enabled to ensure satisfaction to the growers of Wheat, by giving them another desirable opportunity of purchasing for Seed. The change from newly to well warped Lands to any other soil has been invariably attended with the most beneficial results. The various light and strong soils of the extensive Counties of Lincoln, York and Norfolk and two of the Scotch Counties, have been well tested with a change of Wheat from the warps, and abundant and superior productions have invariably rewarded the purchasers....' Every facility was offered to buyers to enter the ground to thresh their wheat and credit on agreed joint security was offered until 3 February 1844, on a discount of 6 per cent for prompt payment.[33]

From such sales fortunes were made in the villages east and west of the Trent in the early nineteenth century. Potatoes were in great demand in London and in the markets of Doncaster and Rotherham. River and coastal shipping provided transport that was both cheap and accessible to the growers and the return of night soil from London and Hull in the empty vessels meant that the market

[33] L.A.O. 2TGH 1/31/4/3–14.

was helping to maintain the fertility of the land from which it was supplied.[34] The cost of warping varied from £10 to £20 an acre in the early nineteenth century but when the value of the land could be raised from a few pounds to anything between £60 and £100 an acre, the outlay and the succeeding crops were well worth it. Public warping drains in the Isle of Axholme enabled quite small occupiers to tap the silt-laden water of the spring tides by making cuts to their own land. As long as they paid for any damage done to the fields of others by uncontrolled movement of water, they could warp for as little as £2 to £3 an acre. Patience was required in the first few years because oats and seeds were usually sown and then two years of grazing by sheep to allow salt to drain away elapsed before say three or four years of wheat could follow. When a regular wheat, potatoes cropping was adopted, with occasional variations of beans, flax and vegetables, then the generous rewards accumulated.

The 1820s and 1830s saw the culmination of a number of improvements, each of which affected the Isle's economy. John Smeaton had reported on the rivers of the Isle of Axholme as early as 1764, after the Idle and Torne rivers had broken their banks the year before. From then on, with moves to bring in enclosure, both draining and warping were undertaken, though the results were not always immediately beneficial. Epworth was enclosed in 1791 and Crowle in 1813. In 1816 a measure to amend the Crowle enclosure Act allowed the commissioners to have right of entry to warp certain lands in Belton called the Pilfry and at Crowle and Luddington. Some 2,000 acres were warped at £25 an acre. By 1838, after building sluices at Amcotts and Keadby, the work was completed. Meanwhile the opening of the Stainforth and Keadby canal after 1793 meant that the Isle had access to the coal, lime and stone supplies of the West Riding, while the urban markets of south and west Yorkshire took the fruit, corn, potatoes, carrots and onions from these fertile parishes. The river Don and its region was now in touch not only with the Isle but with the Trent and the Witham through Fossdyke. The Stainforth and Keadby canal charges give an early indication of the importance of the apples, pears, onions, potatoes, peas and beans which, it was expected, would move westwards from the Isle villages.[35] One local writer was in no doubt that better transport, drainage and warping had transformed the

[34] J. A. Clark, 'On the Farming of Lincolnshire', Prize report, 1852, pp. 120, 110–11; Ralph Creyke, *Some Account of the process of warping*, *JRAS.*, V, 1845 pp. 398–405.

[35] G. Dunston, *The Rivers of Axholme*, London, 1912, pp. 99–100; W. Peck, *A Topographical Account of the Isle of Axholme*, Doncaster, 1815, p. 135.

Axholme parishes in 40 years. The Revd W. B. Stonehouse, writing in 1839, went into detail about the effects of warping areas like Crowle Moor after 1816 and the beneficial effects of cart-warping. Provided that over-cropping was avoided and two loads of good manure per acre were spread, well-managed warp land could produce the value of the fee simple in a particularly good year.[36] The acreage capable of such profit was small and the hazards of bad seed and dry weather after sowing the money-spinning onion crops made the process a risky one but industry in keeping the fields clean did pay off even when prices fell. The profits on crops of flax, carrots and onions in the late 1830s depended upon good transport from the Trent-side wharves and good access by road to them.

One acre of flax after wheat stubble

	£.	s.	d.		£.	s.	d.
Seed	0	15	0	Value of 35 stones per acre at 9s. per stone	15	15	0
Weeding	0	8	0	Expenses	13	0	6
Pulling	0	6	0	Profit per acre	£2	14	6
Leading, Retting	0	5	0				
Getting it out of the dikes, spreading turning	0	12	0				
Taking up and leading home	0	7	0				
Rent of the land including ploughing	6	0	0				
Hackling	4	7	6				
	£13	0	6				

Carrots per acre

	£.	s.	d.		£.	s.	d.
Rent of land prepared by deep ploughing	7	0	0	Sixteen tons at 25s. a ton	20	0	0
Seed, six pounds at 2s.	0	12	0	Expenses	14	17	0
Drilling	0	9	0	Profit	£5	3	0
Weeding	2	0	0				
Pulling, leading and delivering	4	16	0				
	£14	17	0				

[36] Revd W. B. Stonehouse, *The History and Topography of the Isle of Axholme*, London, 1839, pp. 27–31.

Onions per acre

Rent	10	0	0	Value of seven hundred pecks of onions at 1s. a peck	35	0	0
Seed, twelve pounds at 4s.	2	8	0	Expenses	21	14	0
Sowing	0	6	0		£13	6	0
Weeding	3	15	0				
Pulling	1	5	0				
Dressing	3	10	0				
Measuring and getting on board vessel	0	10	0				
	£21	14	0				

An onion crop of 1,000 pecks per acre was considered to be very good and the price of 2s.6d. per peck was high, but in such conditions it would have been possible to raise most of the purchase price of a small piece of land in one crop. Prospects such as these must have kept alive the competition for land.[37] Small owners attempted cart warping by hauling 400 loads per acre of warp from the Trent foreshore. They paid 3d. a load acknowledgement to the owner of the land facing the river and 1s. a mile for each load. Like marl, the warp consolidated peat soil, and where small acreages of up to 10 acres were involved, carting had its advantages over drain-warping. Transport costs for cart-warping meant, however, that small owners at a distance from the Trent were excluded and they had to rely on the public warping drains. Borrowing charges rested heavily on some of the smaller owners, especially when there was a fall in prices. Even so, the determination to acquire a few roods was kept alive and when say 4–5 acres were put together, then the owners enclosed privately. Though some of the smaller owners lived worse than the day labourers on the large farms, hopes of land-ownership always held out better prospects.

'... When in consequence of the open fields being subdivided amongst such a number of owners, there is an opportunity of making a small purchase, a spirit of emulation arises even amongst the day labourers, who have laid by sufficient to pay in part for one or two roods of land, while the remainder of the purchase money is borrowed ... such little plots of ground, being prolific, and being cultivated at extra hours or when the owner has little else to do, will, if he continues to work for hire, and does not depend entirely on his bit of land for support, produce him excellent crops of potatoes, wheat and other things and add very much to his comfort.'[38]

They were, however, particularly vulnerable to the weather. A

[37] Op. cit., pp. 29–32. [38] Op. cit., p. 33.

wet summer could be a disaster on newly warped land but a long, dry period such as the one from February to early September 1826 could produce six quarters of wheat per acre on a small farm at Butterwick Moor.[39] Yet in 1828 the wheat was hardly worth reaping at the end of a wet season. A dry summer also benefited the small farmer in that the Trent waters carried more warp and as it deposited more quickly it was ready for use in perhaps less than three summers.

New causeways of Yorkshire stone had been built between the Axholme villages to allow horses to make their way to deliver corn. During the period of high prices in 1810–13, great progress appears to have been made but not until the influence of McAdam produced roads of 16 to 18 feet in width in the 1820s were road surfaces much improved. Spurn Point boulders were brought up by water and then crushed for use as a cheap and effective alternative to the old flagged paths that had linked Epworth, Belton, Crowle and Luddington with Owston and Haxey in a continuous walk way. It was estimated that now the menace of mud was removed, one horse and a cart could do the work of four horses and a waggon and that costs had been reduced to 25 per cent of their former level. Haxey and Epworth would not have been able to grow and market their potatoes and carrots without this improvement in their roads.[40] In the Isle of Axholme as in the Fens, steam-power eventually joined in the fight against flooding. In 1837 Sir Robert Sheffield had a steam engine erected to drain Butterwick South Moor. It was replaced by a more efficient one in 1854. In 1846 the Rush Carr and Newland Farm engines came into operation.[41] So by 1850, draining, enclosure, warping and improved water and road transport had combined to produce a new outlook for Axholme's farmers. By 1848, after starting in 1839, Doncaster at last provided better accommodation for its market-stall holders in a response appropriate for the town nearest to Lincolnshire's market garden.[42]

Some 12 miles to the east, on the Ancholme carrs, similar extension of the quantity and the quality of the land was being attempted in the 1820s. The scene of the great draining scheme of the seventeenth century was now to be subjected to improvement for arable rather than a pasture system. In 1766 a report on the original draining of the Ancholme by Grandy, Edwards and Smeaton condemned the state of Ferriby Sluice. At Glanford Brigg, the Humber waters had been allowed to deposit silt so that the outlet channel

[39] Op. cit., p. 44. [40] Op. cit., p. 46.
[41] G. Dunston, *The Rivers of Axholme*, London, 1912, p. 52.
[42] C. W. Hatfield, *Historical Notices of Doncaster 2*, Doncaster, 1868, p. 413–14.

was a mere 15 feet in width instead of 40 feet. A new cut to the Humber under an Act of 1767 produced temporary improvement, but John Rennie had to make a survey in 1801 and not until 1826 was work started on his recommendations. An outlay of £24,000 gave this part of the county a straightened river, now wider and deeper than before, a new west catchwater-drain, a reconstructed sluice at South Ferriby and a lock at Harlam Hill. The achievement of John Rennie junior (later Sir John Rennie), this work was completed by the rebuilding of Ferriby Sluice which remains today much as he left it.[43] Once the improvements of the late 1820s were completed a change in the use of the carrs could begin. Turf was pared and burned, rape seeds were sown and wheat, oats, seeds for two years and then wheat could follow. Claying to strengthen the peaty soil was achieved by deep ploughing and as the clay was nearer the surface than in Holland, the relatively expensive holing, digging and spreading were unnecessary. Yields were good as in the Fens and on the Isle of Axholme, with 10½ quarters of oats per acre on a farm at Worlaby as early as 1796, but there was to be here a maintenance of much more grazing land than in the other areas.

The Humber could still menace the Ancholme lands and the demands of river transport meant that levels in the Ancholme river itself had to be kept high. The Ferriby Sluice was not at first quick enough in discharging water from the river to keep levels so low as to save the carrs from some flooding. After a few years of crops, many acres appear to have been put down to grass again. The explanation probably lies in the layout of farms in the region, for the carrs were part of occupations with a mixed husbandry, linking the pastures beside the river with some of the high ground to east and west. Excellent for stock raising, the newly drained lands either remained under grass or returned to it after a regime of seeds, wheat and oats.

Farther to the east on the coastal Marshes, the pressure to increase cultivated acreages took two forms. One was to drain the low-lying fields behind the sea walls and the other was to reclaim land from the sea. The water which flowed to these acres from the Wolds could be safely conveyed to the sea by gravitational means.[44] If dykes and outfalls were kept clean then there was nothing like the drainage problem of the Fens with their sinking levels. Unfortunately neglect of outfalls and banks often led to flooding, and it

[43] L.A.O. *Archivists' Report*, 25, p. 45.

[44] Arthur E. Kirkby, *Humberstone, The story of a Village*, Lincoln, 1953, p. 148. Dikereeves were rarely appointed after 1773 though the Constable had drains cleared of snow in 1830.

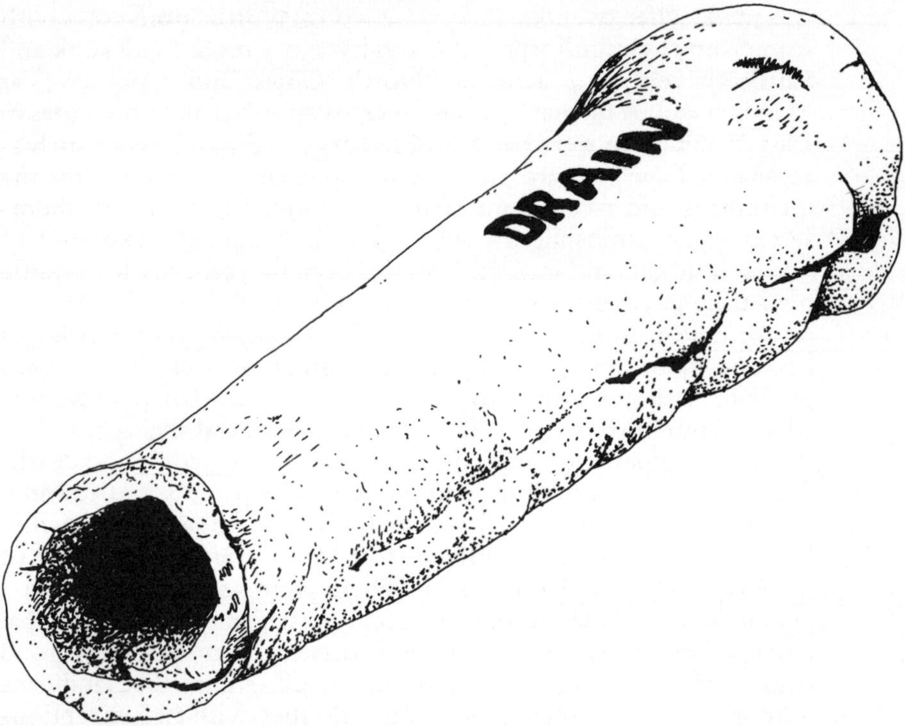

Figure 5. Before the widespread use of Thomas Scragg's extruding machine, invented 1845, hand-made tapered drain pipes were shaped by pressing wet clay round a wooden former. After 1826, pipes stamped 'drain' were exempt from the tax on clay building products, 1784–1850. This specimen, in the Museum of Lincolnshire Life, measures approximately 14 inches long, and the aperture is some 4 inches wide at its narrower end. Drawing by Miss H. Lubin.

seems that only heavy losses to farmers through sheep rot in the 1830s and 1840s forced the necessary action. Underdraining in the fields first by tiles and then by pipes improved the condition of the Marsh farms by the middle of the nineteenth century. In the other battle against water, reclamation from the sea, the stretch of coast from Grimsby to Saltfleet was the scene of some substantial acquisitions of land. These were made in two phases. From 1778–9 about 630 acres were taken in at Tetney and the observations of Arthur Young and Thomas Stone mention schemes at Winteringham, where land was still being won from the Humber, and at Humberstone. Between 1840 and 1858 quite impressive progress was made when over 600 acres were won at North Somercotes with some land at Grainthorpe, followed by 250 acres at Skidbrook and Saltfleethaven, 450 acres at North Cotes and 446 acres at Marshchapel. A further 153 acres were won at North Somercotes in 1863.[45] Yet there were patches of lethargy and indifference such as at Marshchapel, where small working farmers led only by the incumbent and two tenant farmers struggled to maintain themselves in an atmosphere polluted by the stagnant dykes full of leaves, dead cats and sewage. This had been the scene of a legal battle over tithe payment between the incumbent's father, who was the impropriator of the tithes, and a small farmer, an event which had bearing upon the 1836 Tithe Commutation Act. The region presented a dismal picture to Ayscoghe Floyer, the curate of Marshchapel from 1846 to 1872. The sickening odour of the dykes filled the dwellings and he believed caused ague in the people and deaths from disease in cattle, pigs and poultry. The parents and children were ignorant and the locality lacked spiritual and social leadership. Like Ireland, the district suffered from 'the extreme indifference of the large (absentee) landowners'. There were 520 souls 'without a person of independent property except myself and the two principal tenants, one of whom is a violent dissenter the other (a) good supporter (according to his means) of the S.P.G.F.P.'. The landlords 'seldom come near their property nor do they with two exceptions support a single charity in this place'.[46] Ayscoghe Floyer was to supply the want of spiritual, social and even political leadership in a ministry which overcame ill-health to effect improvements in draining, local government, education and schemes of self-help against sickness, fire, poverty and general misfortune. Even here improvement came, though late by the standards of the Fens and the warplands.

Two historians, one modern and the other a nineteenth-century writer, are convinced that Lincolnshire's taming of the element of water led to changed ways of life by the 1830s. Both make the statistics and plans of draining and warping live in human terms. Of the Trent lands and the Isle of Axholme the Revd W. B. Stonehouse wrote in 1839 of the diet of small farmers and the style of servant girls.

'They lived chiefly on bread, butter milk, eggs, and flour puddings; sometimes, but not constantly, they had malt liquor. About forty or fifty years ago this was generally the routine: Sunday,

[45] Thirsk, op. cit., p. 252.

[46] L.A.O. Marshchapel Parish 23/4, 18/4; *Archivists' Report*, 21, pp. 40–2.

bacon, sometimes butchers' meat; Monday, ash-heap cake, with butter in a hole in the middle, and milk to drink with it; Tuesday, pudding made of milk, wheat flour, and eggs; Wednesday, bacon; Thursday, ash heap cake, and butter milk to drink; Friday, hot bread and butter; Saturday, pan pudding, i.e. a pudding made of flour, with small bits of bacon in it of which, said my informant, "A man thought himself very lucky if he got two bits".'

In many instances women wore the same gowns and cloaks which had served their mothers; and nobody could remember a farmer having a complete new suit of clothes. A servant girl of the best class had forty shillings per year wage, when the most homely and necessary articles of wearing apparel were much dearer than they are at present: she got up at three o'clock in a morning to spin, and was clad chiefly in linsey woolsey garments. 'Could she see a servant of the present day, decked out on a Sunday afternoon in a straw bonnet trimmed with silk ribbons, a gauze handkerchief round her neck, a printed muslin gown, a silk shawl, and a pair of white cotton stockings, with the Adelaide boots, verily I believe she would drop down dead with astonishment.'[47]

In a passage which must surely be a classic in agrarian history, Dr Joan Thirsk wrote in 1957 of the revolution in the Fens.

'In the fenlands of Lincolnshire, more perhaps than in any other part of the county, the agricultural revolution was a real revolution, which transformed the landscape, and began a complete reorientation of the fen economy. When death removed the inhabitants of the fen villages who had specialised in rearing thousands of geese and catching fish and wildfowl, their children and grandchildren got a living from the same lands in a quite different way—as ploughmen and labourers on rich cornland. The cranberries which had been gathered by the stone in the fen grounds of Friskney and East Fen disappeared with the drainage and were replaced by corn. New parishes were carved out of East, West and Wildmore fens and given uncongenial names such as Eastville, Midville, Frithville, and Langriville. In a matter of a little over a hundred years, the ambitious sheep farmer on the fen commons, who had vowed to bring the number of his sheep up to 20,000 and to have twenty shepherds with silver sheep hooks, was a mythical and fast becoming an incredible figure. Conditions of life were in some ways healthier and safer; the ague was less troublesome; ... Some of the

[47] Revd W. B. Stonehouse, *The History and Topography of the Isle of Axholme*, London, 1839, p. 47.

fen villages even began to be frequented as pleasure resorts. Already in 1790 Fosdyke was a well-patronised bathing and tea-drinking resort for Sunday afternoon excursionists . . . The unhappy travellers of the seventeenth century who had observed the "sad life" of the fen people with mingled repulsion and pity would hardly have recognised the altered scene.'[48]

Figure 6. Warping sluice, Isle of Axholme

[48] Thirsk, op. cit., pp. 235–6.

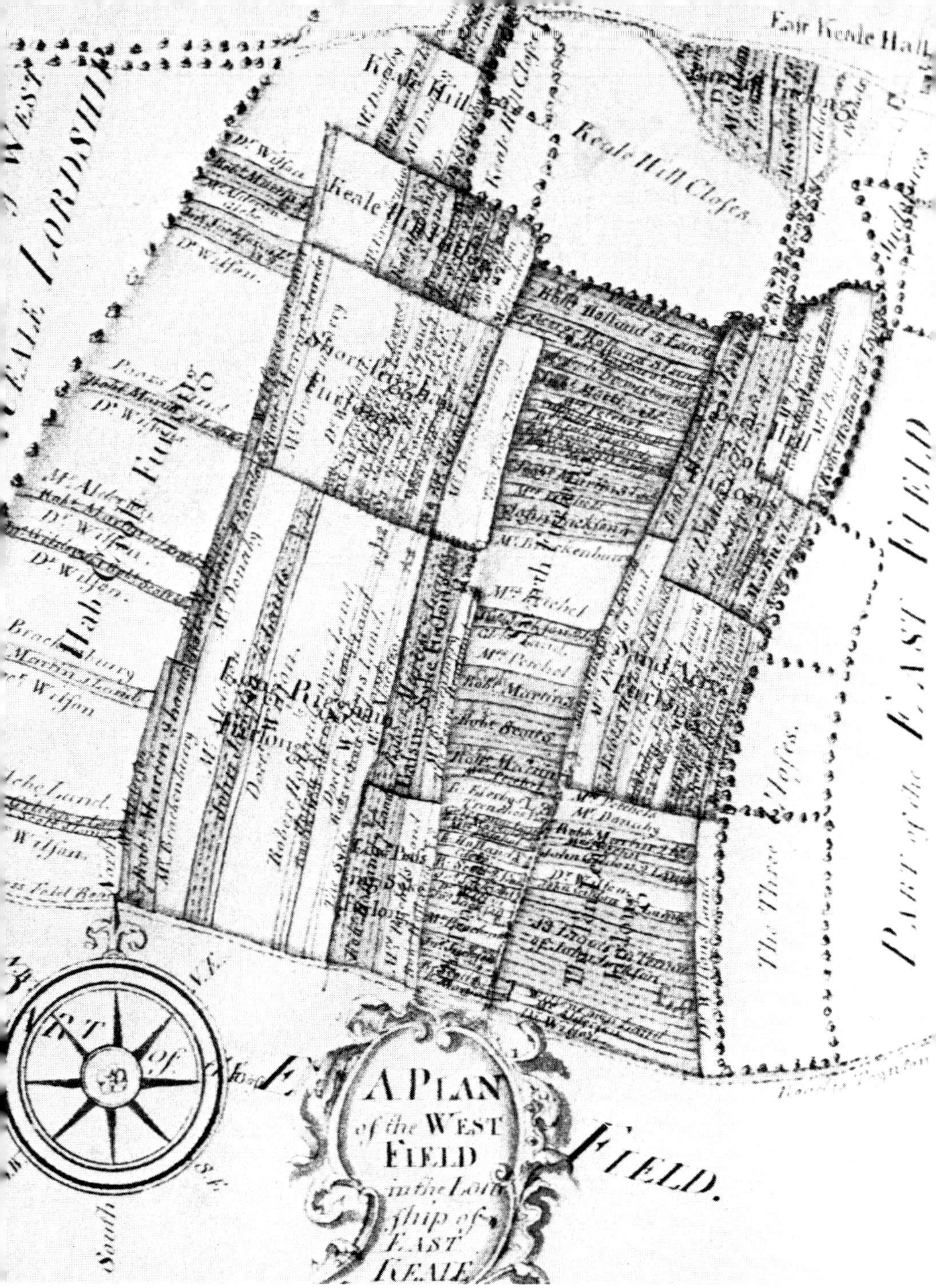

1. WEST FIELD AT EAST KEAL *near Spilsby, from a survey book made in 1757 for the owner John Short by John Grundy of Spalding: L.A.O. Misc. Dep. 2/1. There were three other open fields in the parish, North, Mardin and East. The shaded strips belonged to John Short's estate. The map shows the complexity of the open field system for land valuers and surveyors as well as farmers. The low land in West Field lay at the foot of the map, the higher ground to the north where East Keal Hall stood. Evidence of early enclosure may be seen near the Hall in Keal Hill Closes.* See page 26.

a) Crop marks at Blyton near Gainsborough, showing warping channels between the areas of woodland. There were many enthusiastic warpers on both sides of the lower Trent in the early nineteenth century.

2. WARPING IN THE LOWER TRENT VALLEY.

b) Crop marks at Wildsworth. Although the channels are not as distinct as at Blyton above, this view suggests the link between the tidal Trent and the well-farmed warplands beside it. See page 72.

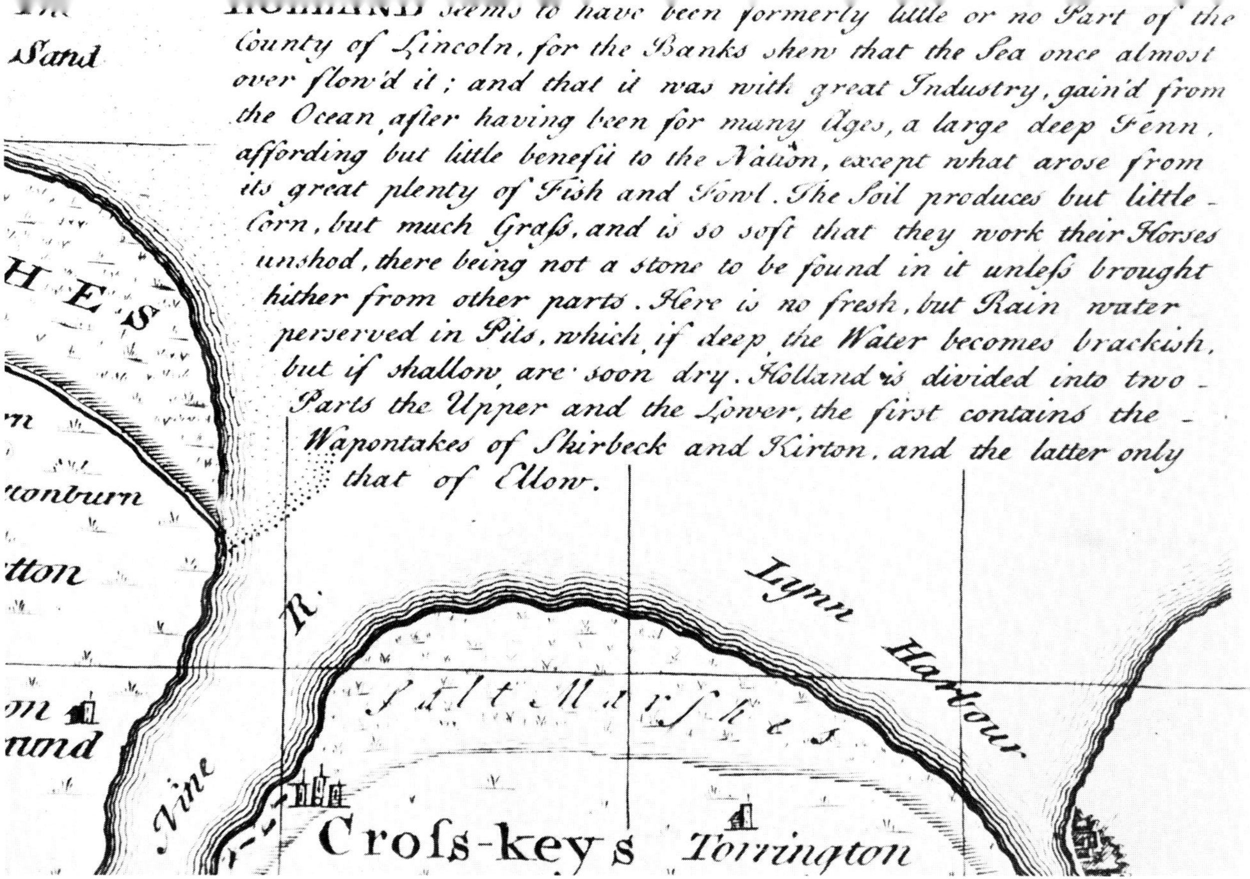

3. HOLLAND *as described on a map by Bowen in 1753. Within 75 years of this comment Holland had become a great wheat producing area, and from Boston and Spalding large quantities of grain were shipped to customers in many parts of the kingdom.* See pages 62–71.

4. THE RIVER WITHAM *from Lincoln to Boston: Bowen's map of Lincolnshire 1753. Compare the unimproved condition of the Witham fenland and Wildmore, West and East Fens with their appearance on the map of 1804 opposite.* See page 62.

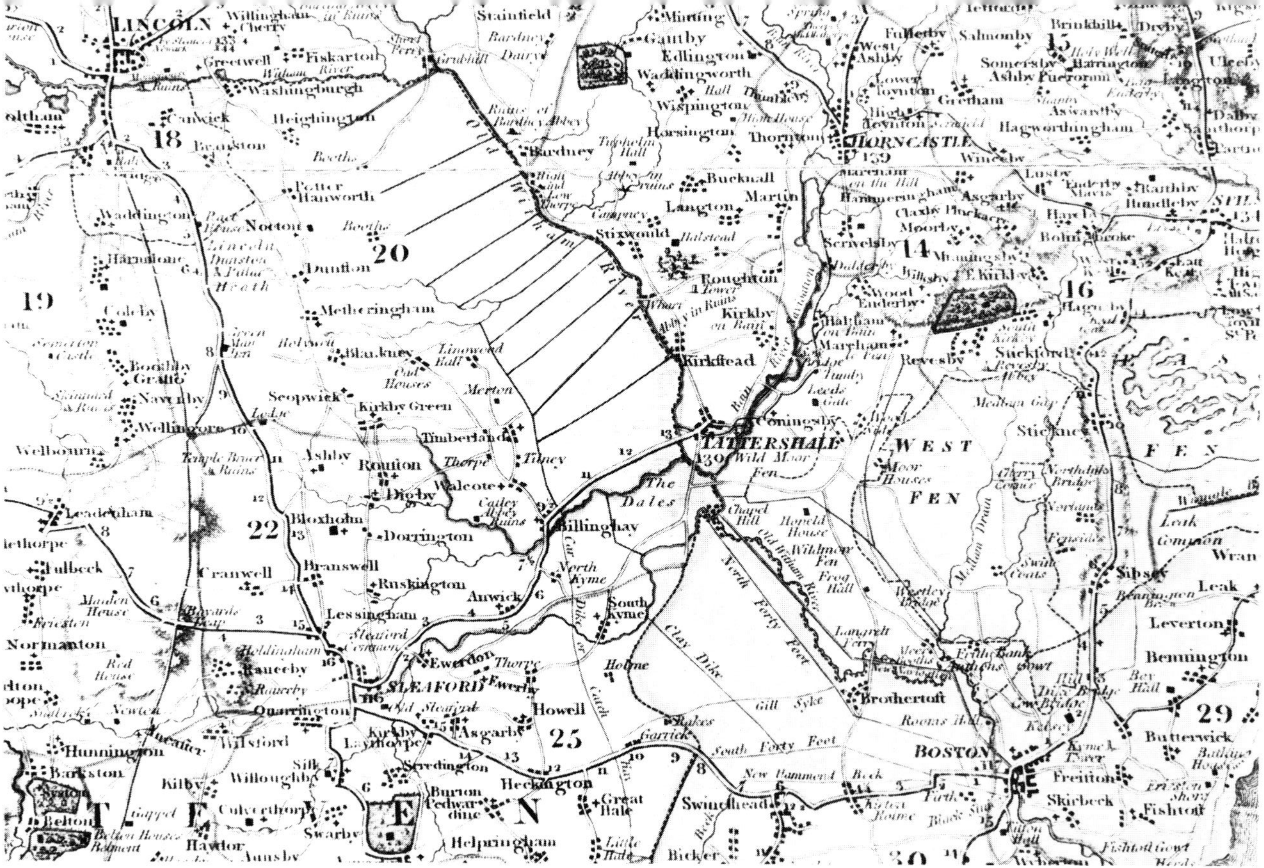

5. THE WITHAM FROM LINCOLN TO BOSTON: *part of a map by Charles Smith, 1804. The improved fenland awaits much of its later new settlement, for example at New Bolingbroke and Frithville in the 1820s. The landscape of parks, woodland, estate villages and country houses is shown as well as the line of settlements running north along the edge of the Heath from Carlton Scroop to Lincoln.* See page 62.

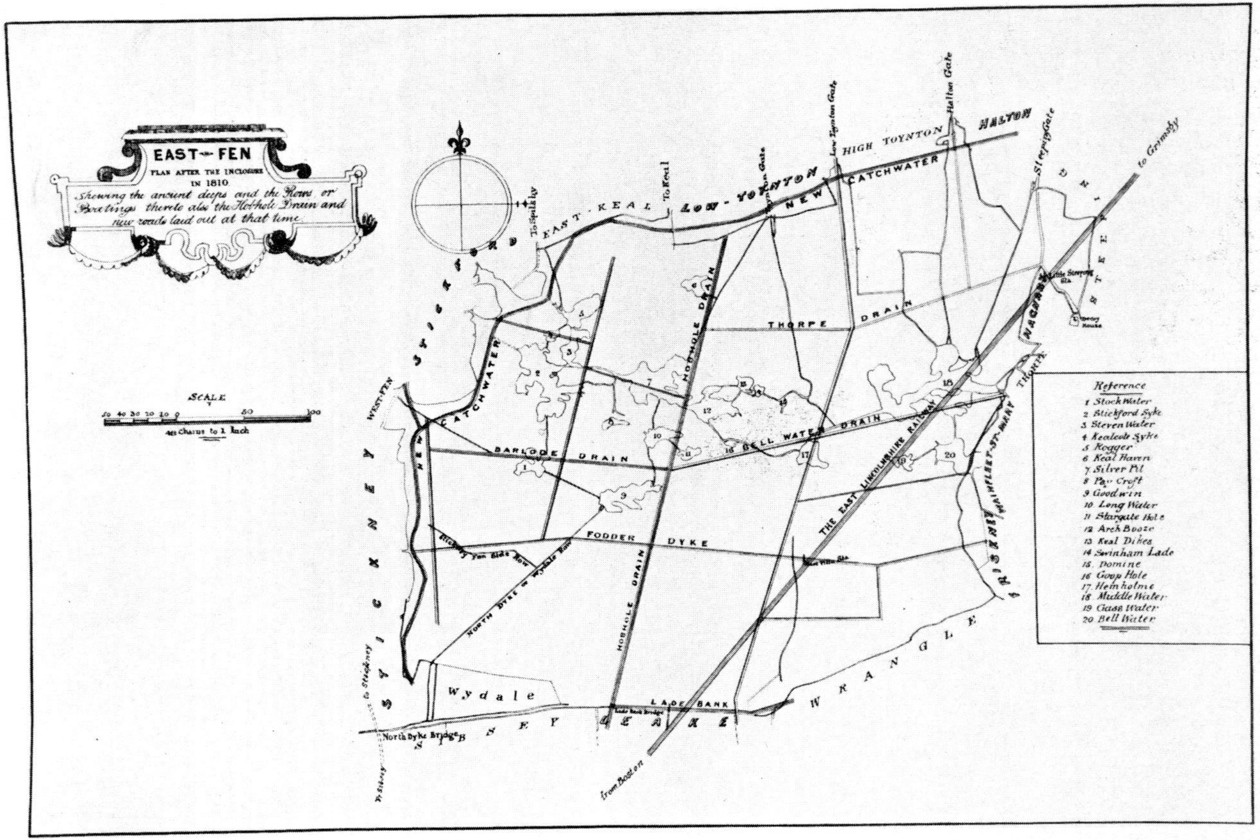

6. PLAN OF EAST FEN *after the enclosure of 1810, showing the old rows or boatings and the new roads laid out at that time, as well as Hobhole Drain. The line of the East Lincolnshire railway from Boston to Grimsby has been added to the map at a later date. The engineers encountered great difficulty in putting the line across the improved but still 'quaking' fenland.* See page 66.

a) MYER'S MILL, *one of four tower mills in Alford. Built in 1827, the tower was raised in 1889 giving it an odd shape ('the high-waisted lady'). The cap with its ogee shape is typical of Lincolnshire. This mill was dismantled in 1952. Most of the surviving windmills in Lincolnshire were originally used for corn rather than for drainage purposes.*

b) An 1856 Bradley and Craven beam engine, working in 1938 in the pumping station at Dogdyke: an example of steam power in the battle against water, it drained 1500 acres in Tattershall and Tattershall–Thorpe parishes.

7. WIND AND WATER POWER.

a) This substantial Dutch barn of 1778 at Fillingham on the Cliff is probably the earliest surviving example in the county.

8. FARM BUILDINGS.

b) A range of 'gothick' farm buildings at Fillingham from 1778. They are probably the result of a conversion of an earlier barn. See page 214.

5

Lincolnshire's social and commercial fabric on the eve of the agricultural revolution

DRAINING schemes owed much to the initiative of landlords and their influence in Parliament. How much did they affect other extensions of Lincolnshire's cultivatable area in the agricultural revolution? Was the structure of landowning in the county conducive to expansion and from whom did the initiative come for attacks on waste land within the unenclosed villages and upon the fens, warrens and poor pastures on their boundaries?

Small landowners predominated in the county and on the whole the aristocratic influence of the great estates was not strong. Yet because of Lincolnshire's size and diversity no sooner is a generalization made than important qualifications have to be registered. In some parts of the county one large landowner dominated a whole region or a number of titled proprietors had estates near to each other and by being resident upon them they exerted an influence over farming practice across a wide area. In North Lindsey the Earl of Yarborough held 55,272 acres by 1873.[1] The property was compact, well-wooded and provided for its owner all the advantages of a classical estate; seclusion, sporting amenities and scope for influence in the social and business life of a great tract of country. The only other titled families possessed scattered estates of about 10,000 acres each in Lindsey. Neither was resident in the nineteenth century. The Willoughbys, Lord Willoughby d'Eresby, and the Earls of Scarbrough could not, in Lindsey at least, wield influence to rival the Yarborough estate centred on Brocklesby. From Barton-on-Humber south to Market Rasen and Louth and across the

[1] R. J. Olney, *Lincolnshire Politics 1832–1885*, Oxford, 1973. The following discussion of landed proprietors is based on Dr Olney's valuable analysis of political interests in Lincolnshire in the mid-nineteenth century.

Wolds, the Yarborough property extended with only the Tathwell estate of the Chaplin family and the 9,000 acres of the Sheffield family at Normanby to compare with it. South and west of the Yarboroughs, however, there were some important concentrations of land in the ownership of the Angersteins with about 11,500 acres, the Tennyson d'Eyncourts at Bayons Manor with some 3,500 acres and the estate at North Willingham belonging to the Bourcherett family of 5,800 acres. The Heneage family owned nearly 11,000 acres around Hainton and in Grimsby, while the estates of Sir Montague John Cholmeley of 6,000 acres and the Vyners' 14,500 acres with a country seat at Gautby completed the list of medium-sized estates in Lindsey in the hands of influential county families. Near the coast at Alford was an estate of some 7,000 acres held by Robert Adam Christopher, later Nisbet Hamilton while much of Spilsby town and 11,000 acres were in the ownership of Lord Willoughby d'Eresby.

In Kesteven in the early nineteenth century no estate led the way as did the Brocklesby concentration in Lindsey, but there were a number of wealthy proprietors with estates ranging from 7,000 to 20,000 acres. Most of them lived there and they looked to Lord Brownlow and Lord Willoughby d'Eresby for political and agricultural leadership. They were represented by the Heathcote, Chaplin, Thorold, Welby and Whichcote families. At Belton, Lord Brownlow presided over 17,000 acres in Kesteven while to the south, around Lincolnshire's greatest house, Grimsthorpe, lay the estates of the former dukes of Ancaster. The 20,000 acres of this property were to be linked with an extensive estate of 17,500 acres to the north belonging to Sir Gilbert Heathcote. Between Grantham and Newark were three medium-sized estates. Sir John Thorold of Syston held about 11,000 acres with another 1,500 in Lindsey, Sir Robert Heron had 2,500 acres around Stubton, while around Caythorpe some 4,000 acres belonged to George Hussey Packe. A number of Kesteven landowners like Lord Brownlow held land in Holland, but this division of Lincolnshire lacked the social, sporting and scenic amenities of Kesteven and Lindsey and although some corporate owners were influential here through their agents, Holland remained the domain of the small proprietor. A few graziers who later became wheat growers in the region between Spalding and Boston stood out. The Everards of Fulney and Gosberton, the Moores of Spalding and the Tunnards of Frampton together with the families of Berridge of Algakirk, Gleed of Donington and Calthorp of Swineshead formed a group who in wealth (though not in acreage) could equal larger proprietors in other parts of the county because their soil was by the mid-nineteenth century highly fertile and relatively safe from flooding.

Lincolnshire stood low on a list of counties in order of the density of country seats within them in 1865. Out of 39 English counties, Lincolnshire ranked thirty-eighth. In the order of counties with great estates over 10,000 acres excluding waste, however, Lincolnshire was twelfth out of 39. It had, in company with Yorkshire and Durham, 28 per cent of its total area occupied by great estates, yet few landed families with the means to create country seats had chosen to make their homes in it. Although some families held great estates in the county, few were resident in Lincolnshire. Its reputation for remoteness, not entirely deserved surely even in the eighteenth century, may have been a cause. Scenic and family attractions in other counties may have added their weight. Lincolnshire was the county from which some families drew their rents and sold off timber and land to keep indebtedness at bay or to finance building, amusements or political activity elsewhere. Perhaps even fashion in landscape played a part. The Wolds, untransformed from bleak, lonely sheep walks and warrens to well-tended arable would have little attraction.[2]

Barbara Savile, wife of the fourth Earl of Scarbrough, preferred the seclusion and wooded beauty of Sandbeck in South Yorkshire to Glentworth Hall below the Cliff. Although Glentworth remained the administrative centre of the Lincolnshire, Durham and Yorkshire estates, the family moved its seat to Sandbeck in the 1760s. When land sales were necessary, 1782–1807, the family turned to Winteringham to capitalize on what was for them an off-lying property that had come into the Lincolnshire collection through marriage. Other scattered holdings were sold in 1784–5 with a temporarily serious loss to the rental. At Winteringham the land to be sold was valued at £52,197 for 2,422 acres. This sale marked a significant decline in an estate's influence in North Lincolnshire and at the time an important addition to the supply of land on the market.[3] Yet, though the Lincolnshire rental fell by about £2,100 a year to £6,653 in 1793, with no more land purchases, it climbed back rapidly to nearly £7,000 in 1800, to £9,000 in 1803 and to £12,000 in 1814. This was a tribute not merely to high wartime prices but to the accumulating benefits of enclosure and the

[2] F. M. L. Thompson, *English Landed Society in the Nineteenth Century*, London, 1963, pp. 30–2, 113–17.

[3] Sir Christopher Wray had owned it in 1589. His daughter Elizabeth married a Saunderson and the possessions of that family came into the hands of Thomas Saunderson the third Earl of Scarbrough.

many improvements associated with it. These rent increases were shouldered by the tenants with remarkably few arrears.

Some families appeared to value Lincolnshire as a source of game and to visit their estates perhaps once a year for hunting or shooting.[4] The county supported many reputable packs of hounds, which, though founded by old families, depended upon the help of tenant farmers for their success. They walked the puppies and later hunted with their landlords. In the time of the second and third Earls of Yarborough it was said that 70 or 80 tenant farmers could turn out in scarlet.[5] With the Belvoir, Blankney, Brocklesby, Burton, Cottesmore and the Southwold, Lincolnshire could be termed 'The home of the Horse and the Hound'. Mr Charles Pelham and Sir John Tyrwhitt had packs very early in the eighteenth century. The Belvoir's hound lists went back to 1758. The third Lord Monson hunted with the Burton from 1774 to 1806. Viscount Lowther brought hounds from Westmorland to the Cottesmore country as early as 1695 and from them Lord Gainsborough's family built up a renowned pack from about 1732 to 1788. Landowners could not hunt without being aware of the condition of the farms and villages through which they sped. Comparisons were made, improvements noted, awareness increased. The numbers of farmers turning out provided a barometer of agricultural fortune which linked with the other semi-social event, the rent-day dinner, served to keep landowners in touch with their own and their neighbours' estates. Lincolnshire then for all its lack of country seats was not a region neglected by its landowners whose incomes in any case depended in some measure upon the success of their agents and tenants to whom they seem to have delegated considerable power and influence.[6]

An example of a family which moved away but did not abandon its Lincolnshire interests was that of Lord Delaval. After inheriting Doddington in 1759 he promoted drainage, enclosure of moorland, the planting of Scotch firs and hop cultivation; this last was a rare activity in Lincolnshire at the time, though it was common across the Trent on the Nottinghamshire clays. In 1771 the family moved to Seaton Delaval in Northumberland on the death of Lord Delaval's brother and Doddington was left to the care of a Scots steward, William Porteus, who remained there until his death in

[4] Sir Osbert Sitwell, *The Scarlet Tree*, London, 1951, p. 185, gives an account of Christmas at Blankney.

[5] *Lincolnshire Magazine*, Vol. I, 1932; G. E. Collins, *Fox-hunting in Lincolnshire*, London, n.d.

[6] See Chapters 8 and 9 for a discussion of land agents and landlords' and tenants' improvements.

1813. He used income from the sale of hops, which in a year like 1788 could amount to £808 to pay off Lincoln tradesmen, to stage a rent-day dinner and to settle the bills of saddlers, butchers, coopers, innkeepers for post-horses, grocers, stationers, flax merchants, waggoners, timber merchants, upholsterers, farriers, plumbers, glaziers, a brazier, a brewer, a hardware merchant, a paint-maker and a druggist. Decorations to the Hall, including the papering of walls which the upholsterer held up until the severe frost ended, were paid for and preparations were made in the woods to open up views and rides for shooting. In July 1789 the family stayed at Doddington for about ten days en route from London to Northumberland. They crossed the Trent by Dunham ferry after leaving the Great North Road. In December of the same year they received in their Portland Place home a basket sent up by Porteus in a fly containing a turkey, two fowls, two woodcocks and a brace of snipes.[7]

Absenteeism did not necessarily mean neglect but amongst the lesser landowners, residence and participation in county social life probably helped to sustain an interest in improvement which took the form of increasing the cultivatable area. Lincolnshire had 23 per cent of its area covered by estates of from 1,000 to 10,000 acres and ranked thirty-fifth in the county list of 39 in 1883. The average for all England was 29·5 per cent. Again for the estates of the 'greater gentry' that is, owners with estates of from 3,000 to 10,000 acres, Lincolnshire was below the national average of 17 per cent with only 13 per cent of its total acreage accounted for by this class of landowner in 1883. About 10 per cent of its acreage was owned by the 'squirearchy' of 1,000 to 3,000 acres each against a national average of 12·4 per cent. Only with small landowners does Lincolnshire touch or exceed national averages with estates of less than 1,000 acres and here their numbers may well have increased in part as a result of the pressure to extend the area which was fit for cultivation as common rights became translated into allotments of land and as people who had made capital in the industries associated with agriculture sought land in which to invest their savings.

A glance at the land market in Lincolnshire suggests that the county could attract buyers who wanted a good investment and who were likely to respond to initiatives even if they themselves failed to make any to increase the county's productive acreage. Indeed many of them had made the capital they sought to invest in landownership by involvement in the schemes which had increased

[7] *LNQ*, Vol. 15, p. 27–59.

the cultivatable area; enclosure, draining and warping or in the provision of the utilities which were essential to the agricultural revolution such as turnpikes and canals. The variety and vitality of the Lincolnshire land market in the eighteenth century have been described by B. A. Holderness, who saw in Lincolnshire itself quite powerful and hitherto little-examined pressures for land acquisition.[8] Tanners, butchers, innkeepers, country attorneys, bankers, physicians dealt in land and helped to swell the numbers of small owners who figure so importantly in the late eighteenth-century land-tax returns. Intermarried with the lesser gentry and the farming community, these wealthy tradesmen and professional men, who inhabited the country towns which were the service-centres for the developing agricultural activity of the county joined with land agents and clergy in land purchase. Merchants whose wealth came from quite small towns included William Long of Barton-on-Humber, Thomas Howgrave of Horncastle, Richard Popplewell of Belton in Axholme, John Moody of Spilsby and William Alvey of Sleaford. Each became an 'esquire' with land to support the dignity. Richard Popplewell was an Axholme wholesaler, shopkeeper, land steward and money lender who from 1695 to 1715 established the largest residential estate in the Isle. St. John Wells, a tanner of Alford, Thomas Linthwaite of Stamford a brazier, bought land early in the century but in the last quarter many more shopkeepers turned to land as an investment. Charles Beaty, ironmonger of Louth, Thomas Hayward a builder of Lincoln as well as the Huttons and Dealtrys of Gainsborough bought large properties. The Dealtrys were merchants and founders of the port's oil-milling industry.

Lawyers and country bankers had money to spare for investment in land. They were in an advantageous position as holders of mortgages and as money-lenders to know of forthcoming sales. The business records of men like David Atkinson of Louth, Benjamin Smith of Horbling, George Tennyson of Grimsby suggest that land could be acquired by first giving mortgages on it. Carr Brackenbury (*c.* 1665–1741) from a family of estate accountants and clergy acquired land near Spilsby including the manors of Lusby, Donington-on-Bain, Skendleby and Hogsthorpe, to join the many lawyers and estate stewards or rent receivers who bought land for

[8] B. A. Holderness. 'The English Land Market in the Eighteenth Century: the Case of Lincolnshire'. *EcHR* XXVII, pp. 556–7. Much of the following discussion is based on his findings. The demand side of the land market was not confined to Lincolnshire, of course. London, Hull and the developing West Riding and Nottinghamshire made contributions.

themselves and their descendants.[9] 'At least two dozen estates in excess of 500 acres were founded by lawyers between 1700 and the early years of the nineteenth century.'[10] Bankers' interest in land is illustrated by the acquisitions of the Ellisons of Lincoln who, as partners with Robert Smith at the Lincoln end of the great Nottingham bank of the Smiths, were by the 1790s established as landowners at Boultham and Sudbrooke. The founder of the Sleaford Bank, Anthony Peacock, added a Witham-side estate to his family's possessions before the end of the century. Bartholomew Claypon, Abraham Sheath and William Garfit, bankers at Boston, were interested in land deals before 1800 and by 1850 some of these families had placed landowning before banking in their business activity. Even physicians entered the land market with Francis Willis, who calmed George III so saving Pitt from political eclipse and the country from an early regency, snapping up freeholds to the anger of Lord le Despencer in Dunston.[11] Samuel Gordon of Newark bought Halverholme Priory near Sleaford and obtained a baronetcy in the 1760s, and another physician, Gervase Gibson, joined in a plan to purchase Earl Fitzwilliam's Kesteven estates in the 1770s.

Given the removal of tithes in many parishes and the allotment of lands and corn rents to the clergy in their stead it was to be expected that the more prudent clergy would appear in the land market. Some Lincolnshire clergy emerged as important landowners in their parishes and where one family provided the incumbents for say three generations then consolidation of landholding could be achieved. The Bassetts in Glentworth, though not landowners, acquired considerable influence there in the late eighteenth century as incumbents and as agents for and tenants of the Earls of Scarbrough. The Lintons of Freiston and the Curtois family of Branston held livings for three generations and built up estates in the process. Few clergy appear to have been using inherited wealth for their excursions into the land market and their wide distribution from fens to clays and the uplands seems to rule out mere opportunism or professional influence. They appear to have had funds to invest and sufficient interest in farming to acquire land. After all, the enclosure movement had revolutionized their involvement in agriculture and given them an improved social and material condition. The age of vicarages built of Georgian brick with sash windows, a study and

[9] L.A.O. *Archivists' Report*, 2, p. 17.
[10] Holderness, op. cit.
[11] See Chapter 2.

more ample living quarters had arrived.[12] They invested in draining, turnpikes and canals. They took up mortgages, lent money and financed annuities. Land purchase was for them, too, an investment, a security for their descendants and a legitimate use for their surplus money. A few were leading diocesan clergy, like the two prebendaries Timothy Heardson and Henry Best, but others were schoolmasters like Francis Bacon of Grantham and William Emeris of Louth, clergy who were connected with the universities or simply parish priests with no family links in either the aristocracy or the gentry.

Farmers, too, invested some of their surplus cash in land. B. A. Holderness observed 'Data from land tax and estate surveys reveal both that a great deal of land remained the property of farming families and that, after a setback to the peasant proprietor in the seventeenth century, a considerable revival took place in the later eighteenth century.' Farmers were involved with builders, shopkeepers, attorneys and others in the buying and selling of small plots of land and buildings; probably in the heart of the old enclosed parts of villages in what seems to have been a particularly active market in the eighteenth century. A survey of the small Simpson property of some 300 acres at Haxey, Epworth and Belton by William Ware in 1791 showed that the prospect of enclosure could put land on the market. One or two pieces were deemed so small as not to be worth enclosing and were therefore to be sold. Other pieces were worth enclosing if they could be warped effectively, in which case they should be added to the Belton estate. Twenty-one acres were sold in Haxey West Carr for £300 to John and William Curtis who were Haxey cordwainers. So in the Isle small tradesmen had an eye for land where competition for it was considered to be fierce.[13]

Farmers were also anxious to acquire summer grazing in the Marsh and purchase of land there had an attraction. Landlords wishing to offer eligible farms to tenants in upland parts of the country would buy summer grazing land to attach to the holding and charge a higher rent for it. Both William Dixon of Holton le Moor near Caistor and Thomas Elmhirst of Stixwould purchased land in the Marsh for grazing to put to the farms they rented on the Wolds. There seems to be no particular geographical pattern to this purchasing by substantial farmers and it continued throughout the century. Edwin Austin established an estate at Gedney from 1690 to 1740, and at the end of the century Philip Skipwith and William

[12] Barley, *Lincolnshire and the Fens*, 1972, p. 110 and *LNQ*, Vol. 14, p. 72. Ulceby Rectory 1707 had earthen floors in three low rooms and a thatched roof.

[13] L.A.O. BRA 833/2.

Wright started their accumulations in the 1790s. Some tenants bought their farms when their landlords were short of cash. John Grant acquired the manor and estate at Oxcombe in the Wolds from Bennet Langton in 1783 in such circumstances. Philip Skipwith, a tenant on a farm at Aylesby near Grimsby, added to his income by enclosure-surveying and road-building. By 1810 he owned an estate at North Kelsey and his son by 1840 could command some 5,000 acres. John Bourne of Dalby, a tenant farmer in 1730, had by his death in 1761 become the owner of many small freeholds there and the long lease of the Beverley Minster land so that he dominated the whole parish. His family consolidated their substance by acting as land agents for other owners. Tennyson's Northern Farmer (old style) insisted he had plenty to occupy him 'Meä, wi' haäte hoondred haäcre o' Squoire's, an' lond o' my oän.' He had also 'managed for Squoire coom Michaelmas thurty year'.

Some purchasers from out of the county were content to visit their lands infrequently and to leave their management to local agents. London's influence was less obvious in the eighteenth century than it had been from about 1570 to 1670 but it was to produce between 1700 and 1730 the Chaplin family at Blankney, the Reynardsons at Holywell, the Vyners at Gautby, the Batemans at Well and between 1730 and 1770 Sir William Smith and Sir Jacob Wolff at Paxton and from 1770 to 1880, J. J. Angerstein at Stainton le Wold.[14] Lord William Manners was to establish himself near Grantham and to purchase Buckminster Park in Leicestershire in 1768. From the West Riding John Beckett, a Barnsley grocer, linen-draper and land-jobber, acquired land in the county and his son, a Leeds banker, bought Somerby near Gainsborough in 1786. The Wilsons of Barnsley, linen-drapers with a Gainsborough agent, took up mortgages and bought land in the 1750s and 1760s. Kelstern manor fell to the Denisons of Leeds in 1759 while another branch of the family acquired land at Binbrook after 1800. Pemberton Milnes of Wakefield bought Timberland near Sleaford in 1783. From Hull, families such as the Hetheringtons, Wilberforces, Jarratts and George Crowle continued a long tradition of involvement with Lincolnshire land purchase. John Livesley of Blackburn, Lancashire, bought 5,000 acres in the 1770s and 1780s, while bankers such as Abel Smith and Ichabod Wright of Nottingham, John Davys of Loughborough and William Pocklington and John Godfrey of Newark joined with some modest purchasers of Lincolnshire land from Worksop and Doncaster. A formidable buyer was, of course, Joseph Banks of Sheffield, attorney and money-lender, who laid out

[14] For a full list, see Holderness, op. cit., p. 560.

£40,000 between 1705 and 1727 to establish his line at Revesby Abbey.

The steady flow of investment into land ownership in the eighteenth century, which seems to have received little or no check from wars and trade recessions, was both a sign of Lincolnshire's own underlying prosperity and its attractiveness to buyers from beyond its borders. It helps as well to explain how the county enjoyed a structure of land-ownership and management which gave scope to a wide variety of people to exercise their talents and to express their ambitions. It reminds us too of the capital resources which the county created or absorbed so that a relentless pressure could be mounted upon the wastes, the Fens and the unpromising Cliff and Wolds and how those acres, once broken in, were to be husbanded in ways and with effects that were to leave observers in the mid-nineteenth century astounded but, fortunately for us, articulate in their admiration for the leading farmers of the several regions of the county.

The land agent had an important role in the improvement of estates especially where the owner was an infrequent visitor. Some thought that agricultural advance would result from long leases; others believed that tenancies-at-will gave both occupiers and landlords a freedom that was essential especially when cereal prices had fallen after 1813. The land agents' work was significant whether the tenants were under long leases or annual agreements. He had to see that the terms of the leases or agreements were observed and that the land was kept in good heart. His interpretation of the wishes of tenants about covenants and rents, when relayed to the landlord, could affect estate policy; his explanation and execution of that policy affected the farmers' response. If like Robert John Atkinson of Brocklesby, agent to Lord Yarborough, he gave evidence to a Select Committee, his observations could influence not only the thinking of the legislature in his own day but the writing of historians long after it. Atkinson's comment that '... I never saw better farmers in any part of the kingdom than the Wold farmers of Lincolnshire. ...' echoes down the years.[15] Their attempts to collect information for their landlords on rents, prices, methods of farming and new practices formed a kind of county network, keeping their employers in touch with the agricultural changes of the day. We need to know more about their education, their backgrounds and their influence generally, but by the nineteenth century a clearer distinction appeared between the agent who occupied a few acres under his landlord and the older tradition of farmer-rent collectors

[15] BPP, 1836, op. cit., Q. 5973.

of the early eighteenth century.[16] Loyalty to the landlord rather than to fellow tenant farmers was the hall-mark of the good agent, together with qualities like honesty, industry and familiarity with accounts and surveying. Theirs cannot have been an easy position, standing as they did between landowners and farmers, though when the Lincolnshire Wolds were becoming arable in the early nineteenth century one is struck by the seemingly passive role of the stewards and agents. They look like observers rather than participants in an active scene which was dominated by energetic, independent tenant farmers.[17] Not all of them worked from offices as well-appointed as the Revesby offices of Sir John Banks' estate which so impressed Arthur Young.

'His office, of two rooms, is contained in the space of thirty feet by sixteen; there is a brick partition between, with an iron plated door, so that the room in which a fire is always burning, might be burnt down without affecting the inner one; . . . There is a catalogue of names and subjects . . . so that whether the inquiry concerned a man, or a drainage or an enclosure, or a farm, or a wood, the request was scarcely named before a mass of information was in a moment before me . . . The first room contains desks, tables and bookcase, with measures, levels etc. and a wooden case, which when open forms a bookcase . . . when closed, forms a package ready for a carrier's wagon. . . .'[18]

Some stewards such as John Parkinson were agents to a number of landowners and included their sons in a partnership, so providing for their training. A letter from him at Asgarby to Sir John Dashwood in 1808 throws some light upon the training of land agents and their delicate relationship with the farmers:

'. . . I feel much gratified with the attention and regard you are pleased to pay to my son John. I think him very honest, industrious and worthy of the service he occupies as a partner in the stewardships I hold and I have the satisfaction to say his eldest brother is equally as ? and prudent as John with a superior education, serving his clerkship in the law with the Town Clerk in Lincoln, after that with ? and Miller in London for a year and two years after with Mr. Shadwell the conveyancer and councillor in Town and my only reason Sir John for giving him the preference is as yours is a new mode of letting land in this county it would not degrade a lawyers' Office, when it might affect the reputation of a man in my country sphere of life, and as my son John is well known to be a joint partner with me in my other stewardships, made me afraid I might not keep

[16] T. W. Beastall, *A North Country Estate*, Chichester, 1975, pp. 121–9 and 217.
[17] Arthur Young, *Gen. View*, 1813, pp. 21–2. [18] Op. cit., p. 23.

clear of being blamed for introducing the mode of letting farms by auction.'[19]

Some agents had stewardships in a number of counties and they relied upon clerks to attend to the day to day running of affairs. In 1841 Mr D. Martin of Holbeach wrote to Lord Brownlow asking for work as an agent. He had been the personal secretary to Lord Farnborough after working in the Paymaster General's Office. His master had made him a trustee to his will and as a sign of his estimation of him he left him £800. He was, at the time of writing from Teignmouth, agent for the Duke of Somerset's estates in Lincolnshire, Cambridgeshire, Buckinghamshire and part of Devon; he could take on another 'estate or two' if they lay near the Duke's lands.[20] When an agent's assistant was being considered for the Dashwood estate in 1777 a prospective applicant was described as 'a good penman . . . young and bred to accounts'.[21] Ability to deal with accounts and to supervise contractors engaged in building seems to have been more important in an agent than knowledge of farming methods or progressive practices. Skill in drawing up leases and agreements, ability to insist on their observance, care in collecting information about the mood of tenants and the activities of other landowners and their stewards; these were the most valued qualities. Advice from an experienced steward about how to handle tenants was expected as well, though it was not always acceptable or acted upon. Sir Francis Dashwood was told in the 1760s '. . . if you get a set of good tenants it will be best to continue them for it is neither good for the landlord, tenant nor the estate to be often shifting'. A general discharge of the tenants in bad times would only throw them together.[22]

A degree of social distance from the tenant farmers was sometimes an advantage. Samuel Ullet was refused the position of under-steward on the Willoughby estates in 1831 because he was thought to have too many acquaintances and relations around the estate.[23] Thomas Dungworth, agent to the sixth Earl of Scarbrough, was called upon to advise his employer about the rent reductions in 1815 of Lord Monson, the Earl of Yarborough, Lady Wray and Sir Thomas Whichcote, to say whether Lord Scarbrough's Lincolnshire farms had been over-valued in a recent survey and valuation and by how much the farmers wanted their rents to be reduced. When the leading farmer on the Lincolnshire estates made the journey to Lord Scarbrough's Yorkshire home to appeal

[19] MSS., D. D. Dashwood (Bucks.) F 7/13/8. [20] L.A.O. 2BNL. 23/37.

[21] MSS, D. D. Dashwood (Bucks.) B/19/6/21.

[22] Ibid., B/19/5/26 and B/19/6/23. [23] L.A.O. 3 ANC 7/23/25/81–3.

for a rent reduction in 1815 without telling the agent of his intention a great stir was caused and matters were made no better by the agent's appearing to take the tenants' part when he himself was an occupier of a holding worth £152 a year. The occasion produced one of the sixth Earl's pungent comments on the habits of farmers in the war years.

'Had not they been lifted out of their sphere by the great agricultural meetings at the Duke of——, My Lord—— (which has totally destroyed that most useful member of Society the *Industrious*, working farmer). Had they not given dinners, with different sorts of wine, drove their gigs, and sent their daughters to boarding schools at 40 and 50gs. a year instead of teaching them to be good housewives at home, they would now have had something to spare for worse times and not endeavour to make the *whole* burden fall on the landlord.'[24]

Thomas Dungworth was expected to coax rents out of the reluctant tenants rather than to advise on new management, though he did explain why farmers were hard pressed. His correspondence reflects some of the independence of many tenant farmers in the post-war years. His predecessor on the other hand, Richard Bassett of Glentworth, had been a friend to the family as well as the steward. He offered to invest some of his savings in the Lumley colliery enterprise of the 1770s, and he lent, at 5 per cent interest, £800 towards the enclosure of Hackthorn.

One steward, John Higgins, born in Shrewsbury in 1796 rose to fortune and fame in South Lincolnshire by the time of his death in 1872. He settled in Lincolnshire in 1819 when he secured the agency of General Manners' estates and in 1824 he managed the small estates of the Darwin family. His employer was Dr Robert Waring Darwin, father of Charles Robert Darwin, author of the *Origin of the Species*. By the 1840s Higgins was an authority on complex tenurial, rating and tithe matters in an area of east Lincolnshire from North Somercotes and Grainthorpe down to Orby and Burgh. His knowledge, accumulated during the work of tithe commutation after 1836, made him a natural choice for numerous incumbents and lay improprietors and in time they made up the greater part of his clientele. He worked as an enclosure commissioner for Alford and neighbouring parishes and in 1840 or 1841, Samuel Forster of the London firm of solicitors, Frere, Forster and Co. which acted for the Well estate of the Christopher family, gave Higgins charge of his Great Carlton property. Through this firm he acquired agencies in Norfolk, Northamptonshire and Middlesex in the 1850s. The Well,

[24] Beastall, op. cit., pp. 123–4.

Alford and Bloxham estates of the Christophers had been in his care for some time as he had been associated with part of them from his first coming to the county to work for George Manners. When in 1852 R. A. Christopher became Chancellor of the Duchy of Lancaster he assisted Higgins in taking up the receivership of the northern division of the Crown estates and the stewardship of some royal manors. After fund-raising for Alford parish church in 1865 and helping with the maintenance of national schools he enjoyed the esteem of land-owners, clergy and tenant farmers. His fortune, accumulated during 50 busy years, was invested largely in railway shares. His surviving children were to receive about £4,000 each at his death. Two of his sons continued his business, another took up land agency in Scotland while a fourth son entered the Church. Two daughters married Lincolnshire farmers, one married a clergyman and two remained single. The agent for non-resident landlords, John Higgins had been in the parishes with which he was most closely associated, the substitute for the squire. In Alford especially he was respected as a Churchman, a Conservative and a leader in the community; a reputation that rested upon his industry and his residence in the locality and not upon his landownership.[25]

It is difficult to establish how much influence an agent had upon farming practices. By bringing the tenants together for bi-annual or annual rent day dinners he could provide a context for them to exchange views. By supervising their performance of the covenants in their leases or annual agreements he could protect an estate from over-cropping and the effects of negligent farming. He could promote the building of cottages, introduce draining schemes, encourage better accommodation for stock on farmsteads either by drawing up plans or arranging for tenants to be assisted in improving their own farm buildings. Landowners sometimes pressed new ideas upon their agents or stewards in the expectation that they in turn would recommend them to the tenants. Lord Willoughby d'Eresby urged the use of Scottish hedge bills, and the attractions of the 1838 Glasgow cattle show upon his Lincolnshire agent and sub-agent.[26] George Booth his sub-agent took an interest in the 'Scotch method of sowing turnips upon ridges' in 1836. That most agents were involved, albeit at one step removed, from agricultural improvement is clear from their correspondence and memoranda and it is more on these than the few written sources from practising farmers that historians depend for their knowledge of farming development. Their contacts on other estates and their oppor-

[25] L.A.O. *Archivists' Report* 25, pp. 66–8.

[26] L.A.O. 3 ANC 7/23/33/44, 7/23/34/55, 7/23/37/17.

tunities for travel put them in a good position to understand and to encourage, for example, the mixed farming which in South Lincolnshire and Lindsey was at the centre of the agricultural revolution. Their knowledge of tenant right customs, the attitudes of farmers and forms of tenure put them in an influential position to encourage the developments which in the second quarter of the nineteenth century were to transform the county's agriculture.

Changes in public utilities such as roads, canals, ports and markets accompanied advances in farming methods. No account of the agricultural revolution can ignore them or their effect on the social life of the county. A decline in the marked regional differences in farming within Lincolnshire was a feature of the developments that took place between 1700 and 1875 and though it is easy to overestimate the influence of better communications in the process, nevertheless better roads, canals and later, railways each played a part in facilitating improved contact between the producers of wool, mutton, wheat, barley and vegetables and their customers both within and outside the county. There was a pressing need for improvement. The land-lighthouse at Dunston was a monument to it in both communications and agriculture. The enclosure of open-field villages gave a new definition to roads which had become wide rutted tracks as travellers had avoided pot-holes in their uncertain progress across the country. Where turnpiking accompanied or preceded enclosure, roads were built up above the surrounding fields to afford a clearer, safer route. In the last quarter of the eighteenth century these ramparted ways were included in Lincolnshire's vocabulary as well as its scenery for the 'ramper' was a landmark, sometimes as a parish boundary, more often as a highway and a means of communication with other villages lying off it. The Brigg turnpike trustees had the Lincoln-Barton-on-Humber road ramparted with limestone and gravel and a section near Caistor was raised with flints.[27] Over areas of open field, warren and heath a rampart was a welcome definition, as at Ravendale Field and across Ulceby Field where the Dexthorpe trustees raised the level and between Lincoln and Sleaford. There were fewer fords as the century progressed and enclosure and draining schemes went ahead. The *Gentleman's Magazine* for May 1774[28] affirmed that the wealth of Lincolnshire was displayed in its good roads but Arthur Young was not impressed with them.[29] Loss of direction on a heath must have been uncomfortable and certainly frustrating. As late as

[27] Charles Brears, *Lincolnshire in the Seventeenth and Eighteenth Centuries*, London, 1940, p. 153.

[28] *The Gentleman's Magazine* 1774, p. 207. [29] Arthur Young, *Gen. View*, p. 405.

1821 it was possible to lose one's bearings at night in Grimsthorpe Park. Robert Dyer, domestic physician to Lady Willoughby, lost his way in a chaise hired at Stamford in which he was completing his journey from London. Only attention to the chimes of the castle clock saved him and the post-boy from travelling round all night.[30]

In the east midlands at large some of the earliest evidence of a concerted attempt to improve roads comes from the Great North road which left most of the county untouched; from the Wragby district where improved links with Rotherham through Bawtry were sought; from the Wolds where the movement of cattle was important, and from the Deeping Fen drainage commissioners who as early as 1666 exercised turnpike trustees' rights on a road near Spalding. In 1725 a turnpike trust was set up for a portion of the Great North road between Spittlegate Hill, Grantham and Little Drayton in Nottinghamshire.[31] As a result of another measure in 1725, milestones were erected and improvements made to the stretch between Stamford and Grantham. In 1738–9 the road from Langworth Bridge to Wragby was repaired and in the 1750s roads around Lincoln received attention. Access to the city from the Dunham and Littleborough ferries, from Waddington over the Witham at Bracebridge and from Canwick Hill was put under turnpike trusts. The road from Lincoln to Peterborough was turnpiked and with the coming of peace with France in 1763 there was an onset of road improvement which made the 1760s a decade of, on paper at least, significant advance. In 1765 access to the West Riding was made easier by a scheme affecting the road from Hainton to Bawtry, while the links by ferry with Selby, York and Hull were brought nearer to Lincoln when the road to Barton was improved. The Lincoln to Newark road was to be turnpiked in 1772 in a scheme which Newark interests had put forward, but the plan fell through and the Lincoln trustees worked only as far as Potter-hill.

Large capital sums were needed to gain permission to bring in a Bill and then to carry out the terms of an Act authorizing a turnpike trust. Resources do not appear to have been slow to come forward. As with land purchase, there were groups of families who had money to spare to invest in road development though improvements were at first uncertain because of lack of expertise in building, lack of suitable building materials or poor management. After a request from the Postmaster General, the Brigg trustees consulted neighbouring magistrates in 1822 and looked for a surveyor to advise on McAdam's principles of road building.[32] His advice

[30] LH vol. 1, part 7, 1951, p. 293. [31] Geo. 1. *c.* 16.

[32] Brears, *Lincolnshire in Seventeenth and Eighteenth Centuries*, p. 156.

was used in 1826 on the Leadenham to Mansfield road and he was surveyor for the Grantham to Nottingham highway. Yet it was long after the first turnpike had been laid down that clear evidence of technical advance, social benefit and economic use appears. Of the 29 trusts in Lincolnshire, the returns of 1840 indicate that though two were in a poor state, the others were enjoying increased revenues from tolls showing that more traffic was moving. But by then the railway age was at hand.[33]

Sir Joseph Banks had shares in the Sleaford and Tattershall road and bridge and in the Grimsby turnpike by 1793. His holdings were to extend in the early years of the new century to the Horncastle Navigation, the Fossdyke Bridge Committee and the Witham Navigation.[34] Indifferent and even dangerous communications were a matter of concern to landlords and their agents. The Rector of Welbourn asked Lady le Despencer to direct her letters to him via 'Mr. Green's the Chemist' in Lincoln as sending them through Grantham was uncertain, but a little later in the same year, 1767, he was advising the Grantham direction again as the Lincoln arrangement was proving unsatisfactory. Postal robberies, or rumours of them, interrupted the forwarding of rents in 1772 on the Dunston estate.[35] In a letter to Sir Francis Dashwood about the Witham improvement Charles Chaplin explained his eagerness for action. It was a matter of public utility; many were involved and somebody had to risk appearing officious to push the plan. He was concerned by the indolence of many who would benefit and he ended with the hope that Parliament would give it proper attention. 'I hope this provincial concern will not be thought too minute and inconsiderable to deserve the attention of the Legislature.'[36] In 1770 he wrote to Lord le Despencer apologizing for failing to meet him in October about plans for an enclosure on Dunston Heath; he had 'taken' the Witham but a lock was out of order and he had to go to an engineer who could not remain long in the county.[37] The scarcity of engineering advice probably inhibited rapid progress in water as well as road transport. Yet some villages were clearly much improved by a turnpiked road. The Sleaford to Tattershall scheme of 1793 broke down the autumnal and winter isolation of the fen villages like Anwick, North Kyme and Billinghay. Land values increased and villages like Burton Pedwardine and Ewerby Thorpe benefited from the remaking of their roads with a firm, gravel base,

[33] Brears, op. cit.
[34] L.A.O. RA 2/A/1/4.
[35] MSS., D. D. Dashwood (Bucks.) C.5. B11/5. and B19/6/7.
[36] Ibid., B19/7/7. [37] Ibid., B19/8/8.

even though they were not turnpiked.[38] Sometimes a bad road to a waterway was enough to deny to farmers and others the benefits of better transport by water. In November 1790, 5,000 poles and rails awaited transport to the Fossdyke from the Doddington estate, yet rutted roads to the waterway held up dispatch. The good level of water in Fossdyke was an advantage, for shipping could move well, but the hop gardens at Doddington on the same level were under water. At that time there was no ready sale for timber as this was the lull between the two great surges of enclosure; the steward at Doddington observed in January 1791 that '. . . the spirit for enclosing seems to be again revivin' in this county'. He had sold timber for the Clayworth enclosure over in Nottinghamshire but Trent flooding and bad roads had made delivery difficult.[39]

Traffic on the Fossdyke did increase in volume and value after the scheme for its improvement, started in 1762, had taken effect but it was towards the end of the Napoleonic wars before the trend was marked. By 1767 a vessel was leaving once per fortnight bound for Leeds with wool and new wharves were being cut and built at Lincoln.[40] Although there were complaints of depression the Fossdyke revenue rose from 1746 to 1750 when it ranged between £400 and £600 a year to £1,370 in 1764 to over £2,000 in 1789. Thereafter except for 1794 it never fell below £2,000 a year and in 1814 it reached nearly £6,000.[41] In 1781 the Glen and Bourne Eau were scoured, so providing a link between Bourne and Spalding. In the next decade the Grantham canal and the Sleaford Navigation were built to put Grantham in touch with the Trent and Sleaford with the Witham. In 1792 an Act was passed for Horncastle to be linked with the Witham. Louth developed as an inland port after its link with Tetney Haven was made between 1763 and 1770. John Cragg of Threckingham on tour in the autumn of 1799 was impressed by Louth's river basin, a quarter of a mile to the east of the town. Spacious, with 50 ton vessels in it, the basin had warehouses for wool and wheat. A slip was being built there amidst a thriving trade in corn, coal and wool. The town had a woollen manufactory employing many children on 20 machines, worked by water power for carding, spinning and reeling the wool. A carpet factory was visited at the same time.[42] Market towns such as Horncastle, Louth and Boston were made more accessible to farmers, who had now a

[38] David Grigg, *The Agricultural Revolution in South Lincolnshire*, Cambridge, 1966, p. 44.

[39] *LNQ*. vol. 16, p. 26.

[40] Sir Francis Hill, *Georgian Lincoln*, Cambridge, 1966, p. 134.

[41] Hill, op. cit. [42] L.A.O. Dixon 12/4/4.

more reliable means of sending their wool, wheat, barley and oats to markets. Farmers' wives in the Fens used small rowing boats or schoutts to make their way to towns along the drains which ran past their farmsteads. Improved waterways opened up the county to the rest of the country, at a time when its cultivatable area was increasing and its production per acre was about to soar. For bulk cargoes like timber, stone and coal the Trent had always been important but now these heavy, slow-moving loads could move farther into the county along Fossdyke and the Witham and from these waterways to connecting canals. Nottingham, the West Midlands and the West Riding were brought nearer to the Lincolnshire producers by improved waterways; from the middle 1820s, market intelligence reports on a weekly basis were available by post for Lindsey farmers from Wakefield, Leeds, Hull and Nottingham, giving facts about the prices of wheat, barley, beans, oats and livestock with comments upon the state of trade.

James Green Dixon of Caistor and Rothwell added a corn merchant's business to his farming in 1824. He stored the purchases made from the north Wolds farmers in warehouses at Brigg, Brandy Wharf, Louth and Grimsby. Some he sent to London but his main artery was the Aire and Calder Canal to his factors Thomas and Richard Binney of Wakefield and James Hirst of Leeds. In return he purchased coal from dealers at Horbury Bridge, Flockton and Lofthouse. It was shipped from Wakefield to the Ancholme and distributed in small quantities to domestic consumers around Caistor. Rape cake, linseed and bones were carted from the canal for local customers.[43] Kesteven and Holland, meanwhile, looked west and south for their markets. Butchers from Manchester, Sheffield and Wakefield drew their supplies from the beef and barley country in Kesteven and West Riding wool spinners bought regularly from the farmers on the Heath. Much of the grain from the new arable lands of the Fens was sent through Spalding and Boston for shipment to London. The capital's stables had an enduring appetite for Lincolnshire oats. In 1811 Boston market provided London with one-third of its intake of oats and for the first half of the nineteenth century it held its place as one of the three leading corn markets in the country.[44] Smithfield attracted livestock on the hoof from South Lincolnshire and then the railways took up the trade. That landowners and their agents were quick to see the beneficial effects of improved transport is illustrated by the appeal in 1766 of the agent on the Drake estates at Croft for his employer to support plans to

[43] L.A.O. *Archivists' Report*, 24; Dixon, p. 21; 3 Dixon 3/2, 1824–5.

[44] Grigg, *Agricultural Revolution in South Lincolnshire*, p. 46 and table 5, p. 7.

widen and resurface the Boston–Wainfleet and the Partney road. Wool from the Croft estate was sent to Boston for shipment north and south along the east coast while cattle en route to Smithfield used these roads. Turnpiking would enable wool to be moved at any time of the year whereas the present condition of the roads meant that it could only be moved with safety in summer. William Drake, convinced by his steward's arguments invested £500 in the venture.[45]

Philip Wright, the Spilsby sheep breeder with whom Arthur Young had discussed the merits of the New Leicesters, sent his sheep to Boston market. An account for one of his journeys survives.[46]

Charges at Boston, May 30 1760

Grass at Stickney for 60 sheep	2s.	
Boy's drink		5d.
Breakfast		6d.
Help	1s.	8d.
Toll bar for 60 sheep and mare	1s.	7½d.
Toll bar for 60 sheep and mare	1s.	7½d.
Spent		2d.
Pens for 60 sheep and bands	5s.	2d.
Grass for 60 sheep	3s.	
Help	1s.	8d.
Mare		6d.
Dinner	1s.	2d.
Supper	1s.	2d.
Breakfast		6d.
Dinner	1s.	2d.
Spent		7d.
Toll bar		1½d.
Spent		2d.
Hostler and mare		7d.

Some allowances were made to local people for the use of improved roads and waterways. There were no tolls for farmers from Gedney Dike and Gedney Marshes making for Lincoln and Boston markets to buy cattle. Trustees of turnpikes allowed the payment of fixed sums instead of tolls. In 1772 Louth residents riding on Dexthorpe turnpike were charged in this way. Brigg tradesmen paid 7s. 6d. a year for their saddle horses on the Brigg turnpike and Lord Monson compounded for his saddle horses and equipages at Riseholme Hedge at 1½ guineas per annum.[47]

By 1815 Lincolnshire had a network of turnpiked roads and

[45] L.A.O. Tyr. 4/1/48..

[46] L.A.O. 2 Chatterton, 1/438, and Arthur Young, *Gen. View*, 1813, pp. 379–80.

[47] Brears, *Lincolnshire in Seventeenth and Eighteenth Centuries*, p. 153.

canals which put producers in closer touch with their customers than ever before, though much remained to be done in the 1820s to improve the quality of roads under the guidance of McAdam. By 1796 many of the market towns of the Wolds had outlets to the sea or a major waterway. Caistor was linked to the Ancholme by 1794. Grantham had access to the Trent at Nottingham by 1797 and Bourne by 1781 had an outlet along the Eau to its junction with the Glen. Though traffic was interrupted by floods, by lack of water in dry seasons such as 1797 and 1798, by defective locks and ice in winter, the waterways contributed to agricultural progress. Yet in time, rising expectations rendered the canals inadequate and in some cases traffic declined or returned to the roads. The financial state of Lincolnshire's turnpikes was not entirely satisfactory, however. Labour costs were low but many of them could not make a profit. James McAdam said that paupers were set to work on road repair in the county in 1824 and between 1825 and 1829 wages were 1s. and 8d. or 2s. a day. In the West Riding they were 2s. and 6d. a day but in the southern counties they were below the Lincolnshire rate. Even so in 1821, 72 per cent of the county's turnpiked road mileage lay under the management of trusts whose financial state was adverse. By 1837 there had been an improvement and 40 per cent of the mileage was controlled by trusts with a favourable financial state.[48]

After 1815 at least it was much easier to move in and out of the county. One Lincoln coach and waggon owner who ran a service to and from London made enough to retire in 1796, helped by his subsidiary trade in rum and brandy. Turnpiking had made possible better passenger services to Bawtry, East Retford and the ferry at Dunham. It had taken four days in 1723 to reach London from Barton-on-Humber. By 1786 the journey from Lincoln to London took 30 hours. A mail coach superseded the old stage-coach between Lincoln and Boston in 1804. The toll-gatherers received 1s. extra per day to attend to it. A London–Boston service started in 1807. By 1818 it was running forward to Louth and by 1827 direct to Grimsby. When in 1838 Usselby House was advertised to let, the good communications of Lindsey were listed in its attractions. Offered at £70 a year with or without 17 acres, the house stood in parkland past which the mail from London through Boston to Hull ran both ways each day. Market Rasen on the Louth–Sheffield mail route was only three miles away. The post and market town of

[48] Grigg, *Agricultural Revolution in South Lincolnshire*, pp. 44, 45; William Albert, *The Turnpike Road System in England, 1663–1840*, Cambridge, 1972, pp. 158, 165, 235.

Caistor was only six miles distant and there was excellent hunting with the Brocklesby and the Burton packs.[49]

Saltfleet and other coastal settlements advertised the pleasures of the seaside long before the railway age. By 1812 T. Russell ran a coach to Boston from the Black Boy in Nottingham three times a week for the use of seabathers.[50] From 1787 Skegness had attracted bathers and provided a tavern for them but in 1845 there was greater provision for tourists. 'Skegness during the summer months is frequented as a watering place and for which there are Bathing Machines, two inns called the "Old" and the "New" Hotels which are suitable and with accommodation of the Table d'hote is tolerably comfortable—there are also a few lodging houses . . . The sea is bold at high tide but it recedes and leaves a large space of land behind until its return.'[51]

Travellers entered Lindsey for business and pleasure. Brigg Fair attracted 200 people from Hull by boat in June 1794.[52] Better roads no doubt helped to draw in more hunting families to the Brocklesby district. John Parkinson observed that in November 1787 a number of country people had told him near Brigg that the hunt was to pass. It was '. . . the finest sight they had ever seen' with 150 horsemen including the Earls of Effingham and Scarbrough, looking in their scarlet like a troop of cavalry. He thought that this 'style of hunting is very different from ours in Lincolnshire'. In 1793 the company at Brocklesby for hunting included Lord Monson, Lord Bourcherett, Lord Exeter, the Vyners and the Aufreres.[53] Meanwhile, in more business-like vein, a meeting was held in Lincoln at the Guildhall to establish a fat stock cattle market. Twenty-nine gentlemen, graziers, farmers and 'others' including Major Thomas Preston, Richard Parkinson, Benjamin Codd and Richard Ellison reasoned that pens should be erected and charged at 'the same sum as is now paid at the like markets in Rotherham . . .'[54] The growth of local and regional banks was a sign of an increasing economic activity though their variations of fortune indicated too that progress was not without its uncertainties and temporary failures.

In 1775 Smiths the bankers of Nottingham opened a Lincoln branch. Richard Ellison and Abel Smith who were associated with it had invested in the Sleaford and Horncastle navigation and a number of turnpike trusts. When Lord Carrington (formerly Robert Smith) retired in 1778 from the Lincoln bank it had a note

[49] L.A.O. 2 TDE. D/1/18. [50] *LRSM*, 10 May 1799, and 6 July 1821.
[51] Lumley MSS., Downes Report, EMS/39, L.A.O. TYR 4/1/141.
[52] L.A.O. Dixon 16/14. [53] L.A.O. Dixon 16/4/22, 16/8/5.
[54] Lincolnshire Library, Lincoln, 5020.

circulation of £116,000 and an annual profit of £9,867. By 1816, under genteel and clerical patronage, Lincoln had seen the opening of a Savings Bank which, despite the financial vicissitudes of the post-war period, was prosperous enough in 1836 to purchase new premises. After the removal in 1826 of restrictions on joint-stock banking, new services were offered and farmers gradually made more use of them. Bank stoppages such as those which clouded the peace celebrations of 1814 in Lincoln, Boston, Leicester and Derby, however, justified their suspicions. Philip Wright, the sheep farmer, lost £670 when the Spilsby bank failed. John Steel and John Wray the bankers, were declared bankrupt, but the debts of nearly £30,000 were paid off under a commission set up to investigate the collapse.[55] Even so, banking had made an impact upon Lincolnshire farmers and had come a long way since the 1770s when agents on the Elwes estates in Lindsey were ordered to trust to merchants' bills to remit the collected rents rather than to place confidence in the Hull banker.[56] The uncertainty of country banking was, however, an element in the change from leases to annual tenancies in the 1820s. The instability of banks added to the air of apprehension in the years after the wars and in that climate the freedom of an annual tenancy was attractive and many farmers as well as landowners preferred it to long leases.

Improvements in transport, markets, banking and postal services were, however, only part of the changing fabric of the county as the agricultural revolution ran its course. The extension of the cultivated area and its more intensive use were the real revolution and this development depended upon sources of power in the form of wind, steam, horses and human energy.

[55] L.A.O. 2 Chatterton, 6/11.

[56] L.A.O. *Archivists' Report*, 1957–8, p. 22.

6

Lincolnshire Labourers

VILLAGE studies and exploration of social evidence now combine to give a sharper picture of the farm labourers upon whose efforts so much of the agricultural advance depended. Though there was more unease and discontent beneath the surface than the traditional view would lead one to expect, Lincolnshire labourers escaped the grinding poverty of farm workers in some of the southern counties without attaining the relative but fluctuating affluence enjoyed in some northern industrialized villages.[1] Arthur Young was impressed by the comparative comfort of Lincolnshire farm workers in the final quarter of the eighteenth century. The provision of cow-gates was thought to be the cause. In 48 parishes in Lincolnshire and Rutland there were 753 cottagers with cow-pastures and they owned nearly 1,200 cows. These kept the labourers off the parish authorities and in consequence the poor rates were under half of those found elsewhere.[2]

The Earl of Scarbrough, Sir John Sheffield, Lord Carrington, Mr Chaplin and Mr Goulton were among the Lincolnshire landlords who provided small plots of land on which cottagers could keep one or sometimes two cows. The cow rather than the pig in the eighteenth century made the difference between need and a degree of comfort in the farm workers' domestic economy. At Blankney, on the edge of the Heath, a village where a labour force was kept for estate development and maintenance as well as for direct farming, the cottagers had a cow each and a croft to provide hay for winter feed. Where a garden and room for a pig were allowed as well, they were contended; the poor rate at 8d. in the pound compared well with the 1s. 3d. in neighbouring parishes. At Hackthorn the rent of a cottage was 20s. a year, but where accommodation for a cow was provided it rose to £3. 10s. There, women were spinning flax for 3d.

[1] B. A. Holderness, 'Open and Close Parishes in England in the Eighteenth and Nineteenth Centuries', *AHR*, Vol. 2, 1972, part II.

[2] G. E. Mingay, *Arthur Young and his Times*, London, 1975, p. 115.

a day to add to the family income. Farther north at Glentworth, on the Cliff, where the cow-gate provision was to elicit favourable comment in estate surveys as late as 1845 and 1862, the cottagers had land in a ring fence which they attempted to cultivate. Arthur Young considered that grassland should be set aside as the cultivation of arable was too much for the spare time and energy of farm workers. At Kirton two allotments, one of 28 acres and another of 22 acres, were grazed and mown for hay alternately. Valued at £50 a year for 50 acres, the occupants were paying 28s. each to the overseers so a profit of 8s. an acre, combined with satisfaction for the cottagers, helped to keep down the poor rate. Sir John Sheffield and Lord Carrington had bought up the cottages, making the occupants their tenants and so removing them from the possible ill effects of holding their cottages from the tenant farmers. In the 1790s with low rents, land for two cows and the room to keep two or three pigs, they impressed observers with their clean, good clothes, good beds and furniture and their care of their children. There was only one public house and the farm workers seemed to be sober and orderly. At Roxby on the Elwes estate, good cottages usually had two acres each for winter feed for cows and one and a half for summer grazing.

At Winteringham and at Humberstone Lord Carrington held the cottages in hand and provided cow-gates and gardens. Independent of the large farmers, the Humberstone cottagers had the use of 60 acres a quarter of a mile from the village. This was divided into a plot for summer pasture and another for winter feed. The cottagers manured the meadow land for more hay and then changed the plots round after three years. With rents lower than they could have expected from the farmers, security of tenure, possession of little paddocks and gardens near their houses as well as use of the grassland, they enjoyed a degree of independence and respectability which at the time was enviable. Similar arrangements on the estates of Messrs Skipwith and Lloyd at Aylesby and on Lord Yarborough's were noted with satisfaction, but even these slender means for comfort were thought to have their drawbacks; when after the War ended prices fell in the 1820s to lower levels and prospects were less inviting, the prejudices against land occupation by farm workers took the form in some villages of cottage demolition and the removal of cow-gates. It was noted in parishes where cow-gates were numerous that the children were not ragged but they were not made industrious and with the pigs they filled every quarter of the village. At Burton in the new cottages Arthur Young thought that 'The women are very lazy; I have noted their indolence in spinning; Mr. Goulton's expression was "they do nothing but bring children, and eat cake;" nay the men milk their cows for them; but the men very sober and industrious."[3]

Shepherds were the aristocracy of the agricultural labour force on the Wolds in the eighteenth century and their pay and conditions of service reflected their special position. In 1776 Richard Ranby agreed to work for a year from May Day for £10.10s. with permission to keep six couples of ewes and lambs and to winter the lambs upon turnips. He was to keep two cows and two pigs in the cratch yard in winter and one in summer. He was to have his cottage rent free and his fuel without cost.[4] These conditions seem to have been typical on the Wolds in this period. In 1789 to 1790 Peter Story was hired for £11.11s. a year with permission to keep a ewe and lambs. By 1799 £13.13s. a year or even £15 were offered for good shepherds with the usual payments in kind. Meanwhile a waggoner in 1785 would receive £10.15s. a year, 5d. as a fastening penny and 1s. for a drink on the day the bargain was struck with perhaps a rent-free cottage and a load of fuel a year. Stephen Windly was taken on as a labourer by Mr Dixon in October 1778 to start on May Day 1779. No money wage was recorded but he was to have a house, garden and a pig yard rent free. For fuel he was to have two loads of furz and a load of coal from Grimsby for payment of the road toll only. He could keep a pig in the cratch yard to go in at threshing time and to remain there until threshing was over. Work was to be provided for him all the year round. He was to thresh all the winter at a fair 'county's price' and his wife was to work on the farm at hay and corn harvest, during 'muck knocking' and at turnip dragging time. Her husband appears to have been responsible for all the mowing of grass on the farm. Here was probably an example of a worker engaged to mow and thresh on piece work done by gangs which he would gather and pay. He would be then the leader of a private gang. Arrangements for housing and fuel provision together with allowances for the keeping of sheep, cows or pigs did not always ensure continuity of service. Joseph Brocklesby engaged in March 1791 to work until the next Lady Day for £8, with 5s. fastening penny and permission to keep a couple of ewes and lambs, left in September 1791 by agreement. He was 'always out' especially on Sundays. The isolation of the living-in farm servants must have been an influence in their changing farms and seeking a degree of independence as early as possible in marriage. One farm servant paid £11 a year from May Day 1785, got married in grass mowing

[3] Arthur Young, *Gen. View*, 1813, pp. 459–64.

[4] L.A.O. Dixon 4/1, f. 21.

time and fled the farm at 3 a.m., leaving all the doors open in his haste.[5]

In 1792 Dixon paid unskilled single labourers £5.5s. a year with 2s.6d. as a fastening penny, and gave them a pair of boots and a greatcoat. Sometimes a waistcoat, a hat and a pair of breeches were added. A groom and waiting boy on a large Wolds farm received £4.4s. in 1798, 2s.6d. fastening penny and a suit, waistcoat, breeches, hat, girdle and a coat. By 1799 indoor female servants were receiving £5.5s. a year whereas in 1788 £4.10s. with 5s. fastening penny were usual. Judging by the strictures upon them many of the female servants found it hard to settle in what seems to have been a kindly if perhaps frugal household. 'Jane Trout was hired for our grass farm, from May Day 1776 to May Day 1777 but she went from her place before her time was up.' She lost 3s. 10d. by being away. Her employer commented 'She behaved amiss.' Her wage was £4 a year. Another servant on £3.3s. a year in 1779 was given 2s. by her mistress when her mother died in July 1779, one shilling for a drawn tooth and 3s. for Caistor fair at Michaelmas 1779. She was given a pair of pumps, two pairs of shoes and five yards of cloth at 14d. a yard 'for shifts'. Fastening pennies of 5s. handkerchiefs, gloves, ribbons, caps and second-hand gowns were not, it seems, of much avail for the female servants continued to leave early and were docked some of their wages for doing so. Their characters did not escape comment from their disappointed employer who found one Judith Hall, employed for £5.5s. in 1782 to 1783, to be '. . . a very rude, ill-behaved girl, dirty and idle and impertinent to the last day'. She appeared to be 'addicted to lying'.[6]

Perhaps the monotony as much as the hard work and low wages drove servants to early departure. Fairs, markets, races and feasts upset them for days, showing how much these comparatively infrequent diversions were in fact needed. The Nocton steward wrote in July 1765 'This two Feasts of Hanworth and Dunston has so Turn'd our labourers Heads from Work that we have not been able to get all our Hay mown last Week as I Expected and Designed.' He claimed later that month that the horse races slowed down work among the haymakers, who were idle and out for money only.[7]

Thomas Dixon of Riby employed William Johnson from 1757 to 1765. He was lent 10s. and 6d. for the Militia and given a prayer book and a Bible valued at 9s. and 6d. Between the middle 1750s and

[5] L.A.O. Dixon 4/1, f. 25.
[6] L.A.O. Dixon 4/1, f. 25.
[7] MSS. D. D. Dashwood (Bucks.), B/19/5/16, 17 and 18.

the late 1790s the wages for all grades of farm employees rose from levels like £1 a year to £15.15s. for men and from £1 to £5.5s. for women. When the allowances in kind are costed then the total for a shepherd could be impressive by 1798 but much extra work was expected to make the allowances of value and perhaps the time and energy required made both the farm worker and his employer think in time that a landless labourer was better off, that is, if he were to be paid a living, money wage. William Barnard's conditions of service for January 1797 made up a total of £31.18s. a year but they imposed burdens upon the shepherd if he were to turn his allowances to account.[8]

	£.	s.	d.
To wages in money	16	16	0
To keep two pigs in the cratch yard	1	1	0
To keep a cow of his own and to let him have the milk of mine but I am to have the calf	10	0	0
House yard and garden rent free and clear of all assessments	1	10	0
To give him a chaldron of coals and leading	1	5	0
To give him two loads of dead furz		10	0
To give a strike of wheat 5s. 6d. Strike of malt 5s.6d.		11	0
Fastening penny		5	0
	£31	18	0

Labour supply in the period of the agricultural revolution was a problem for farmers. They required reliable and if possible long-serving shepherds, foremen and, as the crew-yard because of the manure it provided for hungry wolds land became vital to the farming process, 'garth-men' or stock-keepers. Their wives needed female servants to live in the farm house. Again as the Wolds went increasingly under the plough, the head waggoner became a leading figure in the farm's labour force and he needed young, usually unmarried waggoners, to make up his teams. These single men were required to live in the farm as they had to rise early and finish late, after feeding and bedding their horses. How to separate their sleeping quarters from the female servants' presented a problem which some households failed to solve with resulting bastardy and misery. The men were hired for a year and they could change their employment at the Caistor, Binbrook, Louth or Market Rasen hiring fairs and escape the consequences of their adventures. A

[8] *LNQ*, Vol. 19, p. 100.

supply of casual labour was difficult to command without encouraging over-population in the villages with its attendant pressure on the poor-rates. 'Finding him employment' throughout the year was a sign in an agreement that a worker was on a higher level than the day labourers, who could be put off or sent home when work or weather conditions paid the farmer to dispose of them. Yet landlords and farmers feared the emergence of villages and hamlets with many cheap and accessible cottages, for they attracted settlers who, though useful at hay and corn harvest, might fall upon the parish at other seasons. Where a landlord did not take the cottages in hand and let them out himself, as indeed a number of Lincolnshire landlords did, then the large farmers, grazier-flockmasters in the early eighteenth century or influential mixed farmers by the 1850s, came to hold great sway. Their policy, tolerated by absentee landlords was to pull down empty cottages, to buy in beast gates and to restrict cottage building and repair so that the labour supply was controlled. These demands led gradually to the creation of 'closed' parishes, where all or nearly all of the land and housing were owned by one landlord, and 'open' parishes where accommodation was owned by a wide variety of tradesmen, professional people, farmers and miscellaneous speculators or investors of savings or legacies. These open parishes were, or grew to be, the small country towns or large villages of a thinly-populated countryside from which farm workers employed as day labourers had to travel to their employment on foot or on donkey back. Their homes were in rows of cottages tucked away behind the small shops, warehouses, larger dwellings and the churches and chapels of such places as Binbrook, Louth, Market Rasen, Brigg and Caistor. These and many parishes like them were to staff the gangs, which were recruited to supply labour in great quantity and as cheaply as possible in times of maximum demand. Meanwhile here and there as at Blankney, Digby, Edenham and Brocklesby neat, well-housed communities were growing up beneath the eye of interested landlords whose need for labour for estate improvement and maintenance and for the home farm was combined with a determination to create a model village.[9] With a firm social structure and a clear focus for community life based on the great house and the church, these aesthetically pleasing settlements could provide only limited supplies of extra labour to the tenants who farmed beyond the park gates. Turning to the open parishes for labour, the

[9] For a description of a comfortable 'close' parish on the Heath in 1801, see W. H. Hosford, 'Digby in 1801, the Anatomy of a Lincolnshire Village', *LH*, Vol. 2, No. 3, 1955–6.

farmers helped to create the gang-system and to attract seasonal workers from Ireland.

The beginning of the division between open and close parishes is seen as early as 1711 in South Ormsby. There the forward-looking landlord, Burrell Massingberd, decided to limit the cottages on his estate to the needs of himself and his tenants for labour. Even earlier, Roger North's *Discourse on the Poor* (published in 1753 but thought to have been written before 1690) drew attention to the fact that 'Gentlemen of late years have taken up a Humour of Destroying their Tenements and Cottages ... This is done sometimes barefaced, because they harbour the Poor that are a charge to the Parish.'[10] Arthur Young noted the same trend in 1774 and so did a number of late eighteenth-century observers.[11] The Settlement Acts made landlords unwilling to maintain cottages which were not absolutely necessary, for too much accommodation in relation to employment meant higher poor rates. Squatters' settlements were brought within the influence of estates by charging a small annual acknowledgement on them to the Lord of the Manor and by improving them when they were vacated. Later they could be demolished as part of a rationalization of the estate. In the late eighteenth century small cottage holdings of a few acres were gradually removed on some estates, though in Lincolnshire more detailed work needs to be done to establish the speed and timing of the process. It seems clear that enclosure had little to do with this reduction in cottage holdings. Indeed, ownership was what counted, and demolition, like amalgamation of small farms, could go on when vacancies occurred whether the parish was largely unenclosed or not.[12] 'By 1750–70, the "pauperization" of the agricultural labourer in many parishes of upland Lincolnshire was virtually complete.'[13] Surveyors and valuers of estates seem to have been at pains to urge 'laying to' of farms or the division of others so that remaining holdings could be completed by being given a more balanced allotment of arable, meadow and pasture land and this involved the removal of land surrounding cottages and the destruction of cottage holdings. Comments that cottages were too numerous was perhaps the hallmark of the advanced valuer of the time. His recommendations were not always acted upon, however, for he had sometimes to contend not only with a resident landowner

[11] Holderness, op. cit. [10] Holderness, op. cit.

[12] L.A.O. Hen. 3/43. In the 1789 valuations for Clee and Cleethorpes where enclosure was advocated it was also insisted that amalgamation of three farms of 71 acres, 10 acres and 32 acres should take place anyway when they fell vacant.

[13] Holderness, op. cit.

anxious for his reputation for fairness, but with an estate steward unwilling to admit indifferent management or to embark upon unpopular clearances. When there was pressure through soaring poor rates, however, then the spur to action was acute. At Hainton on the edge of the Wolds in 1789 there is evidence of the buying out of beast-gate owners by farmers who were engaged upon draining the Beast Pasture. Edward Cash was to receive 18s. a year in lieu of winter beast-gate rights in that pasture, as the four tenants who together were sharing the breaking of the Sheep Walk were also draining the bogs in the low part of it and in the Beast Pasture. The estate steward at Hainton thought in 1789 that the cottages were too numerous and ought to be pulled down when the tenants died and two beast-gates should be taken in hand from two tenants when the landlord set up residence. At South Willingham, Barkwith and Benniworth the farms were considered to be too small and the cottages numerous. Yet progress in reducing their number seems to have been slow and uneven.

At Benniworth there were 27 occupiers in 1761 with farms or holdings from 339 acres to three acres. In 1789 there were still 27 from 301 acres to an acre; 16 had less than ten acres each. In 1796 the figures were unchanged but by 1836 there were only fifteen tenants, six of whom appear to have been relatives of the tenants of 1761. At Sixhills in 1814 there were 21 units or occupiers, including 14 acres in hand for 1,941 acres. By 1837 the total acreage was only slightly less at 1,936 acres, yet there were 31 occupiers. Torrington, for an acreage of 429 acres in 1789 had 6 occupiers, 4 in 1814 for 511 acres and 5 in 1837 for 509 acres. Legsby for 654 acres in 1789 had 10 occupiers, 8 in 1814 for 734 acres and 9 in 1837 for 731 acres. On the Heneage estates the influence of the resident landlord may be reflected in these figures. At Hainton where his park of 286 acres was created and in 1834 a Roman Catholic chapel was built, the units of occupation changed very little from 1789 with 25 for 2,090 acres to 26 in 1837 for 2,236 acres. The number of occupations of 10 or fewer acres did fall, however, from 9 in 1789 to 5 in 1837.

Generally the trend towards limitation of cottage accommodation went ahead in Lincolnshire between 1811 and 1821 in a reaction to the provision of cottage beast-gates which writers in the last quarter of the eighteenth century recommended.[14] Labourers had enjoyed at least a vestige of security and a degree of independence resting upon the landowner rather than the tenant farmers. Farm amalgamation could go on without unpopular clearances and yet a

[14] Holderness, op. cit., p. 130, reference to Census Enumeration Abstracts, 1801/5, vol. II, p. 49, note b.

labour supply was ensured for estate development and the labour-intensive improvements of the period such as enclosure, draining, marling and claying. When the collapse of prices and confidence in farming came after the peak prices for wheat in 1813, it is likely that farmers and many landowners began to resent former leniency in granting settlements to those who claimed a cottage holding. John Parkinson believed in 1816 that a reaction started to clerical influence in the local magistracy.[15] Well-meaning clergy on the bench had been too generous in allowing settlements; now hard-pressed, rate-paying farmers looking round for ways to cut costs, saw in numerous cottages and landlord-backed cow-holdings a source of some of their ills. So cottages were demolished and towns like Louth and Horncastle expanded. In the uplands large villages appeared whose isolation in an emptying landscape provoked surprise in travellers.

Small towns or large villages had their attractions for farm workers: some had open common land with opportunities for stock holding, a choice of shops and a range of employment which, though limited, was at least more inviting than that of an isolated village where the local shopkeeper and the leading farmer had undisputed influence. Binbrook, for example, was to be the centre of a small upland region providing labour on a day basis and attracting farm workers to itself. Not until the 1880s during the depression of farming, or indeed until the coming of the motor bus, were these services in the larger villages substantially diminished. Town and village directories for the 1830s and 1840s record a variety of services suggesting a vitality in some regional centres which must have attracted farm labourers as a compensation for the long walk or ride to work on the outlying farms. Some labourers around Caistor walked 6 to 10 miles to and from work each day.[16] Lincolnshire's uplands shared with the East Riding, Nottinghamshire, east Leicestershire, north-west Norfolk and the Cotswolds an uneven distribution of population which was to give rise to the gang system.

Between 1801 and 1841 population in the 'closed' townships of the Lindsey Marshes, for example, grew by an average of 31·9 per cent, yet the growth for all the townships was 63·7 per cent. In east Leicestershire, Rutland and west Kesteven population growth from 1801 to 1841 was only 16·8 per cent in the 'closed' townships but 30·2 per cent in all the townships examined. Population increases,

[15] Board of Agriculture, *Report on the Agricultural State of the Kingdom*, January–March, 1816, pp. 157–8.

[16] Holderness, op. cit., p. 133.

were taking place in the townships where accommodation, provided perhaps in rows of dwellings by artisans and tradesmen with capital for a small investment, and alternative employment and urban services were readily available.[17] Destruction of cottages and limitations on building were not the only causes of the gang system. The agricultural revolution on the Wolds involved the creation of arable surfaces, the carpeting of bare hills with fertile material bought, imported or created locally and all of it had to be transported and spread. In this sense upland Lincolnshire was a new country, just as new as reclaimed salt marsh and drained fenland. As in the lowland parishes, this development changed the landscape and the building pattern of the parishes. The demand for labour could not be met locally and so the towns and larger villages saw the recruitment of private and public gangs. Labourers from the open parishes were considered to be more efficient than those from close ones—a belief based upon faith in the disciplinary effect of uncertainty of employment—but some farmers found that the donkeys used by travelling labourers in Norfolk and Lincolnshire crowded their yards during the day, were fed at the employer's expense and tempted their owners to steal fodder. The strong, skilled and reliable farm worker usually secured the remaining farm cottage close to his job; so it is difficult to be precise about the quality of farm workers in terms of their living on or off the farm. Of greater concern was the quantity of available labour.

As arable farming expanded on the uplands, every 25 to 30 acres under the plough required one more man. Yet on the claylands between the Ancholme and the Trent unemployment of agricultural workers was acute in March 1851 at the time of the census. In 12 parishes from Alkborough, Whitton and Winteringham in the north to Bottesford and Broughton in the south, employment prospects were poor. There were 24 farmed acres to each agricultural worker in the area, a figure similar to that on the Wolds yet in March 1851 no more than two-thirds of the labourers had work in the region and probably few of them found regular work outside it. Employment opportunities on the small farms were limited. Holdings of less than 100 acres absorbed less than 8 per cent of the out-labourers and only 12 per cent of the farm servants. Half the farms were less than 100 acres so a man's best hope lay in the 100–400 acre farms (39 per cent of the total) and these employed 49 per cent of the day-labourers and 66 per cent of the farm servants. Agricultural labourers in north-west Lindsey enjoyed little security of employment. Only one in five lived on the farm while the rest

[17] Holderness, op. cit., p. 135.

had only day or weekly contracts, severable at will, which for many of them cannot have been full-time. A third of the entire work force (or nearly half the day labourers) was surplus to requirements. Agricultural workers ceased work or died younger than most men in the region and when they did survive to old age they were more likely than anyone else to depend on poor relief. Together with general labourers and paupers, the agricultural labourer had the fewest children at school of any occupational group.[18]

On the uplands it was a story of a strong seasonal demand for labour though it is unlikely that there was a severe and regular shortage of labourers at harvest time. Farmers could take six instead of four weeks to harvest their cereals if labour was scarce and crops were heavy. It was estimated in the 1840s that in a day a harvest worker cut half an acre of wheat in a heavy harvest and two-thirds of an acre in a light one. Workers were drawn in from the claylands of Lincolnshire and from Yorkshire and Nottinghamshire to the Fens and Wolds for harvesting. In addition, general workers, artisans and small shopkeepers and their assistants from the market towns and larger villages turned out to help. In 1837 it was observed of Lincoln '... The fashionable are at the watering places, and the mass of the working population is on the fields.'[19] Regular steamship connections with Ireland in the 1820s meant that Irish workers could easily make their way to the harvest fields of eastern Lincolnshire. By the 1840s over 20,000 arrived in Liverpool each spring to move with the ripening crops from south to north in the high-wage districts of the East Riding and Lincolnshire. By then they were migrating according to itineraries drawn up from farmers' replies to the letters they had written or had written for them asking when harvest was likely to start. They reduced the time in waiting for crops to ripen by travelling in hired horse-drawn carts from one part of eastern England to another. They worked for low wages mostly in the Fens and on the clays; only a small proportion went regularly to the uplands, although the accounts of at least one north Wolds farm show payments to a 'Michael Swainey and Co'. The Newark bankers, Messrs Hendley, with branches in Lincolnshire paid out from £4,000 to £5,000 a year to the home-going Irish in the 1830s.[20]

The 1851 census for Binbrook shows that Lincolnshire itself

[18] P. M. Tillott and G. S. Stevenson, *North-West Lindsey in 1851*, Sheffield, 1970.

[19] *LRSM*, 8th September 1837.

[20] J. A. Perkins, 'Harvest Technology and Labour Supply in Lincolnshire and the East Riding of Yorkshire 1750–1850', *Tools and Tillage III*, 1, 1976; L.A.O. 3 Dixon 2/2; Joan Thirsk, *English Peasant Farming*, London, 1957, p. 271.

supplied the extra workers needed in this region of expanding arable acreage on the Wolds. The returns for Tealby, Ludford, Stenigot and Burwell for 1851 support this view.[21] Of the 1,269 inhabitants in Binbrook, 600 were born in the village or neighbouring Orford, 133 within 5 miles of Binbrook, 214 within 5–10 miles, 186 were born within 10–20 miles and 51 over 20 miles away but within Lincolnshire. Neighbouring counties supplied 35, the rest of England 11, Ireland 10, 'other countries', 1, while in 28 cases birthplaces could not be established. None came from Wales or Scotland. Lincolnshire's population increased just over 100 per cent 1801–71, equal to the rise in Leicestershire and Derbyshire but less than the Nottinghamshire increase. The Fens and the uplands showed the most marked increase though some of it was accounted for by the growth of agricultural industries and urban development. The making of artificial manures at West Stockwith, shipbuilding at Burton on Stather and ironstone works at Frodingham after 1861 helped to cause the Lindsey increase. Engineering at Lincoln and Grantham affected the population figures for the Heath while the development of Grimsby, seaside resorts and fishing helped the marshland areas increase their population. Less industrial development and slower advances in farming account for the more modest increase in the clayland parishes and in the clay vales. Only the parishes near the Trent in north-west Lindsey showed a population increase.[22]

On large upland farms by the 1850s the waggoners, unmarried and living with either the farmer, the farm foreman or the head waggoner, supplied the resident labour. Hired at the annual fairs or statutes in May, on receipt of a 'fezzen' or fastening penny of from one to ten shillings, the man was bound to his master for a year by law. Absconding could lead to an order for arrest.[23] George Vicars, a farm bailiff at Roxby, had in 1851 five unmarried male servants living in his house, their ages ranging from 21 to 16 years.[24] The tenant of Binbrook Hill farm in the 1830s had three young waggoners living in the farmhouse. A sale catalogue of 1832 listed four bedsteads in the servant men's room, each with a chaff bed, mattress, bolster, two blankets and a carpet rug.[25] On this farm by 1851

[21] PRO, HO, 107/2115, Tealby: HO, 107/2112, Ludford: HO, 107/2112, Stenigot: HO, 107/211, Burwell.

[22] Thirsk, op. cit., pp. 197–235.

[23] *The Hull and North Lincolnshire Times*, 14 June 1870.

[24] Ian Beckwith, *Roxby, A Lincolnshire Village in the Nineteenth Century*, Roxby, 1967.

[25] L.A.O. Dixon 20/2/5.

the unmarried servants boarded with the farm foreman, but on Hall Farm and Walk Farm, they boarded with the farmer himself, as was still the common practice. About 1860 at Hall Farm, the landlord provided the foreman with a cottage which included accommodation for boarders.[26] At Hill Farm, Binbrook, in 1867 the occupier, John Iles, farmed 1,000 acres of wold land. He employed a large number of 'confined' workers even for such a sizeable holding. In 1867 when he gave evidence to the Parliamentary Commission, he had a foreman, shepherd, garthman, carpenter, blacksmith, seedman and married head waggoner. These were all housed in cottages on his farm and were hired for a year at a time. Taking together payment in kind with money, they were receiving £40 to £45 a year exclusive of a cottage and garden. He had five unmarried waggoners who boarded with his foreman. In addition he employed nine to ten Binbrook labourers by the day. His garthman for the cattle, his carpenter and seedman had been taken on since 1851. On a farm of this size and type in the 1850s there was a fairly clear hierarchy of employees. At the lowest level were the casual workers taken on for specific seasonal tasks. The central role of turnips in the cropping system alone created a demand for workers to weed and single in July and in the winter months to take up, tail and store. Then there was harvesting, mowing, threshing, manure turning, weeding, marling and sheep clipping. Here, day labour was supplemented by gang labour on contract work. Above the day labourers were the 'confined' men hired by the year to see to the daily running of the farm. These were the young waggoners who lived in the farmhouse or with the married foreman.

Above the servants were the specialized workers with a supervisory function. In their ranks something of a revolution had taken place on the Wolds by the 1850s. The shepherd no longer commanded the influence of his grandfather. He was now in charge of an important part of the mixed farm but he had not the responsibility for numbers of younger or less skilled staff as had the head waggoner. The foreman headed John Iles' list of his chief employees in 1867. Admittedly the shepherd came next but the garthman, carpenter, blacksmith and seedman (who was probably a deputy foreman), with the married head waggoner, make up the number. The influence of arable farming with its demand for labour and horse power is reflected in the list. Probably his position in John Iles' reckoning does less than justice to the head waggoner; his function was vital to the farm's economy and his local reputation was gauged

[26] R. J. Olney, ed., *Labouring Life on the Lincolnshire Wolds. A Study of Binbrook in the Mid-Nineteenth Century*, Occasional Papers, 2, *LHA*, Sleaford, 1975.

by the number, size, condition, discipline and turnout of his 'teams' of Suffolks, brown shires and Lincoln Blacks. His remedies for horse ailments were jealously guarded secrets. His authority over the young waggoners was proverbial and was demonstrated in his privilege of appearing for work at 6 a.m.—the unmarried waggoners having been up at 4 a.m. to have the teams ready. As two of his heavier horses could draw two and a half tons he had in his charge considerable power, for on some farms 30 to 40 horses were kept. His saddle room and stables were often a social centre for waggoners from neighbouring farms, who viewed each other's charges with a competitive mixture of admiration and criticism before playing quoits or dominoes to fill in their brief leisure on weekday evenings. His young waggoners had to be in bed by 9 p.m. or 10 on Saturdays and Sundays. After rising at 4 a.m. they would be allowed a break of about half an hour from 9.30 to 10 for 'lunch', then a hot dinner would follow at 2.30. They then attended to their horses for the night and stopped for tea at 6. Spare time then followed, until they 'suppered up' their horses from 8 to 9 when their day finished. On the heavy land below the Wolds, there was even greater need for regular horse power. At Roxby where in 1851 on a farm of 750 acres 30 men and 7 boys were employed, horses were needed to draw loads of potatoes to the lineside at Scawby or Thealby for transit to Manchester. On farms like these, on both the clays and the Wolds, the head waggoner or waggoner-foreman was the doyen of the labour force and for him the gleaming rows of horse brasses were what the silver crook of the shepherd had been a century before.[27]

Day labourers worked from 6 a.m. to 6 p.m. from Monday to Saturday. Sickness or wet days could involve the loss of wages; some farmers sent the men home rather than pay for jobs to be done around the yards and buildings. Wages in the 1850s had slipped from 12s. a week to 10s. and so piecework was sought by the married worker as a supplement. Rent varied from £3 to £4 a year in Binbrook and when 4s. or 5s. a week had gone for bread for a man with a wife and three or four children there was little left for clothes, fuel, furniture, beer or tobacco.[28] Although a Special Assistant Poor Law Commissioner reported in 1843 that 'The Labourers are generally better fixed in Lincolnshire than in any county in England', their diet was frugal.[29] Near Bourne only the head of the

[27] Beckwith, op. cit.

[28] Olney, op. cit., p. 20.

[29] BPP, 1843 (xii) Report of the Special Assistant Poor Law Commissioners on the Employment of Women and Children in Agriculture, pp. 251–71.

household had meat once a week and around Grantham, Boston and Gainsborough, bacon, bread and potatoes were the main items of the diet. The pig provided the margin between hardship and a passable degree of comfort. The bacon dumplings eaten near Louth were just one example of how to make the meat go further and to introduce some variety to the inevitable bread and potatoes. A Brigg butcher reported that a labourer with a wife and children would consume four pounds of mutton a week but the sop, bread, treacle and tea three times a day which was the fare of many of the women sounds as dreary as it must have been to eat.[30]

Allotments could bring vegetables into the labourers' diet; by the 1840s farmers and landowners saw in them a means to self-help and thrift preferable to the old cow-gates, which were thought to divert too much time and energy from the work of the farm. Usually of only one rood in extent, allotments drew favourable comment from sources near Holbeach, Boston, Spilsby, Grantham and Spalding. The possession of an allotment '... leads to a savings bank and there's no saying what good mayn't follow from it' said one witness from Sleaford. To be of use, the allotment needed to be near the labourer's home and on good soil. Many occupiers of these plots of less than half an acre near Boston would hire a plough and then grow corn or potatoes. A farmer from Spilsby thought that they were best cultivated by the farmer for his men as when they were held as gardens they occupied too much time. Others lent ploughs to reliable men so that they could grow corn but at Bourne one-rood allotments costing 10s. to 12s. a year in rent were kept in spade cultivation, or in some cases underlet, to provide an increased income.[31] Contract workers had an even more uncertain domestic economy than day labourers; they might be unemployed between hay and corn harvests and when the turnips had been drawn and stored. Luckily weeding and stone picking on the Wolds and pulling couch grass or twitch in the Fens provided a more regular demand for labour organized in gangs. Private gangs recruited by the farmer worked beside public gangs organized by a gang master who often operated from a town or a large village. Entries in farm accounts such as 'Danby & Co', 'Gibson & Co', clippers, Binbrook, in the 1820s suggest the variety of tasks for which gang labour was useful; threshing, mowing, weeding and sheep clipping. The fact that men, women and children worked together in these gangs eventually disturbed the nineteenth century conscience. Bad words, habits and minimal education for the children were the evils which attracted most concern, as well as hardship and occasional cruelty.

[30] Ibid. [31] Ibid., p. 261–72.

The system ensured a degree of continuity of work and so it had its attractions for the families who preferred not to deal directly with the farmer. John Iles at Binbrook had his weeding done by a public gang whose master, Neal, worked for nobody else. His picture of gang labour at threshing time given in 1867 illustrates the link between the new machines and the continuing demand for cheap and ready labour.

'Women come to my farm with a threshing machine. They are employed on the "stage" of the machine to cut the bands. There is a man at Binbrook who owns several machines, and hires men and women to go with them to the different farms. The women are hired, because they go cheaper; but they are very ready to go, being better paid than at other work. They get 1s.6d. a day; but it is dangerous, especially to the younger ones of 16 or so, because they are so careless; and it leads to great immorality.'[32]

In the 1850s and 1860s at Croyland in the Fens, children aged from five to eight would set off at 6 a.m. in batches of 40 or 50 to walk two or more miles to the farms to begin a working day which would last until twilight. In winter they reached home after dark. Their day must have been arduous with only the shelter of a hedge in which to eat their cold dinner and drink their cold tea. When sleet or snow showers sliced across the great fields on an east wind, the gang master would allow them in turn to stop work and to run about to recover from numbness. Only when rain or snow became continuous did the gang disband and go home for the day. At harvest time children worked with their families at gleaning and some claimed that they gleaned enough to keep them in bread through the winter. Mrs Burrows whose childhood was spent in the Fens of the 1850s wrote towards the end of her life 'For four years, summer and winter, I worked in these gangs—no holiday of any sort, with the exception of very wet days and Sundays—and at the end of that time it felt like Heaven to me when I was taken to the town of Leeds, and put to work in the factory. Talk about White Slaves, the Fen districts at that time was the place to look for them.'[33]

Young girls went into domestic service or worked at inns when they wanted a more respectable alternative to the gang, and some farmers preferred to employ widows or girls working with their mothers. At Welbourn in the 1840s women working with their husbands and children on piecework earned 3s. a day. The freedom

[32] BPP, 1867–8, XVII, Report of Royal Commission on the Employment of Children, p. 516.

[33] Margaret Llewelyn Davies, ed., *Life as we have known it*, London, 1977, pp. 109–14.

of fieldwork appealed to some who rejected the restrictions of domestic service. Girls could earn 1s. or 10d. a day around Spilsby and Brothercroft and near Louth or even 1s. and 6d. or 2s. a day on piecework. Similar wage rates obtained near Bourne and Spalding. The opening of National Schools may have made some girls more discriminating in employment; they might aspire to positions as housemaids, but the free evenings of fieldwork attracted others. Many must have been used to some fieldwork from their earliest years. At Messingham in potato harvest children of 12 to 13 could earn 1s. a day. Their employment had continued from at least 1825 when the Revd J. Bowstead commented upon it in the early 1840s. There were first-class ploughers of 14 or 15 at Sleaford who could earn £2.10s. a year. At 10 or 11 they had probably started as crow scarers or stone pickers. Near Withcall children of 12 could earn 3d. or 4d. a day at these and similar tasks such as weeding. Although by 1843 the opening of schools had reduced the employment of children; some farmers wanted youngsters who could read and write, the reports on their employment in Lincolnshire include many references to children being put to work as soon as they were able near Gainsborough, Spalding, Bourne and Spilsby.[34]

School attendance was affected by children going into the fields on piecework. Holidays were arranged to coincide with the seasonal demands for labour on the farms and school log-books show that not only field work interrupted attendance. At Horncastle the Wesleyan school blamed poor attendance in September 1866 on the fair. In June Mareham School Feast had caused absences while 'a grand wedding this morning' was responsible on another occasion for poor attendance. A circus and Horncastle cattle fair had, the same effect in October, even though the school had not opened until mid-September to allow for harvest work and family gleaning. At Louth and Holbeach schools had few scholars when gleaning was in progress and on 20 September 1876, the school had a half-day's holiday because so many were still out in the cornfields. Then in October, Holbeach fair attracted many children. Scholars seem to have mixed field work, school attendance and local festivities in a way which at least helped to keep monotony at a distance. Time-keeping was another problem as many children had long distances to walk. At Horncastle the schoolmaster wrote in September 1866 'More than half the School habitually come late.'[35]

It is tempting to see the gang system as an ugly result of the

[34] BPP, 1843 XII, Reports of the Special Assistant Poor Law Commissioners on the Employment of Women and Children in Agriculture, pp. 251–3.

[35] L.A.O., S. R. Horncastle, Louth, Holbeach, Hainton.

creation of closed parishes by selfish landlords and farmers but this is surely to over-simplify. Too few landlords were as energetic as the Earl of Yarborough in building cottages. Some of them perhaps lacked the capital, or were satisfied that accommodation in nearby towns and open villages would ensure a labour supply. Something else though was at work besides indifference on the part of landlords or cost cutting by farmers. A labour intensive agriculture had developed within a short space of time on the Wolds, the Heath and in the Fens. The time lag between industrial take-off and the provision of adequate housing in the towns accounted for much misery which is accepted as an unhappy accompaniment of economic advance rather than as a product of wilful class wickedness. Perhaps in the mid-nineteenth century gang system lies similar evidence of a revolution in agricultural aims and methods; a revolution which produced its social strains as well as its benefits. The gangs which came out in the years after 1800 from Binbrook, Ludford, Tetford, Belchford and Donnington-on-Bain to work with others from larger settlements on the edges of the Wolds like Caistor, Market Rasen, Scalby, Louth and North Thoresby were a response to a new need. In the Witham Fens at Billinghay and farther south at Spalding, Crowland, Market Deeping and Bourne a similar demand for labour emerged in an agricultural economy that was creating its own fertile surfaces from land that had been notorious for the meaness of its promise.

Wider use of labour-saving machinery, the 1867 Gangs Act and the Education Acts of 1870, 1873 and 1876 gradually brought about the end of the system. The virtual elimination of couch grass and the reduction of weeds meant that there was less work for gangs to do in last quarter of the nineteenth century and although it was modest enough Lincolnshire farm workers began to enjoy a higher standard of living than their fellows in Rutland and other neighbouring counties. On the Heath and the Wolds poor rates were generally low at 11d. in the pound whereas on the clays in the 1830s they had been 2s. in the pound. By 1870 wages for men were 17s. a week on the Wolds, and 15s. a week in Kesteven and Lindsey on average. Women on piecework could earn 1s. and 6d. a day and boys and girls under 12 or 13 years received from 4d. to 1s. a day.

That the early nineteenth century saw labour unrest in the county is not in doubt. Its causes are difficult to establish. Local conditions produced different forms and varying causes for it. During the Napoleonic wars scarcity, high food prices and recruitment to the militia lay behind some of the discontent. Then after 1815 and on into the 1830s and, with less intensity, into the 1840s, under-employment, lower wages and fear of the loss of seasonal employment caused by the introduction of threshing machines, led to outbreaks of arson and machine wrecking. Magistrates, overseers of the poor and others with responsibility for order and the relief of distress may not have been effective at all times but they were not inactive.

Potatoes were bought by overseers of the poor and distributed to the needy or potato grounds were made over to them at Algarkirk, Friskney, Bourne and Donnington-on-Bain. The old Lincolnshire potato had been improved by 1800. They had sold for 2d. or 3d. a peck in the 1770s but by 1814 at Little Steeping they fetched 4d. a peck. The Horncastle Overseers of the Poor bought pig potatoes at 2½d. a peck. Potatoes, rye bread and barley were provided in parishes such as Bolingbroke and Sibsey while at Swineshead in times of shortage a water pottage made of water, oatmeal and onions was provided. More nutritious fare was sent by Sir Joseph Banks from London to be sold cheaply to his Lincolnshire poor. Rice and herrings were distributed when wheat prices were high. A huge rice pudding was fed to 110 poor children and 11 women at 1d. each in 1801.[36] From 38s. and 8d. a quarter in January 1800 wheat rose to 113s. in Lincoln and distress measures had to be taken as they had been by the setting up of a fund to provide cheap flour in 1794–5.[37] As well as high prices for bread, recruiting disturbed the life of some parishes and caused unrest. In 1805 Willoughton parish was fined £40 for failing to provide two men for the Royal Navy. Lindsey was 92 men short of its quota of 248. The families of hired men became a charge upon a parish and in 1796 there were riots at Caistor, Horncastle, Spilsby and Boston, against service in the militia. The inhabitants of Brigg, Caistor, Grimsby, Kirton in Lindsey and Winterton formed an association to protect their property from incendiarism in the 1820s and even in a village like Humberstone, noted for its cow pastures, good cottages and generally harmonious conditions of life and labour, there was sheep stealing in 1827. Rewards of 15 and 20 guineas were offered for the apprehension of the killers of sheep in North-West Walk and Clover Close in November. In January 1828, despite the offer of £172 in rewards, 43 sheep were killed on three occasions in the East Marsh of Grimsby; owners set up a voluntary watch. At Holbeach the magistrates provided for a watch in 1827 and at Sibsey a night

[36] L.A.O., Hill 22/1/5/6, 11, 12.

[37] Sir Francis Hill, *Georgian Lincoln*, Cambridge, 1966, pp. 171–4; Charles Brears, *Lincolnshire in the Seventeenth and Eighteenth Centuries*, London, 1940, Ch. 14; F. W. Eden, *State of the Poor*, 2, p. 403.

guard against sheep stealing, cattle maiming and rick burning was mounted.

Free soup-kitchens during the war years were opened in the towns and friendly societies grew up like the Kirton Benefit Society, 'fathered' by Nicholas Dunn, which met in the Court House and the Red Lion. Assisted emigration relieved the pressure in some parishes and gave new opportunities to a few families. Sutton-on-Sea for £63 saw a family off to America in 1822 while in 1826 for £29, Halton Holgate sent one to Quebec. After a life of hard work, child rearing and the boarding of farm workers a labourer could still fall upon a parish and have to submit to examination in order to qualify for relief. Richard Hill at Hemswell on the clays, a labourer born in Waddingham in 1771, applied for relief in 1834. He had become a waggoner in 1808 for Thomas Skipworth of South Kelsey for £10 a year with a house, garden, one rood of land and the keep of a cow and two pigs. The cow, fed on dried food in the crew-yard of his master's farm in winter, was to be turned out two weeks before May-day to graze until November. From May until October his two pigs were to run in the fields after which they were brought in for winter. Richard Hill had married when he was 31 and he and his wife, after a few years on the farm were given two farm servants to board. For them £20 a year was allowed, the keep of another cow and two more pigs and the use of half an acre of potato ground. He stayed on the farm until 1824 but by 1834 he was applying for relief for his family of three children still at home, John aged fifteen, Edward, thirteen, and Ann aged eight.[38]

From 1783 to 1785 the poor rates for the county averaged £43,024 a year but from 1813 to 1815 they ran at £230,191 a year. Potatoes were bought as at Rigby for distribution to the poor. Potato grounds were hired for cultivation by them and straw was purchased to provide bedding at Grimsby workhouse. Wages for agricultural workers declined from 12s. a week in 1813 and 15s. in 1815 to levels nearer 9s. or 10s. by 1825. At the same time rents were in arrears on many farms and for a few years at any rate after the war there appears to have been a decline in services like the postal system. Letters had to be brought to Lincoln from Market Deeping by horseback and the mail coach was not restored until 1822. Yet despite the run on banks in 1825 and the outbreaks of incendiarism in December 1830, there were signs of revival. The preparation of lime and bones for spreading on the uplands meant more work, the Lincolnshire Agricultural Society was opened in 1819.

[38] Brears, op. cit., pp. 174–7; L.A.O. *Archivists' Report* 25, p. 70, Settlement examinations. Lincoln (Lindsey) Petty Sessions, LNPS.

Gainsborough opened a woolmarket and reports in 1821 and 1823 stressed the growing activity in wool, sheep and horse sales at both Stamford and Lincoln.[39] In 1833 labourers' wages were 13s. and 4d. a week and on piecework by 1826, 18s. was usual.[40] Slender though these improvements were, together with garden ground, pigs and cows they gave the Lincolnshire farm workers in the 1830s a reputation for relative prosperity which even William Cobbett acknowledged.

On the Lindsey coast estate of Lord Willoughby d'Eresby, however, the sub-agent complained of unrest in the new era of Free Trade after 1846. The poorer tenants were not asking for drainage tiles and a number of labourers had left for the U.S.A. and many more talked about emigration; parish officers were dubious about assisting them as they left their families behind. In 1849 to 1850 labourers' wages were only 10s. a week in the coastal parishes and there had been a 20 per cent reduction in the wages of estate workmen. He saw incitement as a cause of the many fires around Steeping at this time. 'The poor in this part of Lincolnshire are better off than they are where I have lived in Surrey, Kent and Berkshire since the New Poor Law.' There had been outbreaks of arson since 1830; the Willoughby agents put them down to the reduction of seasonal work by the new threshing machines, the dislike of the New Poor Law, to the work of radicals and to the influence of the 'Toms and Jerrys' or beer houses. Spilsby was thought to be a centre of radicalism, a source from which sprang incendiarism and cattle maiming.[41] Unrest was reported from Barrow-on-Humber, Grantham, Moulton and Kirton Meers, where threshing machines were destroyed between the autumn of 1830 and March 1831. Landlords advised their farmers to suspend the use of the machines and wheat prices rose as so little threshed wheat came on to the market. The *Stamford Mercury* reported 43 fires at this time though there were few riots in the county as a whole.[42] In the autumn of 1830 Lincolnshire magistrates feared that rioting which had been reported in Huntingdonshire would spread north into the county. At Stamford the Duke of Richmond's 'Sussex Plan' was adopted in which a constabulary force of yeomen, shopkeepers and 'respectable' labourers was enrolled, divided into

[39] Sir Francis Hill, *Georgian Lincoln*, Cambridge, 1966, pp. 190–3.

[40] Fifth Annual Report, Poor Law Commissioners for England and Wales, 1839, pp. 18–19.

[41] L.A.O., 3 ANC 7/23/58/27, 34, 37, 58, 67, 68, 90; 3 ANC 7/23/59/51; 3 ANC 7/23/31/13; 3 ANC 7/23/29/9; 3 ANC 7/23/23/4–21.

[42] Rex C. Russell, *AHR*, Vol. 18, 1970, pt. II, pp. 173–5.

mobile sections and sent off to occupy villages before any rioting began. The period of serious disturbance in Lincolnshire from November 1830 to January 1831 was later and shorter than in Kent and Surrey but the outbreaks of arson were alarming between Louth and Boston. There seemed to be links with similar expressions of discontent in west Norfolk and north Cambridgeshire. One of the worst fires was at Stowe Gate in west Lindsey where 200 quarters of wheat, a large rick of beans, four horses and thirteen fat beasts were destroyed in a conflagration which resulted in damage valued from £1,500 to £2,000.[43]

Another expression of discontent came in the form of opposition to tithe payment in the 1830s. When a small farmer at Marshchapel fought the impropriator of the tithes, J. G. Floyer, in the Court of Exchequer, support for the farmer came from a wide area. The character of the opposition to the rapacious tithe owner suggests that the issue had wider and deeper implications than those of Marshchapel. It was claimed locally that the passing of the 1836 Tithe Commutation Act was affected by the petitions sent from the parish. Contributions towards legal costs came from Louth, Grimsby, Cleethorpes, Horncastle, Spilsby and Huttoft. Money was collected at inns and beer houses in small amounts of half a crown and three or five shillings at a time from groups and individuals signing themselves 'A Friend and Brother', 'An Enemy to Oppression', 'Fear Nothing', 'For Freedom's Cause by poor Dick'. Others were recorded as 'An Enemy of Lay Tithes', 'A Friend to the Oppressed' and one donor observed 'May the same cause never rise again.'[44] The period of the New Poor Law, Free Trade and the advance of mixed farming on the Wolds and the Heath had a restless character despite its reputation for productivity. Although conditions in Lincolnshire were better than in most of the southern counties, disturbance and incendiarism had an unwelcome place in the sequence of change.

Railway building was to have some impact upon the economies of the Lincolnshire villages in the 1850s as Lincoln and Boston were connected and the limestone plateau of south-west Kesteven was crossed by the line from Peterborough to York. The effect of migrant labour needed to build the lines was felt in the numbers of lodgers taken in by agricultural labourers' families. In Little Bytham in 1851 there were 15 in one household and in another 11. They created a temporary housing shortage which may have added

[43] E. J. Hobsbawm and George Rudé, *Captain Swing*, London, 1969, pp. 147–8, 168 and 256.

[44] L.A.O. *Archivists' Report*, 21, pp. 40–1, Marshchapel parish.

to other local influences in increasing housebuilding. Although their truck or 'tommy' shops siphoned off some of the demand for food and drink from local suppliers, their consumption of bread, meat and beer was considerable. Mrs Pilkington, one of Lord Willoughby d'Eresby's tenants, was allowed to brew small beer for the one year, 1851, in her house. It took 12 months to turn an agricultural labourer into a navvy but the 17s. a week for the shoveller and the 19s. a week for the pickman added temporarily to the effective demand of south-west Kesteven. The Great Northern railway did not rely on local labour but in terms of men born in Lincolnshire, the East Midlands generally and East Anglia it had an attraction and during 1851, for example, it certainly affected the census returns for villages such as Bitchfield, Brassingthorpe, Burton Coggles, Swayfield, Swinstead, Great Ponton, Great Gonerby and Syston. Railway workers accounted for 58 per cent of the total male population at Castle Bytham, 68 per cent at Carlby and 30 per cent at Witham-on-the-Hill. Local labour was used, however, to cart the sand and timber to the line from the Willoughby pits and woods. At 6d. each, sleepers were moved in batches of 1,500 to 2,000 at a time and in the slack days of a farming winter the extra work must have been welcome.[45]

[45] M. J. Dickson, 'The Short Term Effects of the Great Northern Railway on the Economy of South West Kesteven', 1850–2, *LHA*, Vol. 6, 1971, pp. 103–11.

7

Prices and farming prospects

THE rise and fall of farm prices had a bearing upon the timing and nature of the changes which are known as the agricultural revolution. Modern studies of agriculture have questioned both the seriousness of farming depressions and their delaying effects upon improvements. The very diversity of farming conditions within one county makes generalizations hazardous and the response of the Lindsey farmers on the uplands in the period 1813 to 1837 to falling cereal prices makes essential a rethinking of assumptions about profitability in a depression.[1] Even so price changes did affect relationships between tenant farmers and landlords. They altered expectations and assumptions about the roles of each which in turn affected activity in cropping, building, draining, reclamation and stock rearing. Labour shortages and high food prices affected the social background to farming. Price trends, if maintained for long enough were, like the weather, the stuff of which optimism or pessimism were made and these had their effect upon the pace and timing of agricultural change. Whilst the effect of the French Revolutionary and the Napoleonic wars and the following decline in cereal prices had the most profound influence upon the structure of Lincolnshire agriculture, earlier price movements deserve some brief description if only to indicate their subordinate part in the agricultural revolution.

The middle years of George I's reign saw difficulty and depression in farming. After the long dry season of 1719 land which had let formerly for £1 to 25s. an acre was hard to tenant at any price. At Michaelmas 1723 the price of some wheats had fallen to 28s. a quarter in Lincoln. In November of that year Mrs Whichcot, a landowner on the Cliff, was told by her Harpswell steward that he had not got in £12 in rent as times were so bad. 'There is very great

[1] J. A. Perkins, 'Tenure, Tenant Right, and Agricultural Progress in Lindsey, 1780–1850' and 'The Prosperity of Farming on the Lindsey Uplands 1813–1837; *AHR* Vol. 23, 1975, pt. I and Vol. 24, 1976, pt. II.

Complaint in the Country of the badness of the Times, which Effects every body's Tenants and Consequently yours amongst the Rest....' In February 1726 he complained '... as to the sheep they are so very Rotten everywhere that whoever buys any this Spring must Run great Hazards'. Mrs Massingberd was told by her agents that she would have to abate two-thirds of her rents in 1728. Sheep rot in the Fens in 1730 had caused farmers distress; in 1731 the Duke of Kingston's agent at Langworth complained of the rent arrears which he attributed to sheep rot, even though he had spent money in draining to keep the tenants contented. Yet food prices, for all the complaints of low returns on grain by farmers, even pressed upon a household like the Whichcots' at Harpswell which viewed the high living of the Lumley-Saunderson family at Glentworth with a mixture of awe and resentment, especially when their purchasing of butter in preparation for the entertainment of 300 of their tenants sent up prices in Gainsborough market to 7d. a pound.[2] It is possible that a link existed between the level of food prices and such disturbances as the riots against the removal of the western spires of the Minster at Lincoln, the tumult at Bourne in 1740 when it was feared that wheat was to be exported, and the mob activity at Boston in 1757, the threatening temper of which led to the prudent cancellation of the Lincoln race meeting because the nobility were thought to be in danger of assault. The attack upon the Court of Sewers' dams by a crowd in West Fen in 1757 may have been in part touched off by one of the periodic food shortages of the time.

Graziers were discontented because their wool seemed not to meet with the ready sales they had come to expect; their resentment multiplied against Irish competition and restrictions upon export. In 1726 a Lincolnshire grazier expressed their feelings and called for restraints upon Irish imports and the maintenance of wool prices to encourage English sheep farming. The spending of rents and taxes in London, the investment of profits in public funds instead of in the county seemed to one Lincolnshire grazier to be the cause of the malaise.[3] The seeming bias of Parliament in favour of English woollen goods manufacturers, which prevented growers from exporting their raw material to foreign buyers, intensified the graziers' sense of grievance. In Lincolnshire feeling ran high against

[2] C. E. Mingay, *The Agricultural Depression, 1730–1750, Essays in Economic History*, ed. E. M. Carus Wilson, II, 314 reprinted from *EcHR*, 2nd Series VIII, 1955; C. M. Lloyd, ed. *Letters from John Wallace to Madam Whichot, LRS*, Vol. 66, Lincoln, 1973, pp. 15, 28, 32; Sir Francis Hill, *Georgian Lincoln*, Cambridge, 1966, pp. 105–7; W. O. Massingberd, *History of Ormsby*, Lincoln, 1893, p. 307.

[3] L.A.O. Tyr. 2/2/1.

the apathy of members of Parliament on the issue. The publications of John Smith, a Lincoln clergyman, in 1747 and 1762 were designed to voice the farmers' complaints, to alert Parliament and to censure the landowners for allowing their pleasures to come between them and their tenants in what should have been a common crusade against the woolmen. In 1749 restrictions were placed upon the movement of cattle in an attempt to damp down disease; they had to be owned for 40 days before sales were made. Many farmers had lost profits in the outbreaks of cattle plague of 1746–9. Inspectors were hurriedly appointed by magistrates to make sure that diseased dead stock was buried; fairs and markets in most of Lindsey were forbidden until the summer of 1751. Thousands of animals are recorded as having been buried in the East and West Fens and in Kirton Wapentake and at Donnington, Gosberton, Swinehead and Surfleet. Yet the legislation on marketing stock would cut into profits, it was feared, by forcing producers to send their own representatives to sales rather than by relying upon salesmen or factors. Costs of sales it was predicted would go up from three to seven times by the new method.

Behind all the complaints there does seem to have been a genuine dissatisfaction, at least from 1730 to about 1750, at the relatively low prices for wheat, interrupted only by a brief rise from 1740 to 1741. Rent arrears and abatements were the result; trade generally faltered as farmers had less to spend even if town dwellers benefited from cheaper bread and the labourers' real wages rose. New landowners made their appearance; improved cropping and the beginnings of the enclosure of rabbit warrens and sheep walks pointed the way forward. By the early 1760s prices of wheat were rising and the outlook was changing.[4] Enclosure Acts and improved communications together with higher prices for wheat at Lincoln led the way to raised rents and more confidence in arable farming. Wheat prices per quarter rose from 25s.5d. (1741 to 1750) to 32s.3d. (1751–60), 40s.11d. (1761–70) and 47s. (1781–90). On the scattered estates of the fourth Earl of Scarbrough rents increased in a number of parishes, partly because of enclosure and other improvements but also because cereal prices were thought to justify them. The £809 annual rental at Winteringham of 1765 went up to £1,295 in 1766, to £1,395 in 1770 and to £1,858 in 1777. At Glentworth, Saxby, Skegness, Toft and Newton, Wharton, Blyton, Middle Rasen, Threddlethorpe and Wickenby similar increases took place. In the 1770s Stainton and Reasby and Willoughton had rent increases to take

[4] Charles Brears, *Lincolnshire in the Seventeenth and Eighteenth Centuries*, London, 1940, Ch. XLV; Hill, op. cit., pp. 107–11; L.A.O. Monson, 21/12/2.

account of improvements and higher prices. By 1784, however, two years after the fifth Earl succeeded to the title, the agent had to review the rents and to justify the changes which had taken place since 1775. In 1778 the tenants had asked for a reduction as wheat prices had fallen. In 1775 the rents were raised on the basis of 50s. a quarter for wheat and 20s. to 21s. and 6d. a todd for wool. He thought that as wheat in 1784 was as well priced as in 1775 the present rents were justified but as wool was only worth from 15s. to 12s. a todd, farmers did find the times harder than in 1775. It was decided to adjust rent increases to help the farmers who kept many sheep. When wool prices improved then rents would be reviewed. John Parkinson the land agent and enclosure commissioner calculated in 1786 that for the previous 12 years there had been a loss of 9s. and 4d. an acre out of every 20s. an acre of rent for grazing land in the Marsh, a loss only slightly less than on grazing land farther inland. John Chapman of Marshchapel recorded wool prices of 20s. a todd in 1742 and many years after it. By 1770 wool fetched only 14s. and 6d. a todd and stayed below 18s. until 1777. In 1780 it was as low as 10s. and 10d. and only reached 19s. a todd in 1787. Where ploughing was severely restricted as on the Drake coastal Marsh estate, these trends meant distress produced in part by more and better wool from improved sheep, by the trade distortions of the American and Dutch Wars and by Irish imports.[5]

Lincolnshire's rural economy was dependent upon the production of wool in the early eighteenth century.[6] From being a supplier of short carding wool it was becoming the chief source of long or combing wool for the worsted manufacturers of East Anglia and the West Riding. Before the advent of mixed farming on the thin soils of the uplands, sheep were valuable to fertilize the lower lands under tillage because they were folded at night. Lincolnshire's reputation as a wool-producing county went back to the twelfth century and from the fourteenth its fame had been growing as the home of long-woolled sheep suited to the harsh weather conditions of eastern England. Mutton production, on the other hand, was a secondary interest. Sheep were bred in the more sheltered valleys of the Wolds and the west-facing stretches of the Heath and Cliff and then sent for fattening to the rich pastures of the Outer Marsh owned or rented by the upland farmers. In the eighteenth century the sheep were often sold to farmers who specialized in fattening on

[5] Hill, op. cit., p. 114–16; T. W. Beastall, *A North Country Estate*, Chichester, 1975; pp. 92–3; L.A.O. Tyr. 4/87, 103, 108, 111.

[6] J. A. Perkins, *Sheep Farming in Eighteenth and Nineteenth Century Lincolnshire*, Occasional Papers 4, *SLHA*, Sleaford, 1977.

the Outer Marsh and who came out of their marshland parishes to meet upland breeders at the great sheep fairs at Caistor, Lincoln and Boston. These movements and divisions of activity produced sheep excellent for length and strength of their fleece but ungainly in appearance, heavy-boned and coarse-grained in the flesh. As the county was thinly populated, the local demand for mutton was limited but despite its 'spongy' or course texture, the result of fattening on rich grass, Lincolnshire mutton had a market in London for consumers who found large joints of meat acceptable and who were not too demanding about taste. Prices there were rarely attractive for the sheep arrived in the capital in the early autumn, having been sheared in the summer and undergone a long drove from Lincolnshire just as the general supply of livestock from all parts of the Kingdom was at a high level. Graziers were not paid for their wool clip until the Lady Day of the next year and so they tended to market their animals for cash to pay autumn bills and to buy in new stock. Long-wools from Lincolnshire were not fashionable as their appearance offended those to whom form was important yet their heavy frames carried a valuable fleece, so heavy that in the weeks before shearing shepherds and trained dogs were made to stand by to turn the animals which had a tendency to 'rigwelt' or fall on their backs, unable to right themselves owing to the weight of their wool. Fleeces of 29 lbs. were known; the standard Lincolnshire measure was the 28 lbs. todd but the average weight of fleece was 15 lbs. Occasional recordings of 21 inches in length were made but 10 inches to 18 inches was usual.

There were, however, drawbacks to this long, strong wool. Some tended to be greasy; some cut from near the neck of the sheep tended to 'cot' while coarser grains snapped in vigorous combing. Even so the whiteness of the wool in an age of indifferent dyeing techniques was a distinct advantage for it took dye well and the wool's strength appealed to manufacturers who were intent on supplying the coarse, stiff cloth that fashion demanded and for which heavy combing was essential. The large frame of the sheep gave it a degree of protection from foot rot or liver fluke in areas of bad drainage, while its good fleece and heavy bone gave it a hardiness essential in treeless acreages of the Wolds, Heath and Cliff. When disease struck the national flocks, Lincolnshire graziers enjoyed an advantage in that their sheep were considered safe by purchasers and they sold well in markets which were hastily over-supplied with diseased stock. Until the flocks of other regions revived, Lincolnshire enjoyed a temporary but valuable superiority. Seven to eight sheep could be raised per acre in the summer months in the Outer Marsh as against the usual three to four elsewhere and with little extra feeding above the normal grazing; good meat could be put on in 12 weeks from May to August. The uplands were thought to have too thin or short a bite to fatten sheep yet the Marsh with its 'brackish' water in stagnant, unfenced ditches was considered unsuitable for the breeding of lambs. Hence the concentration on breeding and rearing to first shear in the more sheltered parts of the uplands and the fattening down on the rich pastures of the open Marsh of weaned lambs or hoggetts or newly-sheared sheep from the uplands. Some flocks of small, hardy sheep known as the 'heath' variety were still being kept in the early eighteenth century on the higher ground. They supplied wool for carding that was short, thick and dense. They were valuable as they could roam far and wide in search of grass and they could be driven longer distances to fold than the long-woolled sheep. The alternative, before the turnip transformed the economy of the uplands, was to use the land they occupied as rabbit warrens; although this practice had its attractions and its value, the keeping of the small short-woolled sheep was more profitable.

Most of the Lincolnshire wool, whether of the short or long variety, was bought by middlemen or staplers who visited the same parts of the county each year after clipping in July and did business with the same farmers. They brought that season's price with them for few growers traded their wool independently as they lacked the expertise needed to survive in a competitive market; they relied on trusted staplers who would negotiate a reasonable price and then leave behind a note or bill to represent the rate of interest on the purchase price, to be paid in full the following spring. The bill which matured in November was useful in meeting winter costs incurred in livestock purchase and other demands. The staplers would send sheets and packers to the farms to prepare the wool for its journey to East Anglia or the West Riding and the grazier would provide transport to the nearest wharves. This close relationship between the growers, staplers and manufacturers in Norwich, Wakefield, and Halifax may well have prevented much change in the quality of the clip. This mutually satisfactory relationship and the rural economy that depended upon it were to disintegrate slowly, however, from the 1720s and the grazier interest in Lincolnshire was to undergo a decline until sheep rearing had taken its place in the new pattern of mixed farming.

The slump in wool prices in 1723 was probably the result of an over-production of fleeces and a fall in demand. Freedom from sheep rot, a blessing to graziers, had together with a drought in

1723, increased the numbers of live sheep. Graziers found that pastures were too dry to fatten satisfactorily so they kept alive thousands of sheep and added to the following year's breed. Poor cereal harvests led to more spending on foodstuffs rather than textiles and there was an outflow of specie as our exports of corn fell off. A lack of purchasing power affected the graziers holding large flocks of sheep and faced with a reduced demand. Though there were to be notable recoveries in wool prices in the late 1750s, the 1790s and in the years just after the end of the Napoleonic wars, a decline had set in. No longer was specialized wool growing to enjoy pride of place in the economic life of the county.

One reason for the decline was the competition from cotton manufacture. By the 1820s cottons had taken the lead in the dress of all classes of society and although there was to be for climatic reasons, if nothing else, a steady demand for woollens the change had a serious effect upon the producers of coarse, long wool. By the late 1820s even charities like the Lincoln Dorcas Charity were distributing cotton and woollen 'stuffs' to the needy in the ratio of four to one. For the greater part of the eighteenth century a hard, shining surface to finished woollens was preferred and was produced by pressing the hot cloth made from the fine threads of the hand-spinners. Gradually a preference for softness in the cloth and the feel of a good pile turned attention to the wools produced by Merino fleeces from Spain and in the early years of the nineteenth century from Saxony and Australia. A decline in demand for English short wools set in so that by the 1830s the supply of short wools used for the manufacture of fine cloths was almost entirely foreign. Meanwhile, with the development of mixed farming on the Lincolnshire uplands, fodder supplies increased and the supply of long-woolled sheep rose as light soil pasture went under the plough in response to improved cereal prices. This process was not confined to Lincolnshire so the county's share of the national long wool flock sank from near monopoly to an estimated 44 per cent by 1800. From an estimated 21 per cent share in 1800 of the national wool supply, both long and short, Lincolnshire accounted for about 17 per cent in 1828. The county's share of the nation's total number of sheep of all varieties fell by 1840 to only 7 per cent. By the 1820s it was feared that unless the quality of Lincolnshire wool could be changed to give a silkier texture then buyers would desert the county in even greater numbers. The sheep was now taking its place in a pattern of mixed farming, where its carcass was more profitable than its fleece. Perhaps the changeover in relative values began to take place after the 1730s and 1740s for mutton was very cheap at market then but by 1800 with the growth of an urban population farmers began to look to the flesh of their sheep for profits rather than to their fleeces.

The decline of the grazing interest was long and at times painful; strenuous efforts by graziers to lower costs and improve productivity failed to reverse the trend. They put pressure on Parliament to allow the export of raw wool and to restrict the import of foreign wool. They attempted to promote local manufacture of worsted and hosiery and encourage new uses for wool. They sought to make Lincolnshire consumers buy articles made from local wool by fostering county pride in such products and tried to alter the marketing of wool so that local growers acted together to defend prices and so to break the hold of buyers from manufacturing districts.

It was not easy to cut unit costs of production and to raise productivity if only because labour costs were not excessive and a drastic reduction in the work force at a time of rising population would have raised the level of poor relief and so the burdens of higher poor rates. A shepherd earning only 12s. a week with a cottage, four acres of land and a few perquisites could manage a flock of 900 breeding ewes on Bourne's farm at Dalby in the late eighteenth century. Sheep shearing gangs were not expensive, for they sheared at the rate of 2d. a head about 1800 and at only 1s. 8d. a sheep in 1860. Less injury to sheep in shearing and quicker clipping brought their benefits to the grower. In 1800 a shearer clipped 13 to 20 sheep in a day, though individual champions could tackle more than this, by 1860, 25 to 30 sheep in a day was the usual work load. Even so this had no major effect on production costs. Neither had grass improvement for the pasture of the Outer Marsh was as lush already as it needed to be and any addition to its richness only increased the length and coarseness of the wool.

The improvement of the breed of sheep was, however, to help growers in adverse conditions; and as sheep rearing merged with mixed farming Lincolnshire was to win an international reputation as the home of a breed of sheep that commanded general respect as an all-round 'rent paying animal'. The improved Lincoln was good for both mutton and wool. Another way of facing low prices for wool was to store unsold supplies until the market improved. In this wool had an advantage over other agricultural produce. Even so moth could damage the store and the wool became less pliable and harsher as time elapsed. The specialist grazier could not afford to hold on indefinitely to this, his chief source of cash, and as he went for quick sales of fresh wool whenever he could, storage was not a remedy for low prices and sluggish demand. Here the mixed farmer of the uplands to whom wool growing was only one part of his general activity had the advantage; he could afford to store wool for longer.

Legislative measures to protect the graziers' position were late, insignificant and ineffective. Not until 1825 was the prohibition of the export of English wool lifted and even then only a limited long wool trade with France developed. The manufacturing interest in Parliament, intent upon maintaining work and prosperity in the towns and industrialized villages, was not prepared to levy duties upon imported wool to help the English grower. In 1803 a duty of ½d. a pound weight was imposed on foreign wool, increased in 1819 to 6d. but by 1825 reduced to a mere 1d. a pound weight on wools valued at 1s. a pound and ½d. on those worth less than a shilling. The efforts of landowners like the Duke of Ancaster and Mr Pelham, the future Lord Yarborough, with other Lincolnshire owners had not saved wool from foreign competition or from prohibition on export before 1825. From the 1780s smuggling out raw wool in exchange for wines, spirits and tea flourished through ports like Grainthorpe and Saltfleet but its costs rose as the preventive services became more effective. A major effort to create a wool manufacturing industry in eastern Lindsey was made in the 1780s. Magistrates ordered overseers of the poor to buy wool and the implements necessary to set the unemployed to work on textile manufacture. Paupers and their children were to work up wool before they qualified for relief in money. Children over six were to be taught to knit and those over nine were to spin. The Vicar of Willoughby near Alford, the Rev. R. G. Bowyer, helped to set up a Society for the Promotion of Industry to employ the poor in spinning and weaving wool, a cheaper material than locally grown flax or hemp. Premiums were offered between 1786 and 1790 to encourage children under eight to knit at home while older children were sent to spinning schools. For a few years these experiments succeeded. The Society subsidized a dyer and finisher at Louth. Sir Frederick Eden reported in 1795 though that the spinning schools had been abandoned. Individual weavers were to be found long afterwards at Tetney in 1804, for example, at North Somercotes in 1829, at Brigg in the 1820s and at Louth in the 1840s, but the attempt to provide a lively home market for wool in Lincolnshire manufacture of worsteds had failed except as part of the poor law system. Here it continued in poor houses until just before the passing of the 1834 Poor Law Amendment Act.

Failure seems not have been the result of the application of steam to the industry, coal for which was not found in the county. Decline seems to have resulted from opposition from within the county. Farmers and landowners thought manufacturing was antipathetic to tillage farming which was at that time labour intensive. Women and children, in demand for turnip lifting and weeding, would be drawn into local factories and only higher wages would draw them out again and on to the land. Children, it was argued, would be rendered physically unfit for farm work after spending part of their working lives spinning and weaving. Weak in body and untaught in the skills of farm work, they would be of little use to their employers. Farmers who were often guardians of the poor came to regard the spinning schools as expensive to the parishes and damaging in the long run to arable farming. The guardians at Caistor union workhouse in 1840 opposed the entry of boys into the local brickyards for not only were they centres of vice, the farmers contended, they were also labour intensive sources of employment in competition with tillage agriculture. The milling and crushing industries, on the other hand, were generally capital intensive and as they were closely linked with the supplying the needs of arable farming, they provoked less hostility.

Social pressure was brought to bear upon Lincolnshire people to wear and use worsted cloth to help support the wool growers. Meeting in Caistor in 1802, a group of growers resolved to encourage the use of woollen cloth by themselves and their families. Much earlier, in 1785, the Society for the Promotion of Industry started a 'ball and card' assembly at Alford to which nobility and gentry were invited provided that they wore wool spun and woven in Lincolnshire. The only concession to cotton or silk was in the gentlemen's stockings. The event, transferred to Lincoln in 1788, became the 'Stuff' and later the 'Colour' ball or 'Colour Fancy Ball'. To keep up demand for woollens the colour theme was changed each year. Gradually regulations on dress were relaxed so that by 1807 ladies were admitted if they had purchased ten yards of stuff and by the 1830s dancers were not expected to dress in wool but merely to adhere to a prevailing colour. In the years just after its foundation this social event did set the seal of fashion upon wool and the annual colour change did something towards keeping looms busy but as the attendance was only 200 to 300 persons, the impact was not great. Other uses for wool besides dress were encouraged. At Louth a water-powered factory on the river Ludd supported by Louth Corporation in the 1780s produced blankets and carpets. In 1834 a steam engine was introduced and with continued support from the corporation the mill enjoyed a brief golden age in the 1830s, employing at one time about 1,000 workers. By 1838, however, its labour force had fallen dramatically and its owner combined carpet manufacture with a wool stapler's business. Carpets made from hard long Lincolnshire wool had a market in both China and America in the late eighteenth century and this side of manufacturing prospered in the late 1780s. Sacking and rope provided alternative uses for wool in the Napoleonic war. A manufactory was started in 1808 at Caistor for corn sacks and rope and when hemp was in demand by the Royal Navy, wool was an acceptable substitute for rope making. Unfortunately these were not lasting outlets for Lincolnshire wool and so attempts had to be made to market the raw material in ways which were more advantageous to the grower.

Wool prices were determined by the purchasers and a way of breaking their hold was to open wool markets in the county. From 1823 at Gainsborough wool markets were held on three separate days in June and July while in Kidgate Louth a wool market was held from 1825 until 1843. Gainsborough attracted more wool from Nottinghamshire than Lincolnshire and only outlived the market at Louth by some three years. In a wool market, growers offered their wool fair they went a step further and after meeting together they than waiting to be visited by them on their farms. In their proximity to each other lay some collective strength for the growers but in the wool fair they went a step farther and after meeting together they determined the price before sales began. Ideally this gave them the upper hand over the buyers. Mr C. W. H. Pelham, Lord Yarborough's eldest son, proposed the setting up of such a fair in 1834 along the lines of a successful venture in Norfolk founded by Coke of Holkham. Yet success eluded the venture largely because the growers themselves lacked faith in marketing which departed from the traditions to which they were used. To appear at a market with one's wool was to some an admission of poverty and a certain way to low rewards if not a public demonstration of impending bankruptcy. Others believed that growers could never organize themselves for long to maintain prices in a traditionally competitive branch of farming. By the 1830s Lincolnshire's commanding position in wool growing had been lost. Agents for the growers did market more wool for them as the nineteenth century progressed but at markets like those at Doncaster and Wakefield between the wool growers' farms and the manufacturers' spindles and looms. The Doncaster fair held weekly in June, July and August into the 1880s accounted for perhaps 10 per cent of the Lincolnshire growers' supply and although it was considered to be an important outlet, the bulk of Lincolnshire wool was still sold to West Riding buyers who travelled around the county in the time-honoured way. They visited more often, however, and purchased less at a time whereas formerly they would have bought the entire clip. By the mid-nineteenth century the specialist grower had to store a greater proportion of his wool and to raise a loan on it as security with which to purchase new stock. The old grazier districts of the Outer Marsh were now the mere appendages of upland farms, visited infrequently by their owners or tenants from the prosperous mixed-farming parishes.

Another way in which the ground was prepared for the triumph of mixed farming in the early nineteenth century was the decline in the rearing and trapping of rabbits.[7] An alternative to wool growing on the uplands had been the establishment of rabbit warrens, considered a suitable and fairly prosperous activity for land at a distance from the farmstead. The first references to cony or rabbit warrens date from the early seventeenth century but by the 1780s the largest Lincolnshire warrens displayed a pattern of distribution related to the geology of the county. There were two major groups both linked with light soils, on the sands round Frodingham and on the Wolds in a line from the Humber south-east to beyond Horncastle. The 'right of warren' mentioned in many enclosure awards meant the right to hunt or trap hares, rabbits, partridges and pheasants on an area of land but by the end of the eighteenth century the term meant an enclosure devoted to the breeding and trapping of rabbits for profit. Banks were built of sods of earth which lasted for about seven years, forming enclosures in which rabbits with different furs were bred. Lincolnshire rabbits had a market value because those with black and those with silver fur could be isolated and so with the more usual grey rabbits, three shades of fur were sold. The banks were topped with gorse bushes and strengthened with kidds or stakes at one yard intervals. The cost worked out at about 3s. and 4d. for seven yards.

Estimates of the basic winter breeding stock varied with the quality of the ground. At Withcall a stock of 2,600 couples on 1,000 acres, or five rabbits to the acre, was thought to be usual. Bucks were killed down to about a quarter of their natural number to control the population of the warren. Tenants renting rabbit warrens from landowners usually appointed a warrener with a house and the keep of two cows with seasonal labour to help him when bank repairs and trapping were in progress. Drifting snow

[7] The following discussion is taken from P. S. Doughty, 'The Rabbit in Lincolnshire, a short history', *Journal of the Scunthorpe Museum Society*, Vol. No. 2, 1965, pp. 15–23.

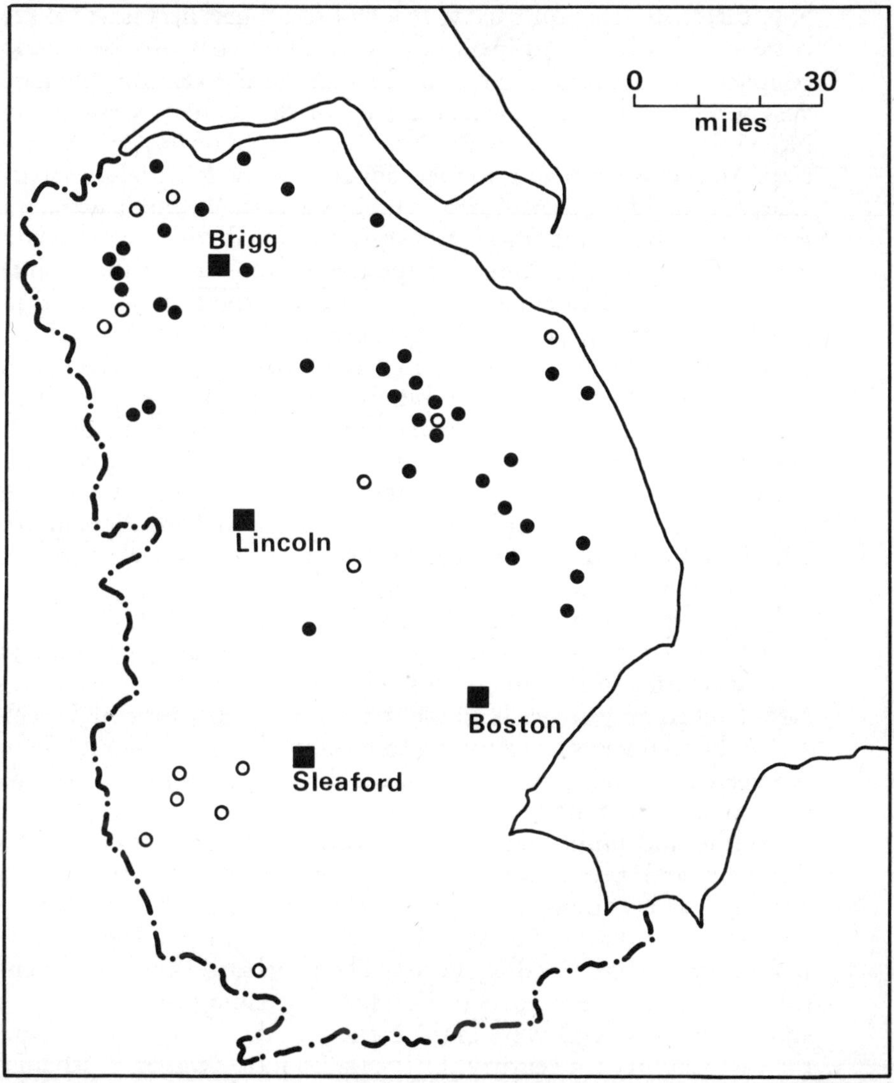

Figure 7. Rabbit warrens in Lincolnshire. The map indicates those warrens which were maintained and run commercially on a systematic basis. There were other areas, especially in the south of the county, given over to rabbits but their breeding and trapping were not undertaken by a warrener. Open circles indicate the occurrence of 'Warren Farm'.

had to be removed from the banks to prevent the rabbits from crossing from one enclosure to another. Fodder of turnips, clover, hay, threshed oats and barley was laid out when necessary; three large cart loads of turnips a day were required to fodder 1,000 couples. Some trapping went on throughout the year but the harvest for furs, the most valuable part of the animal, went on in November and December. Rabbits were caught or 'typed' on a tip trap. An enclosure of about 11 feet square was made with holes in its sides at ground level to allow the rabbits access. Within it was a pit four feet deep and about four feet square covered with a wooden lid resting on a pivot. In August, September and October the rabbits were encouraged to enter the enclosure and the trap was held in place by a catch. Accustomed to finding ample and enticing fodder, they continued to cluster there in November when the catch was released and as many as 400 rabbits at a time could be caught. They died by asphyxiation without damage to their carcasses or their pelts. Other trapping methods involved driving the animals into banked enclosures and netting them. The upkeep of a warren in 1799 on a 250-acre site at Blankney rented by Richard Piers under Charles Chaplin showed that an annual profit of just over £90 was possible because its produce brought in £275.

The market for rabbit fur was unstable but around Brigg at least it supported a fur dressing industry of some importance into the second quarter of the nineteenth century. In the 1790s rabbit carcases fetched only 2d. each. In the 1780s a silver grey fur could reach 1s. 3d. but ten years later, owing to fashion changes, it would fetch between 10d. and 11d. There was a fluctuating demand for this variety in China but mostly they were put on the home market for trimming and lining garments, making muffs and 'beaver' hats. Dressing and preparation were highly skilled occupations and although as a cottage industry they were found in a number of Lincolnshire villages, the main concentration was in Brigg where many girls were trained in the art. The processed skins then went from the small Trent ports to London for making up. Port books show that cony skins were in the cargoes of departing vessels from the early eighteenth century. In 1793 a London skinner, Nathaniel Haram, bequeathed £200 to the Charity School of his home town, Scunthorpe.

By the 1820s the value of the untended warrens was low and even that of the specialized, efficient, supervised ones was falling. Land ploughed, marled and manured made more per acre than it could as a rabbit warren. Few of the warrens listed in the early nineteenth-century directories were recorded in the 1880s. At Risby, however, some 3,000 acres in 1842 were allowed as a warren but by 1882 all but 30 acres were in tillage. Some areas reverted to warren land in the depressed years for arable farming after 1875 and Risby provides today perhaps the best impression of what a warren was like. Commercial workings of warrens had ended by 1900. The difficulty in locating warrens is increased by the use of the term in enclosure awards to mean areas of rough land overrun with rabbits rather than an acreage worked commercially for a crop of rabbit fur and carcasses. From about 1750 to 1850 there were 45 warrens of some size where supervised breeding and trapping was conducted.[8]

With the decline in specialized wool growing and the conversion of many rabbit warrens to ploughland, mixed farming in the uplands began to transform the county's agriculture. Yet in the 1820s prospects were not inviting and it is surprising that so much progress was made in apparently unpromising circumstances. Part of the explanation must be that though times were difficult they were not so depressing that all enterprise was discouraged. Memories of the high cereal prices before 1813 were still fresh yet realism taught that they would never again be so easily achieved. Only by cost cutting and more intensive use of the available cultivable area would farms be made to pay. Some farmers may have left to give place to others with lower expectations and simpler ways of life.[9] Whether they were new tenants or members of long-established farming families with new and more modest aims, the occupiers of the 1820s and 1830s effected changes which by their speed and nature made Lincolnshire's mixed farming an object lesson for the whole Kingdom. Evidence of depression or even gloom is nevertheless abundant. After the failure of banks in 1815 and 1816 there were periodic shortages of credit and bank notes until in the 1830s joint-stock banking brought a welcome stability to the scene. The rentals of the Ancaster, Thorold and Welby estates show that farmers could not pay their rents on time and that 1822 was a particularly difficult year. Arrears and requests for abatements or reductions of rent were frequent until the late 1830s after which, despite a short depression from 1847 to 1852, steady improvement and even prosperity were enjoyed until 1874. Not until 1851 on the Ancaster estates did receipts touch wartime levels and on the Welby property it was 1837 before the pre-1815 figures were reached. It seems then that memories of the good times, together with an intensive use of resources in the bad ones, prepared

[8] See Chapter IX for changing use of upland acreages.

[9] David Grigg, *The Agricultural Revolution in South Lincolnshire*, Cambridge, 1966, p. 117.

the county for an advance in which even contemporaries seem hardly to have believed until the middle 1840s.

That it was possible in the 1840s to indulge in successful speculation in wheat is indicated by the example of two young men one of whom was the second son of Francis Robinson of Frampton.[10] Robinson farmed under two landlords but he owned 'a nice estate' at Wyberton and Skirbeck. His second son, born in 1824, studied surveying after being at school at Grantham. He helped his father for two years and then went to sea and brought back a load of mahogany. He helped his father again but his keep, an account in a savings bank, a clothing allowance, pocket money and payment for extra work were not enough to finance a trip through the British Isles which he and a friend had longed to make. In 1844 they bought the whole wheat crop including straw on 16 acres, 'all something like £8.10s. per acre'. They harvested it at a profit in spite of a setback when a fire caused by a spark from a steam threshing machine, one of the first to be used in that district, destroyed a whole stack. 'We made as little trouble as we could of that' he observed and took some satisfaction that theirs must have been the first fire from such a source. They took a sample of their wheat to Boston, a yield of 6 quarters 2 bushels an acre, and sold the crop at a 'nice profit', the whole harvesting process having been completed in ten days. They kept their money 'until a convenient time, then have a trip with it to seek some information'. Though the 1844 harvest was good and was brought in under dry conditions, 1845 was wet and with 500 wethers on turnips, foot and mouth disease taught him a 'good lesson in dressing sheep that winter'. He saved them all and so, in good spirits, he and his companion began their journey by allowing a stick to fall to point the direction for starting. It fell to the north so they set off to Hull, York, Newcastle and Edinburgh and eventually saw parts of Ireland, Bristol and London. After a time as a merchant in Boston, Robinson in 1859 bought Titton Hall estate from his father's trustees where he had lived first with his sister and then with his wife since 1850.

By 1865 Lincolnshire was the country's leading wheat producer with a surplus of 5,725 (thousand bushels) a year for dispatch mainly by rail to counties such as the West Riding, Lancashire and Middlesex. Lincolnshire's nearest rival was Cambridgeshire with a surplus of 3,192 (thousand bushels). Although Cambridgeshire led the country in wheat yields per acre at 34·67 bushels and Kent was second with 33·57 bushels, Lincolnshire's yield at 32·75 bushels put the county third in the national county yield table, just ahead of

[10] L.A.O. Misc. Don 440, Robinson autobiography.

Sussex, Essex and Norfolk. Lincolnshire's agricultural advance coincided with the railway age and its speed was similar. Wheat from Lincolnshire was drawn increasingly to London markets by the new railway services at the expense of its natural market in the West Riding. Even so in 1865 more Lincolnshire grown wheat was consumed there than wheat from the North Riding. The Manchester, Sheffield and Lincolnshire railway when, after 1849, it reached Lindsey, influenced the movement of livestock and caused the decline of drovers' traffic across the Trent through Bawtry to Rotherham and Sheffield. By 1865 sheep, pigs and cattle were being carried to South Yorkshire and Lancashire markets though the traffic manager of the Great Eastern railway said cattle walking was still competing with the railways for distances up to 40 miles. By 1850 Newgate Market in London was receiving 800 tons of dead meat a week from a wide area of England and Scotland along the Eastern Counties railway. At Smithfield by 1850 the area of supply had been widened by the railways from the Home Counties to Lincolnshire, Yorkshire, Durham, Aberdeenshire and Fife.[11] With demand on this scale Lincolnshire's response was dramatic in the 30 years after 1815. In South Lincolnshire average wheat yields doubled in that time. As mixed farming progressed, regional differences diminished, although on the clays change was slower than upon the Heath and in north-west Kesteven. High demand for wheat and livestock, a willingness by farmers to eliminate waste so as to increase output, a realization that a mere increase in the cultivated area was no longer the way to higher output, linked to landlords' investment and the reward of tenants' investment by tenant-right customs were to be the elements of success. Meanwhile price levels were low enough to convince farmers that efficiency had to be applied to reduce costs per bushel but they were still high enough to encourage investment and to keep enterprise alive.

[11] G. R. Hawke, *Railways and Economic Growth in England and Wales 1840–1870*, Oxford, 1970, Ch. IV, Railways and Agriculture, pp. 107, 109, 116, 119, 134, 142 and 150–1.

8

Tenants' rights; the emergence of a new class

ONE of the reasons for the success of mixed farming in Lincolnshire in the uninviting economic climate of the second quarter of the nineteenth century was the ample reward a tenant could expect by then for any improvements he effected on his farm. At the same time many farmers were working under annual agreements as tenants-at-will, a development which some authorities like Arthur Young and Thomas Stone had deplored as inimical to improvement. Leases long enough to give the occupier time to recover some profit from his investment were thought traditionally to be essential for agricultural improvement. In say, 21 years, a favourite span, justice could be done both to tenant and landlord. In the 1790s Arthur Young and Thomas Stone both condemned the absence of leases.[1] Certainly there is evidence in the eighteenth century of leases for 21, 14 or 7 years to bring limestone cliff land, the Heath and parts of the Wolds into cultivation. With the lease went arrangements of a primitive kind for paying the outgoing tenant for good practices, the award being based upon the opinion of two or three reputable viewers who took as their standard the local custom. Arbitration in farming seems to have a long history though it was only to develop in the early nineteenth century an intricate mechanism for assessing tenants' rights. In 1790, for example, on the Manners estate at Bloxham, William Ingall, an occupier of 392 acres, was to be allowed under the terms of a seven years lease to break up 140 acres of old pasture and to make it into tillage land. He was to have allowances of 2s. and 6d. an acre on land twice cropped and upon turnip land. Fields which had been eaten by sheep after seeds were to be valued by the incomer and two umpires if the new occupier entered in October but if he delayed until February the 2s. and 6d. an acre would be

[1] Arthur Young, *Gen. View*, 1813, p. 64; Thomas Stone, *Gen. View*, 1784, p. 96.

allowed. The outgoer was to be compensated for the last year's manure. At Salmonby a 15 years lease was arranged for a farm of 324 acres with much 'walk' land in it with a view to the increase of the cultivatable area by the tenant. The landlord was to erect a good barn and a stable on the walks and at the end of the lease to buy in crops on any part of the land enclosed for arable.[2]

On the limestone cliff in 1748 a 15 years lease was granted to a tenant of the Earl of Scarbrough at Glentworth. He was to clear 20 acres of 'furr pasture' and to prepare it for cultivation in five acre lots at a time. His corn crop in his last year of occupation was to be valued by independent valuers. The tenant was to be allowed it as a 'following crop'. He was to build a barn at his own expense so that threshing could be done on the newly claimed land. In 1757 a 21 years lease was signed with two occupiers in partnership for 391 acres at Glentworth. They were to enclose four parts of about 100 acres each and to build their own barns, granaries and stables. Their inducements were a low rent of £63 a year and because of their '... large expense of Inclosure and planting with white thorns', they were to have forty acres sown with corn as a 'following crop' for no rent or tithe. At Hackthorn in 1779 similar agreements were made with an occupier who was to have his 'following crop' valued by two independent assessors after he had brought into cultivation an area of poor pasture on the limestone cliff. Richard Bassett, the agent, had to supervise the breaking in of the land now used for tillage and to make sure that the occupiers farmed it according to the recommendations of Parkinson and Fletcher who surveyed the estate in 1793 and wrote '. . . the distant Heath or Warren lands (should be farmed) one quarter fallow and turnips; one quarter barley, one quarter clover or seeds, one quarter pease, wheat... and apply the produce of three crops to manure the fallow and if deficient, to make addition by purchasing Dove manure, feeding oxen on Oil Cakes, or such other Mode of procuring Manure...' Where tenancies had become annual, a change which on these estates was made in the late 1750s, 'contract books' were opened in which tenants signed agreements to keep to certain good practices. In the contracts compensation to tenants for good management was clearly acknowledged. The scale and complexity of these agreements are a far cry from the Lincolnshire custom of the 1820s but they show that the submission of tenants' claims to independent valuers and arrangements for compensation for improvements had grown up long before 1815. At Winteringham in 1763, for example '. . . the said Earl shall pay a full satisfaction for (the farmyard

[2] L.A.O. Hig. 1/1.

manure) as two honest, judicious men to be chosen by each party shall value it at'. At Wharton and Blyton and at Toft and Newton three assessors were involved; two chosen by the landlord and one by the tenant.

Tenancies-at-will appear to have grown in popularity as farming prospects became more unsettled after 1815. When prices were rising, a long lease was a disadvantage to a landlord for he was unable to gain possession of his farm and to raise the rent. Yet a long lease did not guarantee him a steady income when times were bad for a tenant could abandon both the lease and the farm. Given the services of increasingly professional land agents, an owner could manage his farms more carefully when they were let by annual agreements. A substantial tenant on a long lease could make difficulties if assurances of a renewal were not forthcoming. He could even expect a chance to buy his farm at an advantageous price and assume the attitudes of an owner.

William Dawson, the occupier at Withcall on the Wolds near Louth of Lincolnshire's largest farm of 2,300 acres with 6 years of his lease to run was said in 1842 to be putting off would-be purchasers for his farm and announcing that he would spend no more on bones, linseed cake, artificial manure, draining, buildings or fences and that in his last year he would sow the whole acreage with wheat.[3] Perhaps, too, landowners saw that by the 1830s the age of encouraging tenants with capital to break in warren, walk or wold land by long leases and low rents was over and that now a regime of closely integrated crop rotations and stricter management was needed. More buildings were required and this meant on the larger estates the appointment of a clerk of works or his equivalent and a staff of bricklayers and carpenters. The growth of estate works departments deserves further exploration but where tenants had the responsibility for building it seems clear that they could resist rent increases or press for reductions or returns when prices were low. William Downes, a valuer from Essex, observed in 1845 when he examined farms in Lincolnshire that tenants raised the cry 'I built this and that all at my own expense and surely now you will not think of raising my rent.' Perhaps that is why he urged upon the eighth Earl of Scarbrough the need for tile manufacture on the estate and the importance of the landlord's role in building and repair. At Willoughton he came across a tenant whose land was 'infamously' farmed as he spent much time in a public house, yet the land agent defended the occupier by saying that his uncle had built the farm house some 12 years ago '. . . compleat from the ground and at an

[3] L.A.O. 3 ANC 7/23/43/16.

expense of between 3 and 400£'.[4] Such an observation seemed to prove the valuer right.

In the long run, annual tenancies, strict supervision of farming practices and landlords' responsibility for building and draining were thought to be the spurs to progress on estates that were 'classical' in structure, that is a stately home, an estate office and a works department situated near to the holdings of the tenants. Not all properties were of this kind, however, but for the absentee landowner who relied upon the success of a few substantial tenants not only for regular rent but for the maintenance of the fabric of his property there was a value in annual tenancies in that rents could be reviewed each year. Where relations were good, annual tenancies could run on for many years whereas the end of a long lease and the possibility of its renewal would occasion a crisis. The tenant would fear that a change was almost inevitable, the landlord would have to decide on renewal or his replacement or indeed upon sale of the farm. Annual tenancies were by comparison flexible and, it now seems from recent research, in no way a barrier to progress.[5] Leases often precluded the re-arrangement of farms to give better balanced units in terms of soil type and access to roads and farm buildings. Under an annual tenancy system an estate or a group of farms could be regrouped with a minimum of disturbance over a number of years. Farm sizes were not constantly changing but at Beelsby on the Wolds, for example, in 1787, 2,200 acres in the parish had four farms of 300 acres each, four farms of from 10 to 40 acres each and eight small holdings of from 3 to 8 acres each and 70 acres of cottage pasture. By 1817 the parish had two large farms one of 1,086 acres and the other of 1,080 acres.[6]

Leases were favoured by owners who had few opportunities for monitoring the activities of their tenants or who wanted a steady return for a minimum of management cost. The outlying farms of an estate sometimes remained on lease until perhaps the needs of consolidation brought about a sale. Withcall, off-lying from the Willoughby d'Eresby estate, was of this kind. Oxford and Cambridge colleges, the Dean and Chapter of Lincoln Cathedral and institutional owners such as the Charterhouse of London continued leasing into the nineteenth century. Clare Hall, Cambridge let its

[4] Lumley MSS., EMS/39.

[5] J. A. Perkins, 'Tenure, Tenant Right, and Agricultural Progress in Lindsey, 1780–1850', *AHR*, Vol. 23, pt. 1, 1975, pp. 1–22.

[6] Perkins, op. cit., G. E. Mingay, 'The Size of Farms in the Eighteenth Century', *EcHR* 2nd Ser., XIV, no. 3, 1962, p. 470; and A. C. Sinclair, *A History of Beelsby*, London, 1947, pp. 58–61.

Wrawby farm in 1818 on a 22 years lease. Single farms belonging to small owners were often leased after advertisement in county newspapers and the farms awarded in lieu of tithe or glebe farms were sometimes offered on lease like the 194 acres at Horsington let for seven years in 1840 or as long as the Rector should hold the living within that term.[7] For the tenant, however, a lease had the drawback of keeping him to a rent which in times of low prices became onerous whereas a tenant-at-will had a better chance of negotiating a reduction. County custom, public opinion and the wish of landlords to be to seen to be fair and considerate were his protection against eviction. The Chandos Clause of the 1832 Reform Act gave the vote to annual tenants who paid £50 or more in rent and this perhaps helped to make landlords adhere to the annual system which they had first adopted in response to new and less stable price levels. As the 'manufacturing interest' grew in influence, however, tenants and landlords appear to have moved together anyway in a common effort to defend their position. Though political influence over tenants played a part as indeed did a wish to preserve game, it is difficult to see either of these considerations as major influences in establishing tenancies-at-will as the norm. Tenants were probably more articulate and independent after the war with its somewhat heady prosperity and neither landlords nor their agents were prepared for wholesale evictions in defence of political interest or game when a steady rent return was their chief preoccupation.

One of the more outspoken landlords, at least to his Lincolnshire agent, was the sixth Earl of Scarbrough, yet he always drew back from evictions for arrears of rent and ordered that the interest on old arrears should be paid to the tenant as an encouragement. One of his Glentworth tenants, William Danby, illustrated in the years after the war some of the independence which was perhaps more general. He had entered his farm in 1810, and he had spent nearly £100 since then on new stalls for his beasts; furthermore, he claimed he had put in windows to his farm buildings and wintered 50 head of cattle and horses, with losses which but for his improvements would have been higher. In all he had laid out £250 in buildings and when his farm was revalued in 1814 he appears to have objected to the £457 put upon it at Glentworth though not to the £233 charged for his grazing land at Skegness. He took a farm at Cleatham near Kirton Lindsey and began a long wrangle with the Scarbrough agent, Thomas Dungworth, for compensation. He had been asked to shoot by Lord Scarbrough and he now wanted reimbursement for

[7] *LRSM*, 18 September 1840.

the keep of a pointer and for loss of time spent shooting. He was given £10 for the pointer's keep. His tenant right was valued in 1816 at £215.8s.8d. but arbitration continued into 1817, involving valuers from Owersby and North Collingham in Nottinghamshire. Danby observed that his management could not have been so bad as he was offered his present farm by Mr Thorpe of Owersby 'a gentleman farmer', and 'that does not show I am deserving of a bad character, I am sure'. He went on to say that he did not want a reduction for the Skegness grazing, as that land will always do as 'much as anybody thinks of'.[8] William Dawson, the tenant at Withcall wrote to Lord Willoughby's agent in 1829 complaining about the restriction on the growing of two white crops in succession observing that 'It is found out in this neighbourhood that wheat is a good deal finer after oats than clover.'[9] When in 1845 the Rev. Thomas Dupre had criticized Lord Willoughby's tenants for their mismanagement and indifference to the conditions of their labourers, ten farmers signed a letter to their landlord defending their record on both counts and resolving that neither the offending clergyman nor his sons would be allowed to shoot across their lands.[10] Though angry about slow rent payment from his Lincolnshire estate, the sixth Earl of Scarbrough wrote in 1817 when calling for game for a ten day house party 'I would not have a shot fir'd which could injure any of my tenants' Crops.'

Confidence that farms held on annual tenancies would pass peacefully from father to son was high, and on the strength of it many Wolds farmers risked great injections of capital to their holdings. On both the estates of the Earls of Yarborough and Lord Monson family continuity was usual, though the merits of applicants were taken into account and succession was not automatic. Even so, near hereditary tenanting is suggested by the names recorded from 1754 in Lord Yarborough's list of puppy walkers for the Brocklesby Hunt. John Parkinson, a Nottinghamshire and Lincolnshire land agent, believed that leases were unnecessary; fathers were succeeded by sons, and this was the natural order of things.[11] This was one side of the county custom which meant that tenants 'never changed unless they die, or become unfortunate in business, or without there is gross neglect'.[12] After the Napoleonic war, a county like Lincolnshire was conscious of the growing power of the manufacturing interest in national affairs, of the stresses set up in rural society by the state of the poor and by the growing independence of the

[8] Lumley MSS., ETE/13. [9] L.A.O. 3 ANC 7/23/21/23–4.
[10] L.A.O. 3 ANC 7/23/47/119. [11] Perkins, op. cit.
[12] BPP, 1847–8, VII, p. 36.

farmers who now faced an unsettled future but who in certain circumstances began to prosper. Tenants-at-will were treated carefully and encouraged to work their farms each with its individual characteristics of contour and soil type known so well by them and their sons. Social gatherings played their part in the process. Tenants and others celebrated events like the coming of age of an heir as at Burton Hall in February 1830 or at Wragby later that year. Rent day dinners were annual or sometimes bi-annual conferences of management and tenantry at which the agent was expected to assess the morale of the occupiers and draw conclusions from it. They helped towards prompt rent payment for not to appear could reflect upon one's standing as a farmer but they also gave opportunities for voicing complaints. At Limber on the Wolds in the 1820s and 1830s the tenants would dine to celebrate the Earl of Yarborough's birthday in August and the hunting field drew farmers together for sport and at the same time afforded them contacts that were useful in times of rural disturbance like the unrest of 1830–1 when they formed the local volunteer cavalry corps.

The stability and success of farmers had a bearing upon the peacefulness or lack of it in the county generally. Arson or fear of it seems always to have been close to the surface in the correspondence of Lord Willoughby's agent and sub-agents in the second quarter of the nineteenth century and a feeling that the conduct of farmers towards labourers had to be watched appears to have been strong. James Finlay the sub-agent wrote to Lewis Kennedy the agent in 1847 that farmers do not discharge labourers as manufacturers do when times are bad. Had they done so, he claimed, there would have been insurrection in the county.[15] Tenants-at-will were treated well because good tenants were scarce and once they were installed their departure was usually regretted. A newcomer was in a better position to bargain over terms than a sitting tenant. Though many Wolds farmers prospered others possessed of little capital appear to have been demoralized by the advent of Free Trade. 'I was told by a farmer he had lately the offer of ten farms! but he thinks of going to America where they are not in the humour of Free Trade' wrote James Finlay from Willoughby in 1850 in a rueful comment on Repeal and its consequences.[14] Repairs for tenants had a direct bearing upon their success and their ability to pay rents. In 1836 William Jones of Scotterthorpe requested a repair to his barn and the sub-agent commented 'We all know what a Dead ruin it is to offer wheat in a bad condition.'[15] There were social and economic advan-

[13] L.A.O. 3 ANC 7/23/57/9. [14] L.A.O. 3 ANC 7/23/59/70.
[15] L.A.O. 3 ANC 7/23/32/57.

tages to both tenant and landlord in the annual system but a further safeguard for the tenant who expended his capital on improvement and high farming was the Lincolnshire Custom of tenant right which seems to have acquired a refinement and an authority by the second quarter of the nineteenth century so great that it must be counted as a major influence in the agricultural revolution in that period.

The Lincolnshire Custom which was to be the basis of the 1875 and 1883 Agricultural Holdings Acts was a product of the farming situation in Lindsey which occurred after 1815 and although earlier customs and practices had their influence, the Lincolnshire Custom was no mere extension of them. Rather it was the result of a particular set of needs in a light-soil area of the county at a crucial time in farming fortunes. Just as rents had risen to take account of wartime prices a collapse of the price level took place with the approaching end of hostilities after 1813. By this time the limit of the area which it was practical to claim for arable farming was being reached. Attention was turning to increasing output from what was already fit for tillage. The estimation of crops as 'away-going' or 'following crops' had been relatively easy. As alternating cereal and fodder crops in rotations were applied to the uplands in the final decades of the eighteenth century, it was necessary to develop a system for compensating tenants for their outlays and giving them a sense of security. Once established, that made annual tenancies-at-will preferable to leases for both landlords and occupiers. When farming confidence was badly shaken after 1815 there was great need to have cheaper methods for assessing tenants' claims, if they were to be expected to continue or embark upon rotational farming with expensive inputs of fertilizers. Though there was considerable variation from farm to farm on the Lindsey uplands in the cycle of fodder and cereal crops, nevertheless integration of different crops was the common feature of the rotation. Although soil types, the wishes of the landlord and farmers' ideas on what was beneficial and therefore profitable made for different rotations, the idea was common to all that each crop should contribute to the success of the following ones. Fertilizers applied to a turnip crop could affect the quality and quantity of a wheat crop four or five years later.

That crop integration and the close association of arable farming with stock rearing was likely to produce a great increase of yields particularly from the Lindsey uplands was becoming clear at the end of the eighteenth century. Land agents were at pains to see that farms had the correct proportion of their acreages in pasture and meadow so that the arable, again divided so as to facilitate a suitable crop rotation, could receive the right amount of manure to maintain fertility. As cereal prices rose from 1790 to about 1813 the warrens and sheep walks, many of which were already enclosed, were turned over to more intensive arable farming.

Evidence of the trend comes from many parts of the Lincolnshire uplands. Plough houses or sheds replaced cow houses on some farms as more accommodation was needed for waggons, ploughs and carts.[16] Tenants were willing to build new houses and barns, the latter situated on the walks or warrens. Later a crew-yard might be added and a dwelling, making the nucleus of a new farm or a second homestead for the existing one. When 90 acres of warren were enclosed at Welbourn on the Heath a barn was to be built to serve the new enclosure; its cost was to be met from the sale of decayed timber at Nocton.[17] At Farlesthorpe just off the Wolds near Alford where tenancies were annual, a tenant built a new farmhouse for his 150 acre holding in 1798; on four other farms the occupiers had built waggon houses, cow houses and a barn.[18] On the Heneage estates at Hainton and Barkwith on the Wolds above Wragby, according to a survey of 1789, tenants had built new farm houses as they shared in breaking in the walk land piece by piece. When in 1792 Charles Anderson Pelham purchased from Robert Cliffe of Brigg 404 acres near Brocklesby, there was a reference to a newly built farmhouse, some new enclosure and a warren.[19] A lease of 1781 for 900 acres in Worlaby and 700 acres in Ruckland high on the Wolds between Horncastle and Louth, to replace a 21 years lease, provided for three tenants from Little Coates, Theddlethorpe and Ruckland to hold the land in partnership for three years; then if all went well they were to move to an annual tenancy. The Worlaby warren was to have over 400 couples of rabbits and 500 couples of silver-haired rabbits, but the meadows and enclosures were to be protected from their burrowings. Umpires were to assess the stock of rabbits at the end of the tenancy and to allow for an 'overplus' or to insist on the outgoers' making up a deficiency. A new occupier was to be allowed entry at Martinmas, 11 November, to plough up the fallows for turnips. The outgoer could remain until May Day. A following crop of 100 acres of corn was to be allowed, the new-comer having had the right to sow clover in it. He or the landlord was to have the chance to buy the crop on the valuation of two umpires. The outgoers were to have the cost of grass seeds sown one year before the end of the tenancy and the cost of sainfoin which

16 L.A.O. Dixon 4/1 f. 118–19.

17 MSS., D. D. Dashwood (Bucks.) B19/4/12, 1765.

18 L.A.O. Hig. 12/3.

19 L.A.O. Yarb. 3/2/2/1–2.

may have been sown two years before they left. They were to leave all the manure on the farm; they were to fell no timber and they were to give six days per year in 'boon work' for the landlord and to keep their buildings and Ruckland Church in repair. Their rent was to be £333 a year plus tithe and taxes. This is an example of a lease early enough to show the value of a stocked warren and yet late enough to show a move to a tenancy-at-will and the beginnings of compensation for tenants' good practice.

John Parkinson, Lord Yarborough's land valuer, explained to Sir Joseph Banks in 1796 the importance of drawing his farmers away from too much grazing so that they could live better, employ more men and pay higher rents. Many tenants on the Revesby estate because of their landlord's 'indulgence' had saved 'no Money ... with a proper proportion of Arable the Farms will be cheaper to the Tenant than they are now, will produce more Corn and fat cattle for Community and employ more poor Labourers in Winter ...' Yet he believed it would be difficult to get them to change their ways. Some tenants '... have been in the Habit of one Trail of Grazing their Farms in an Old Way with an inferior breed of poor Cattle, a little Arable Ill-managed, have gained nothing perhaps in their Old Way, and therefore seems unable to bear any Advance Altho' an Active Farmer would pay the advance and get Money—those sort of Tenants must be nicely watched ... and by degrees draw them into better Habits'. John Parkinson made an eloquent plea for mixed farming and where land was any good for arable, a tenant ought to be encouraged to plough at least half of his farm, the landlord seeing to the main drains. From 'the ancient appearance' of the parish he believed that there had been much more arable and now it 'does not supply itself'. He urged the cultivation of poor land in certain market conditions 'Perhaps some Men may Observe the Lowest Yield scarcely pay for Cultivation, I have Often given that sort of Land a serious Consideration, and find when Cattle and Wool is a beneficial Artical, the farmers Gain may be greater and on an Average nearly equal, but when it is considered that by Agriculture the Land produces Crops that will preserve Cattle in the severest Winter and Food for so many more Beings than the Master, and also employ 7 Men in Agriculture to one in Grazing and we well know it requires one Acre of Good Land to feed two Sheep when one Acre of medium land will produce 900 pecks of Potatoes or 3 qtrs of Wheat which will give a great deal more food to a Family than two Sheep will do, in fact the greatest error we Farmers have been guilty of, is going to extreme.' He believed that a tenant or his son could plough half an acre each between the morning and evening care of their cattle which would prevent laziness 'I have been long convinced that a proper proportion of Arable does not diminish the quantity of Sheep and Wool because one half of the Quantity of Land will summer as much Stock as the whole will Winter and that Half in Arable contributes to their Winter Support.'[20]

When in 1815 John Burcham valued a farm of 536 acres at £497 a year for Henry Dalton in Walesby on the Wolds between Market Rasen and Caistor, he observed 'This Farm is inconveniently situate, on account of the Tillage land being at a distance from the Farm house, Roads bad and Hilly, there is not a sufficient Quantity of Wold land to this farm to enable the occupier to grow Turnips, sufficient for the support of the Cattle and Sheep in the Winter ... the present Occupier states that he has at his own expense, nearly subdivided the farm with good quick fences, and also erected the whole of the Buildings upon the Wold.'[21] Another plea for a balanced farm and an end to an excessive acreage of grass came in 1829 when the Rev. Thomas Dupré wrote from Willoughby rectory to his patron Lord Willoughby about the state of his tenants. After pointing out that too many homesteads were clustered in the village at a distance from their land he complained that expenditure on the Willoughby High Drain had brought few benefits because there were too few collateral drains. He continued in a request for more arable and an integrated farming pattern 'The Arable, Pasture and Meadow land too bear no proportion to each other, and there is a vast quantity of low wet land with good depth of soil at present of trifling value, which if it were drained and ploughed up would greatly increase your rental ... I know of one farm consisting of near three hundred and fifty acres and only twenty five under the Plough and the consequence is that one third of it is now unstocked and as there can be no straw, the whole never knows the taste of manure. The tenant can never grow cabbages, seeds or turnips, and he can have no other recourse but his grass, and that too much impoverished, for the improvement of sheep and cattle.'[22]

Between 1790 and 1804 on the Manners estate in the parishes of Bloxham, Revesby, Salmonby, Rigsby and Alford there was evidence of walk land being broken in for tillage and the building of new barns and extra farmsteads though here leases were preferred to tenancies-at-will. On a Bloxham farm held on a seven years lease, the landlord was to help with the tenants' costs in hedging, ditching, marling or claying and cropping records for 1790 to 1801 showed that in the arable fields of 20 acres in extent on one 350 acre farm the

[20] BL, Add. MSS., 33979, 43837. [21] L.A.O. 4 TDE F/4/5.
[22] L.A.O. 3 ANC 7/23/21/27.

following course was adopted, barley, wheat, turnips, barley, seeds, pasture, barley, seeds, oats, barley, wheat and in 1801 turnips. At Salmonby the landlord built a new barn and a stable on new arable land on 'the walks' within the first two years of a 15 years tenancy of a farm of 324 acres. Arrangements were made as was usual at this time, for the landlord to buy in, on the assessment of two valuers, the following crop of corn in the enclosed arable. At Rigsby in 1780 arrangements for hedging walk land for arable were laid down in a 15 years lease. The Great Walk of over 60 acres was to be made arable and the landlord was to find the quicks. He was to build his tenant within two years of the tenancy a barn, a fenced-in crew-yard, and to provide him with a pump and a newly dug well. As an addition to the holding's present messuage he was to put up within five years a building consisting of a parlour, bedchamber, garret and cellar. On another Rigsby farm of 443 acres, the Great Walk of 65 acres were cultivated from 1790 to 1801 under, pasture, pasture, pasture, oats, turnips, barley, seeds, seeds, oats, barley, seeds and seeds again in 1801.[23] Although the rotations varied the attack upon the walks and tops was general and it involved the siting of new buildings on the uplands which in some instances later became the main farmsteads. At Doddington between Lincoln and the Nottinghamshire border there had appeared by 1778 farms called Moor, Top, Grange, Brick, Springs, Carr Lane and Carr Farm none of which had been there earlier in the century. These were the new outlying farms whose names tell us of the pressure on the low, wet soils as well as that upon the uplands.[24] By the middle of the nineteenth century there were social reasons expressed for having farms run from sites outside the villages. As James Finlay the Willoughby sub-agent put it 'I consider it very objectionable to have farm premises muddled together in a village and among public houses and beer shops as at Willoughby, it is destruction to many farmers and engenders bad habits among their men.'[25]

On clay soils, in the Fens and on the Isle of Axholme there is evidence of new division fences and new outbuildings and home-steads at this time. A Revesby Abbey estate survey of 1796 stressed the need for the underdraining of the clays so that a turnip crop could be grown. Sandy land near by should be put under oats and turnips for four years followed by seeds eaten on by sheep for four years '... if white clay could be led upon the Sandy land and sand upon the clayey land the crops would improve very much'.[26] On the same estate a pumping engine was at work between 1806 and

[23] L.A.O. Hig. 1/1, 1790. [24] M. W. Barley, *LH*, 1, pt. 7, 1951, pp. 252, 257.
[25] L.A.O. 3 ANC 7/23/64/31. [26] L.A.O. RA 2/B/17.

1807. Bones were purchased and crushed for spreading. A bone mill was at work in 1802 and Revesby Bank pumping engine was fixed with a pair of hammers for bone crushing about the same time for a cost of £28. Engines at Medlam and Revesby drained 175 acres from 1805 to 1806 at the cost of 6d. an acre. By 1818 a new barn, 30 feet long, 15½ feet wide and 14 feet high was being built in brick and tile for £73.10s.[27] for a tenant at Whaplode near Holbeach. At Farlesthorpe, the owner the Rev. H. Kipling, agreed with a tenant on an annual agreement in 1801 to let 60 acres for £36 a year on what appears to have been a new farm. The tenant was to divide the acreage and to sow the whole with corn in his first year. The next year he was to have two-thirds of the acreage in corn and one-third under seeds to be eaten on by sheep. The next year the land was to have one-third fallow, a third seeds and a third corn. The fourth year it was to have two-thirds under corn and one-third fallow, and the fifth year a third seeds, a third fallow and a third corn and so on for the length of the tenancy. At the end of his occupation the tenant could remove his gates, shuttle posts and rails in the division fences and have the eatage of his last year allowed him on the assessment of two valuers and an umpire. Again on this estate there was evidence of tenants building and being given rent allowances even though they were tenants-at-will and the largest farm was only 141 acres. Some of the 14 farms of the estate lay in Marsh parishes at Saleby, Huttoft, Trusthorpe, Manby and Saltfleetby.[28] In the north-west at Belton and Crowle on the Isle of Axholme, enclosure was accompanied by the creation of a new farm in 1798 on the estate of R. P. Steer. 'Goodcrop' farm of 95 acres of the new enclosures on Thornbush Carr and Sandtoft Plains was left in the occupation of Richard Winter whilst his father occupied another holding on the same estate. The Winters were still there as tenants in 1821.[29]

These changes demanded new arrangements for the compensation of tenants when after 1813 farming prospects became uncertain. Farmers on annual tenancies needed the assurance of a custom for the reward of unexhausted improvements. In Kesteven tenant right had probably more to do with the process of entry to a farm. In Lincolnshire farms were vacated on 5 April. Clearly the outgoing tenant had either to let the incoming tenant into the farm prior to this date, or carry out the cultivation for him. In the latter case the incoming tenant could then pay a mutually agreed sum for labour and seed. Tenant right for a wider variety of services could naturally

[27] L.A.O. RA 2/A/1/3, RA 2/A/1/4. [28] L.A.O. Hig. 13/3.
[29] L.A.O. 2 TGH 1/34/5/A/34, 2TGH 1/34/J/A/37.

grow out of this.[30] In Lindsey, too, there were arrangements for easing the take-over of the incoming tenant by a system of compensation assessed by valuers and referred to an umpire if a dispute took place. Damage done to a tenant's holding by game could be assessed in the same way as, for example, on Sir John Nelthorpe's property at Scawby near Brigg but the growth of the Lincolnshire custom after 1815 as the mid and late nineteenth-century commentators knew it owed more to the integrated rotations and arrangements for mixed farming of the period than to entry procedures.

In Lindsey an element of dual occupation by outgoing and incoming tenants appears to have been general. The outgoer withdrew from the land as each crop was harvested and he was free to sell waygoing crops to the highest bidder, not just to his successor. Landlords thus enjoyed a longer interval in which to choose a successor. If the incoming tenant had to enter the farm to sow spring corn, the landlord had only three months from 10 October in which to find a new tenant. Where his old tenant withdrew gradually, he could afford to wait until the late spring when his deadline was the need for the sowing of the turnip crop with its great appetite for fertilizers. There was much variation in the Lincolnshire custom, both within Lindsey and between Lindsey and Kesteven. There were even variations from farm to farm within a single estate, though the differences were related to the nature of the soil, or the location of the holding. On Sir John Nelthorpe's farms, more was allowed to tenants whose fields were sandy but at a distance from the clay deposits than to those with a need for claying who happened to farm near the clay. Those with the lightest of sandy land—and therefore the greatest need for claying—were allowed their costs for a period of twelve years; others on the estate were allowed costs for ten or merely six years. By the 1840s, uniformity of practice and output in the uplands was near; with it came a uniformity in tenant right awards which spread to other parts of the county. Yet the custom was notable for its flexibility in that new fertilizers, for example, could be taken into it. Allowances for guano used on Lindsey farms in the 1840s meant that more occupiers would use it, in the knowledge that if they had to leave their farms they would be compensated for it. Thus innovation was encouraged.

Given the generally good reputation of Lincolnshire landlords and the continuity of occupation of their tenants under tenancies-at-will, there was little movement of farming families unless times

[30] David Grigg, 'The Development of Tenant Right in South Lincolnshire'. *LH*, 2, pt. 9, 1962, pp. 41–7.

were especially difficult. Landlords were anxious not to have to pay an outgoer his tenant-right and then to take the farm in hand because an incomer was not available. At the same time, the custom probably helped in the difficult years after 1813 to consolidate within Lincolnshire farming families who had experience, knowledge of the soil, a willingness to innovate as they made the uplands productive and, very important in a time of massive inputs of labour, power and fertilizers, large capital resources. The custom helped to reduce disputes and to ease landlord-tenant relationships. When, after the Napoleonic wars, farmers were becoming more independent, the custom gave a formality, a ritual even, for their claims to consideration; this encouragement seems to have been socially healthy as well as economically fruitful.

The custom offered an alternative to distraint for non-payment of arrears. When a tenant left a farm his arrears could be deducted from the award. When a new tenant was coming in he could be ordered to pay to the landlord the outgoer's arrears and to deduct the sum from the amount he would be paying to his predecessor for unexhausted improvements. Thus court cases with their attendant publicity were avoided. Rarely, it seems, did landlords refuse to accept the custom as binding even though before 1875 it had not yet the recognition of law. In 1832, however, Lady Gordon of Green Park Lodge, Piccadilly, objected to the claims of an outgoing tenant, Francis Taylor, from her farm at Linwood near Market Rasen. Taylor was a tenant of some substance. His rent was £1,000 a year, he kept 26 working horses, 50 cattle and 800 sheep. After agreeing to a rent increase after the arrival of a new agent in 1829 he quarrelled with him when, contrary to his terms of occupation, 300 hedgerow trees were felled and damage was done to his fences, his corn crops and his eddish crops by the dragging of heavy timber across his land. Taylor gave notice to quit and when his claims for unexhausted improvements were refused by his landlady he went to court for the repayment of rent and taxes on 'land fallowed the year previous to his quitting' and for 'the Tenants Rights ... to which he was entitled ... according to the custom of the country'. The case caused a stir locally for usually compensation was amicably arranged between outgoers and incomers. A special jury allowed Taylor's claims for rent and taxes on his 'summer fallowed land' and 'for fold-yard fences and buildings five or six inches only in the ground' but they rejected other claims for unexhausted improvements not sanctioned by law. After about 1832, however, tenant right became increasingly a matter between incomers and their predecessors as landlords were rarely faced by the spectre they feared most; the necessity of taking an untenanted farm in hand.

After 1815 the leadership of agricultural progress passed from Norfolk with its tradition of long leases to Lincolnshire with its tenancies-at-will, its good landlord-tenant relationships and its increasingly accepted customs of compensation for unexhausted improvements.

9

Progress and productivity, 1815 to 1850

IMPROVEMENTS to livestock were an important aspect of the agricultural revolution in Lincolnshire. The need to fold sheep on the thin light soils of the Wolds as part of the mixed farming system of the nineteenth century meant that enclosure and subdivision of large fields by temporary fencing were essential. Better farm buildings providing protection from the elements helped to raise the number and the quality of good livestock.[1]

The Improved Lincoln which was to be celebrated as an excellent rent-paying animal for mixed farmers by the third quarter of the nineteenth century resulted from the work of a small number of breeders on the light soils of a few parishes on the north Wolds and the Cliff.[2] When wool prices collapsed in the 1720s the response in the uplands was to turn more land over to rabbit warrens and to the buying of Scotch cattle for fattening on better pastures in more sheltered locations. The need for winter fodder for cattle may well have hastened the introduction of the turnip culture which was, after about 1770, to change the economy of the uplands and to allow large-scale sheep rearing. Breeding sheep in the uplands for fattening in the lowlands gave way to an integration of the two on the holdings of individual farmers who were now breeders, rearers and fatteners of sheep as well as arable farmers. Smaller sheep were a better paying proposition than the old, large Lincolns; mutton could be marketed thanks to the winter fodder provided by turnips, in the winter and spring which were formerly periods of scarcity and high prices. Heavy sheep were needed to solidify the land for barley after turnips, so the way was clear for rearing a long-woolled sheep which was a good producer of mutton. The 'Improved

[1] Thirsk, op. cit. pp. 162–4.

[2] J. A. Perkins, *Sheep Farming in Eighteenth and Nineteenth Century Lincolnshire*, *SLHA*, 4, Sleaford, 1977.

Lincoln' was eventually to satisfy the need and to be an international success. Use was made of the knowledge and experience of ram breeders or 'tup-men' who hired out rams and who provided the Lincolnshire farmers with opportunities to experiment with breeds and to guard against inbreeding. Farmers like Bourne of Dalby were offering rams to let before the Disley Society of Loughborough in the 1780s was at work promoting Robert Bakewell's New Leicesters. On the whole, Lincolnshire breeders did not like to use rams from their own flocks. 'In and in' breeding was thought to promote hereditary disorders or infirmities and to cause the animals to run to fat, yet Robert Bakewell based the reputation of his 'New Leicesters' upon 'in and in breeding' or breeding with closely related animals. He remained critical of cross-breeding all his life even though he let out New Leicester tups. It was from crossing that the new Lincolns emerged. They produced good mutton; they yielded wool which lent itself to the making of new varieties of cloth in new techniques of manufacture; they were heavy enough to help solidify the light soils of the uplands and they could withstand exposure in turnip fields through the winter to make the manure needed for the following cereal crops.

The development of the 'Improved Lincoln' lasted from about 1760 to 1830 but the process was not without its setbacks (Plate 10a). Some breeders like Charles Chaplin of Tathwell on the Wolds near Louth crossed his Lincolns with the Teeswater breed in an attempt to increase the weight of his fleeces; others bought Southdowns and Sir Joseph Banks introduced Merino rams. The main improvement came from crossing with New Leicesters, however, and its success, particularly in the 1840s in other parts of England and in the Antipodes, showed that cross-breeding under careful conditions was the way to save the flocks from degeneration. Lincolnshire farmers found that though some breeds from Durham and Northumberland did adapt quite well to the Lincolnshire environment, wholesale purchase of new breeds was not the answer. Transfer of breeds usually involved some losses and the purchase made heavy demands upon a farmer's capital. Lincolnshire farmers relied instead upon selective cross-breeding. The New Leicesters which were to create the Improved Lincolns were probably themselves the result of careful inbreeding of the Old Lincolns by Robert Bakewell. They were at their prime for mutton after the second shear or about 27 months after birth, whereas the Old Lincolns were slaughtered after the third shear at about 39 months after birth. On the uplands it was essential to have an animal which came to maturity quickly to allow a rapid turnover, for the light soils never yielded a rich herbage. The new breed had a low ratio of bone to total carcass weight. In the Old Lincoln, the meat was about half the total live weight but in the New Leicesters it was about two-thirds of the live weight. Until the late 1830s when livestock began to reach London and Yorkshire from Lincolnshire by steamship and in the 1840s by rail, the New Leicesters enjoyed yet another advantage: thcy could be driven long distances and arrive at market in good condition.

It is not surprising that the New Leicesters were not transferred to Lincolnshire to replace the Old Lincoln flocks, for despite their good features their deficiencies, such as small joints, insipid meat and shorter wool, were such as to make them unsuitable as the general breed of the county. Farmers were perceptive enough to understand that the New Leicester rams imparted to their progeny their attributes when put to the ewes of the old breed. The result was the Improved Lincoln.

New Leicester rams were hired by Lincolnshire farmers in the 1760s at costs ranging from 15 to 40 guineas. Benjamin Codd, a tenant of Lord Scarbrough's at Glentworth on the Cliff, was a pioneer in the introduction of New Leicester blood in the 1770s. He crossed his original flock of Cheviots or Northumberland hill sheep with Bakewell rams until in 1785 he found the fees too high; he relied on line breeding from his own stock thereafter. By the end of the eighteenth century the keeping of Old Lincolns was confined to the Outer Marsh parishes. In 1796 a Disley Society was founded in Lincoln for the improvement of the breed and to promote the interests of those farmers who had invested in New Leicester rams for letting out to Lincolnshire farmers; membership was strongest among farmers in the Cliff parishes north of Lincoln and the northern part of the Wolds. Samuel Slater of North Carlton bred New Leicester rams and was able, by the 1830s, to purchase his farm with capital raised partly from the sale of his prize flock. John Dudding of Barton and Philip Skipwith of Aylesby were leading sheep-breeders on the Wolds. The Aylesby flock was probably the longest surviving in the county and one of the most valuable. William Torr paid £1,500 for it in the 1840s and retained it until 1875. He was determined to keep the flock pure as it had been for about 80 years. In 1798 Philip Skipwith had paid 600 guineas for the hire of one ram for one season from an owner of New Leicesters at Holme Pierrepoint (Notts.) who had bought Bakewell's flock on his death in 1796. In 1812 Dudding of Barton and three others paid 1,000 guineas for the hire of a ram from Normanton in Leicestershire. In 1827 Clarke of Canwick on the Heath just south of Lincoln showed two wethers in Lincoln market with fleeces of 24 pounds as against the usual 10 to 12 pounds.[3] The emergence of the Improved Lincolns was comparatively rapid. From the 1790s to about 1810 the New Leicester blood was widely accepted though there were many local variations of the breed. On the north Wolds, the Cliff and the Heath the New Leicester characteristics were most pronounced in the new breed. In the central and southern Wolds parishes the Old Lincoln attributes lingered but it was to be here that the new breed was to achieve its most balanced form by the second quarter of the nineteenth century. When J. and E. Walesby left the ram business in September 1833 it was claimed that their 'Flock goes back 80 years and retains the distinctive qualities of the true old Lincolnshire breed.'[4] The dispersal of a carefully bred flock was a social event providing work for auctioneers, caterers and printers from Louth and Market Rasen.[5]

Henry Dudding of Riby on the Wolds was one of the great sheep breeders of the nineteenth century. Born at Panton in 1838, he and his brother William took over the farming of 2,500 acres at Panton and Lambcroft from their father. In 1876 Henry took his flock of Lincolns to Riby where he farmed 800 acres. Later he took on 500 acres from the Earl of Yarborough at Croxby to which he added 850 acres at Grasby with 120 acres of marsh pasture. Farming a four course system, his operations attracted many foreign visitors for whom he was the 'premier tenant farmer'. His annual sale of stock at Riby was considered second only to Lincoln Show as a social event.[6] Lincoln sheep, improved and refined by the Duddings and others, won their reputation after about 1876 but signs of methodical breeding and the value of certain prize rams went back some 80 years. At Aylesby Philip Skipwith and later William Torr built up a formidable reputation in Lincoln sheep. Torr's dispersal sale in 1875 brought in £44,395. R. and W. Wright sold 950 sheep in the 1890s to Senor Manuel Cobo of Buenos Aires from their Nocton Heath farm for £30,000.[7] J. R. and R. R. Kirkham of Biscathorpe between Louth and Wragby successfully produced good mutton and wool from their flock in the 1850s. Rams were let out at £25 a service but certain prize animals could produce up to £160 a time in fees. The flock continued until 1901 by which time Biscathorpe sheep were in demand in South America.[8] William Dawson of Withcall was producing heavy three-shear sheep as early as 1826 on a farm which in

[3] Thirsk, op. cit. pp. 250–1. [4] L.A.O. Dixon 20/4/9.
[5] L. A. O. Dixon 20/4/13–14.
[6] G. E. Collins, *Farming and Fox-hunting*, London, n.d., p. 38.
[7] Op. cit. pp. 32–5. [8] Op. cit., p. 63.

its day with its 350 acres under turnips was considered to be the perfect holding. It was the Dudding enterprise which represents the late but complete triumph of the Lincoln sheep. 'Dudding was only the greatest of the number of giants in sheep breeding who brought the Lincoln to what was generally regarded as a great pitch of perfection.'[9] When demand in South America and the Dominions was booming the Lincolns were just right for crossing with the Merino to increase size and to give more and tastier meat. In the late 1890s Riby was for a time the centre of the sheep-rearing world, with all of North Lincolnshire on holiday for the sales, with entertainments for wealthy buyers at the Yarborough Hotel in Grimsby and jollification in the big barns for those who had helped give the Riby flock its fame. By the 1870s the Lincoln breed had a high reputation in County Tipperary and in Germany, where a cross with the Merino had made Lincolns more popular in the mid-1860s. It was after 1875, however, that the great demand from Australia and New Zealand had its impact. There it helped to form the Corriedale breed used for high quality carpet wool.

In England the breed successfully transferred to the Midland counties and the East Riding of Yorkshire. Nottinghamshire farmers favoured it because the mining districts of Derbyshire provided a good market for the wool and meat. In Leicestershire itself the Improved Lincoln was to triumph over the New Leicesters by the 1860s and even Bakewell's successor at Disley was to breed it. The sheer quantity of both wool and mutton on the new breed was an unbeatable combination when the flock was integrated with arable production on a mixed farm. The fleece though slightly lighter than on the old breed was finer and was therefore in demand with worsted manufacturers who put up with the shorter staple now its quality was improved. The animals yielded a low ratio of offal to meat and their lean cuts were in increasing demand from butchers. The Improved Lincolns needed no shelter in bad weather; they lost few lambs in breeding and the ewes were prolific, for about a third produced pairs while triplets were common and fours not unknown. They were ready for slaughter after the second shear, 12 months ahead of the old breed yet they were worth keeping for a second shear if mutton prices were low and wool prices were high. In an age when farmers were seeking protection from over-specialization, the Improved Lincolns fitted into a mixed farming pattern as an easy-to-rear, sound producer of wool and mutton.

During the last years of the eighteenth century Thomas Turnell

[9] J. A. Scott Watson and M. Elliott Hobbs, *Great Farmers*, London, 1937, pp. 169–70.

of Reasby near Wragby founded a herd of cattle which was to be the celebrated Lincoln red shorthorn. They were sought after for their good milk yields, their attractive cherry-red colour and their meat. Wolds farmers reared calves for sale to butchers after three or four years or for dispatch to the graziers of the Marsh. Dairying was uncommon despite Arthur Young's reference to Normanby farmers who weaned their calves after ten or twelve days and made the milk into butter for sale in Hull.[10] As well as the calf-rearing husbandry, cattle from Scotland or Wales were fattened in west Lincolnshire. On the Cliff north of Lincoln and in Kesteven this trade had been profitable in the early years of the eighteenth century. Wolds farmers who by the second quarter of the nineteenth century had little pasture left took in stock for the winter only from Marsh and lowland farmers. The owners would help towards the cost of cake while the host farmers provided accommodation, straw and other keep.[11] By 1850, the Lincoln shorthorn was prized as a beef animal. Durham blood from the Collings' herd had been introduced. Thomas Bates of Worlaby had an offer of 1,000 guineas for Duchess, bought at Charles Colling's sale in 1810. The herd was to remain in being until 1850.[12] James Green Dixon of Holton and Rothwell on the Wolds, took great pride in his shorthorn, Young Strawberry, calved in 1827; he had her portrait painted when she was 21. His shorthorns had been recorded in a herd book and he had added to them by purchasing at the final sale of Robert Collings in 1820.[13] (Plate 10b).

Lincolnshire cattle, tall, lean, long, good for draught and pied or white in colour, still retained until the 1780s in the eastern Marshland parishes both the appearance and the name of their Dutch origins. William Torr of Aylesby remarked on the likeness between English shorthorns and the stock he observed at Utrecht fair in 1838.[14] The 'Turnell Reds', however, brought with them some of the advantages of the superior herds from Durham and the Yorkshire border near Darlington. They were small and quick to fatten. Lord Willoughby d'Eresby introduced them at Bourne and farmers such as Messrs Dyke and Coalam at Withern between Louth and Mablethorpe, Baumber at Somersby and Cartwright at Tathwell bred them in the 1830s and 1840s. The Old Welbourn Reds of the

[10] Thirsk, op. cit. p. 274.
[11] J. A. Clarke, 'On the Farming of Lincolnshire', Prize Report, 1852, pp. 146–7.
[12] *British Breeds of Livestock*, Board of Agriculture and Fisheries, London, 1913, p. 45.
[13] L.A.O. Dixon 12/4/2, 12/7/4/19; *Archivists' Report* 24, p. 21.
[14] G. E. Collins, op. cit., p. 28.

south and east of the county were bred into the Lincoln Reds. Charles Colling (1750–1836), with his brother Robert (d. 1820) did much to improve the quality of Lincolnshire cattle by their sales to Lincolnshire enthusiasts. Oastler of Aylesby hired one of their bulls, and at the Collings' Ketton sale in 1810, Grant of Wyham purchased Laura for 210 guineas, Lucilla for 106 guineas and a bull, Major, for 200 guineas. His programme was to cross his Turnell cattle with Collings-bred bulls. At the 1818 sale Philip Skipwith of Aylesby, J. White of Great Coates, Leighton of North Willingham and W. Brookes of Laceby were buying Collings' stock for Lincolnshire. Dudding of Panton on the Wolds gave 255 guineas for a bull at a Durham shorthorn sale in 1829 while three years earlier shorthorn blood had been bought at the Chilham sale. William Torr of Aylesby became the most celebrated shorthorn breeder in the county. He began in 1844 by hiring bulls from John Booth of Killerby and Richard Booth of Worlaby. Believing that it took 30 years to build up a good breed, he was to make the tree in his sale ring at Aylesby near Brocklesby a centre of the shorthorn world until the dispersal of his herd in 1875. At that sale, 84 head of shorthorns sold at an average of £500 each and the £2,160 guineas paid for one of his cows set up a national record. A great traveller in England and Ireland in the company of other Lincolnshire breeders, he made a reputation as an authority on the design of farm buildings and cottages. In his time he farmed 3,000 acres at Aylesby, Riby, Irby and Rothwell under various landlords, including the Earl of Yarborough and Colonel Tomline; he also held grazing at Immingham and Stallingborough. In 1848 he paid £1,500 for Philip Skipwith's flock of 400 ewes, the heirs of about 80 years of breeding in Leicesters.[15] By the 1840s Lincolnshire was a source for improved stock called upon by other parts of the country; its intake of better breeds having been completed about 1815.[16]

Howden in East Yorkshire had by the 1830s given place to Horncastle as the greatest horse fair in the country, drawing buyers from all parts of the British Isles, from Europe and even the U.S.A. In 1832 one of Lord Yarborough's tenants sold six hunters there for a total of £1,000. Horses were bred for the saddle and for coach work in many Wolds villages. At Lincoln horse fair in April 1838 a Wolds farmer sold 23 working horses for 1,700 guineas.[17] In South Holland, breeding mares were kept in large numbers by the many

[15] G. E. Collins, op. cit., pp. 28–34.

[16] J. A. Perkins, 'The Prosperity of Farming on the Lindsey Uplands 1813–37', *AHR*, Vol. 24, Part II, 1976, p. 142.

[17] Perkins, op. cit., p. 142.

smaller farmers of the Fens. Horse breeding here had gone on for some 250 years, the animals finding their way to the coal workings of Nottinghamshire and the lead mines of Derbyshire.[18] At the Lincoln meeting of the Royal Agricultural Society in 1854 the quality of the hunters on show for Lord Yarborough and Lord Henry Bentinck and used by the South Wold excited favourable comment.[19] Robert Howard of Rise Farm, Nocton was among award winners for a black Lincolnshire stallion while 'Beauty' belonging to Charles Bayles of Riseholme and bred by J. Knowles of Langworth was the outstanding black cart filly.

Recent work on the history and pedigree of the Shire horse has revealed how much this breed owes to its Lincolnshire origins.[20] The name Shire comes from its association with the middle and eastern English counties between the Severn, the Humber and the Cam, but the breed appears to date from the birth in Lincolnshire in 1800 of Honest Tom. This horse dominated the breed, for his descendants by 1924 numbered 105 of the prize winners at the London show of that year out of a total of 133 winners.[21] In the late eighteenth century there were two kinds of heavy horse in Lincolnshire, the sorrel sometimes called the Suffolk or Punch and the Lincolnshire or Leicestershire Black. The Fen blacks were renowned as heavy, slow but reliable workers sometimes called Dodmen from the Norfolk word for a snail. The Lincolnshire blacks with their coarse and profuse hair, their black skin with the occasional pink patch were the animals upon which, when they were at their prime of five years, the real work of the agricultural revolution fell. In the Wolds at least, they moved vast quantities of natural and artificial manures to the thin soils of the uplands, and tons of harvested wheat and roots. Enclosure, the generally favourable price structure for farmers of the 1790s and then the high prices of the Napoleonic Wars encouraged the large-scale breeding of shire horses. They were in demand in the wars and then in Europe when hostilities were over. The development of railways and an insistent home demand led to a confusion of breeding between sorrels and blacks so that the era of high farming saw the use of many mongrels. They were, however, light, active and suited to the plough team.[22] The quality of the shire fell off and only a minority

[18] Thirsk, op. cit., p. 32. [19] *JRA. Soc.*, Vol. 15, 1855, report XII, pp. 379–82.

[20] Keith Chivers, *The Shire Horse, A History of the Breed, the Society, and the Men*, London, 1976.

[21] Chivers, op. cit., pp. 563, 215, 58.

[22] J. Burke, 'Breeding and Management of Horses on a Farm', *JRA Soc.*, v. 1845, p. 519.

of breeders, mainly in the Fens, strove to maintain high standards. Meanwhile the opposite trend was affecting cattle with the publication of herd books for shorthorns in 1822, for Herefords and Devons in 1846 and 1851, followed by registration for the Aberdeen Angus in 1862 and the South Wales Blacks in 1875.

The movements of one noted brown stallion between 1817 and 1824 gives some idea of the work and life of the owners and their horsemen. Fred Dixon's 'Waxwork' travelled a county route which lasted a week. The charges were £1 per mare covered, payable at mid-summer. On Mondays the stallion was at Whatton in Nottinghamshire, at Long Bennington in Lincolnshire and then at Balderton in Nottinghamshire for Wednesday night. He was then brought back through Lincolnshire villages to Foston and Great Ponton for Saturday. His progress was a welcome break from rural monotony in the villages and the arrival of a stallion and his groom was an occasion for interest and activity among farmers, innkeepers and farm workers. John Savidge of Bassingham, who by 1820 was farming under Sir John Thorold at Carlton Scroop near Ancaster, was one of the owners of a stallion which represented some of the best shire blood. On his introduction card he stated that for one guinea a service his 'well-bred Black Horse' named 'Useful' would cover mares. The stallion was bred out of one of the best black mares in the county sired by a famous black horse from Bicker Fen. Between 1820 and 1828 John Savidge worked from Barrowby Vale near Grantham. Although his stock was never entered in the Shire stud book opened some 60 years later, it now seems certain that his horses had much to do with the keeping up of good Lincolnshire blacks.[23] Later in the century the Mountain family of Saleby near Alford were to breed some outstanding shires like 'Mountain's Champion' in the late 1850s and to sell colts to the U.S.A. in the 1880s. Enoch Goodson was a notable Lincolnshire-Leicestershire border horse breeder, specializing in brown shires in the 1860s while near Alford, J. Bassitt of Willoughby and Walter Raunsley of Well Hall in the same period were producing animals like 'Lincolnshire Lad II', a leading example of a heavy shire. Lincolnshire provided a leader of the Shire Society (founded 1884) in William T. Lands of Welbourn, a farmer of 350 acres. His geldings were sold for town work at three to five years. The impact of these Lincolnshire breeders was considerable and in an age when interest in the Shire horse has revived, it is worth noting that almost every good specimen of the 1970s is traceable in the direct male line to one or two famous horses bred in the Fens over 150 years ago.[24]

[23] Chivers, op. cit., p. 68–9. [24] Chivers, op. cit., pp. 215, 657, 209, 76.

Arthur Young considered Lincolnshire pigs to be of little value. They were of a mongrel sort, the result of little care in breeding. Yet, late in the day, Lincolnshire was to make a contribution to pig breeding by the production of curly or woolly back pigs. Owing to the absence of woodlands, except in central and western Kesteven, the county had enjoyed little repute for pig-breeding in the eighteenth century. Few were ever kept on the Fens in this period and though more were reared in the Marsh and on the clays, it was not until the last quarter of the nineteenth century that pigs, with poultry, took their place in the farming economy; the province of farmers' wives and daughters. Young found some good black pigs at Brothercroft, Kirby and Owersby where crossing had improved the lop-eared, long-haired, coarse Lincolnshire varieties. Good white pigs and a herd of Chinese blacks were discovered at Osbournby on the eastern slope of the Heath near Sleaford and an Owersby farmer's individual feeding system attracted his approval. At both Frieston and Kirmond large black and sandy pigs were bred with commercial success.[25] By the 1860s smaller farmers were starting to excel in pig-breeding. The Duckerings of Kirton Lindsey, the Rowlands of Wainfleet and H. Caudwell of Midville had built up county reputations as breeders. It was 1907, however, before the Lincolnshire curly-coated pig with its record of early maturity, rapid growth, good pork and quality bacon was put on show in the county and 1908 before it was accepted at Smithfield as a separate breed. The Lincolnshire pig had made progress since the 1850s when at Lincoln fair dealers caused a scandal by filing their animals' teeth to falsify their ages. For the rural labourer the pig was by the late nineteenth century what the cow had been a century earlier, a guarantee of some small margin of comfort, important enough to be insured in a village club against loss, injury and disease.[26]

Improved livestock alone would not have produced the rise in productivity and profit of the second quarter of the nineteenth century. On the Cliff north of Lincoln, an area of about 110,000 acres and on the chalk Wolds of 260,000 acres, increased yields from thin soils in hitherto unimproved country were to make the reputations of many progressive farmers and their fortunes as costs were reduced in relation to the prices of produce. New arable land was made to support more stock and higher yields of cereals more than

[25] Arthur Young, *Gen. View*, 1813, pp. 427–8.

[26] G. E. Collins, op. cit.; *British Breeds of Livestock*, Board of Agriculture and Fisheries, London, 1913, pp. 113–14; J. A. Scott Watson and M. Elliott Hobbs, *Great Farmers*, London, 1937, p. 207.

compensated farmers for lower grain prices. From an average of 20 to 24 bushels of wheat per acre in the late 1790s for a sowing of up to 4 bushels of seed, yields were up by the 1830s on the Wolds to 28 to 32 bushels per acre. The Lindsey uplands became a permanent supplier of cereals to the nation's markets instead of an occasional contributor when local supplies happened to be abundant. When cereals in turn suffered price falls after the Napoleonic war, a system of farming had been so successfully devised and applied in relatively large farm units on both the Wolds and the Cliff, that occupiers were able to go on reducing costs and raising output.

Given good landlord-tenant relationships and an increasingly respected tenant-right custom for the reward of unexhausted improvements, farmers in Lindsey were prepared to spend £8 or £9 per acre, about 15 to 20 times the unimproved annual value of the land in the late 1790s, to convert the Wolds from pasture to permanent arable. The land was 'pared and burnt' by gangs using breast ploughs to lift the turf so that wireworms and other pests were reduced and to fertilize the land ready for turnips. Then 'marling', the spreading of soil which was a mixture of clay and sand took place. Dressing with chalk at 80 cubic feet per acre to give solidarity and 'sweetness' to the land was undertaken to stop the turnips putting down tap roots or 'fingers and toes', which they were prone to do in light soils. There then followed a dressing of 60 bushels of bones per acre on the first turnip crop in the rotation. Fodder crops then had to be included in the rotation to continue the process of raising the soil's fertility so that two or three cereal crops could be taken every five years. Each time turnips were grown, usually every four or five years, a dressing of bones at 20 bushels per acre and a generous application of crew yard manure were applied. Every 20 to 25 years the land was given a dressing of chalk. The ratio of livestock to acreage steadily increased until by the 1830s there were at least three sheep kept to the acre on land which 50 years before had supported only one. The profits made by Wolds farmers in the second quarter of the nineteenth century are difficult to determine with accuracy owing to the rudimentary, and in some cases, unintelligible character of the farm accounts which have survived. It seems though that they calculated firstly in terms of the primary charges upon tenant-farming: rents and tithes. Secondly, outlays on labour, depreciation of deadstock, parochial and county rates and the expenses of the farm family were allowed. Finally, net profit, over and above the farmer's interest on capital and living expenses, was calculated.

Francis Iles in the 1830s ran his 957 acres of Wold land in this way.[27] One of Lord Yarborough's farms of 1,020 acres, 840 acres of which were permanent arable and 180 of permanent grass, yielded in 1836 £4,730 a year from sales of produce. Of these sales, livestock and associated products accounted for over 40 per cent of the total of the returns. The rearing of sheep and the consequent sale of mutton was the leading item in the livestock sales, wool accounted for only 10 per cent of the annual value of produce sold from the farm in 1836 although in other years it could rise to 30 per cent. Cattle were valuable for making dung on this as on other Wolds farms. The permanent arable would have been cultivated under the five-course rotation usual on the Yarborough estate. Some tenants were able to raise as much as 60 bushels of barley per acre in the 1830s and 1840s. The tenant had capital for this farm of £8,600, just over £8 an acre; £6,000 of this represented the fixed capital of cattle, sheep kept for breeding, horses and implements, £2,600 the farmer's circulating capital for working the farm, of which £1,300 went on rent and tithes. The rest was absorbed by labour costs, fertilizers, repairs, depreciation of live and deadstock, parish and county rates and miscellaneous charges. Expressed as a return on the farmer's capital of £8,600 his profit was 25 per cent. Allowing 5 per cent for a return on his capital which he could have earned by investing in Consols, his return for risk and farming skill was 20 per cent on capital outlay, and when living costs of his family were allowed, 19 per cent.[28]

New methods in Lindsey were not confined to a narrow farming community. The high general standard of farming struck many nineteenth-century observers. Lincolnshire compared well with its rival East Lothian; there only the best land was farmed to near perfection but in Lincolnshire the fine crops of the Heath and the Wolds were clearly the result of man's ingenuity in using the poor soils. On the Cliff, one could travel 40 miles without seeing badly-managed land but for the occasional neglected field.[29] Lincolnshire in the 1840s stood comparison with any other county because so many farmers reached high standards on unpromising soils. Lindsey farmers, in answer to an Anti-Corn Law questionnaire in 1839 stated that 'With respect to the breeding and management of sheep, and the application of bones and tile underdraining, we deny (the Scots') superiority; bones and drain tiles were

[27] L.A.O. Yarb. 5, discussed by J. A. Perkins, *AHR.*, Vol. 24, pt. 11, 1976.
[28] Perkins, op. cit., p. 142.
[29] P. Pusey, *JRA Soc.*, Vol. 3, 1843, 'On the Agricultural Improvements of Lincolnshire', pp. 288, 299.

extensively used in Lincolnshire long before they were used in Scotland.'[30] James Caird, the great nineteenth-century observer, had reservations about the progress made by Lindsey farmers. He was prejudiced in favour of leases and mistrusted some tenant-right customs. He complained that few swedes were grown, yet the land was too light for them. Swedes were hard on the teeth of sheep and lambs folded upon them, and the relatively high cost of Lincolnshire labour meant that raising and slicing them before feeding to stock was expensive. He thought Lincolnshire farms less neat than their Norfolk counterparts, yet again, labour costs were an influence and the appearance of a farm was not always an indication of its profitability. Even he allowed, however, that the speed of Lincolnshire's advance since 1815 put it in the first rank of well-farmed counties and that the generally high standard was remarkable. Giving evidence in 1848, Major F. Brown, familiar with land management and farming between Grantham, Lincoln, Sleaford and Newark, said that Lincolnshire farming 50 years ago was 'in a wretched state; and I do not mean to say that the improvements having progressed gradually; I think we have made a very rapid stride....' John Parkinson, the Lincolnshire and Nottinghamshire land agent, believed that Lincolnshire's wastes had become highly productive in his lifetime.[31] William Hesseltine of Worlaby said that on his family farm the period 1812 to 1826 saw rapid advance not only on his holding but on those of his neighbours as well. Thomas Calvert Beasley, who farmed near Grantham, said in 1838 that only 35 years before then large areas of the Heath were just rabbit warrens.[32] For South Lincolnshire as a whole and upon the Heath and North-west Kesteven '... it can reasonably be contended that "the agricultural revolution" ... occurred in the thirty years after the end of the Napoleonic wars, when the general adoption of the new methods doubled average grain yields'.[33]

In Kesteven the new productivity did not involve much structural change. Higher output did not depend upon the creation of larger farms. Labour saving and mechanization were not yet important influences, but new rotations and fertilizers were, and were applicable on small as well as large farms. The post-Napoleonic war years brought a realization that the limit of marginal land was being

[30] L.A.O. Monson MSS. (Mon.), 25/13/10/2/7; J. A. Perkins, *AHR*, op. cit. p. 134.
[31] BPP, Select Committee on Agricultural Customs, 1847–8 VII, Q. 7226, 7355.
[32] Ibid., Q. 355, 499.
[33] David Grigg, *The Agricultural Revolution in South Lincolnshire*, Cambridge, 1966, p. 191.

reached and that only more intensive use of the soil would enable farmers to live with lower prices for both grain and stock. High grain prices in the areas of South Lincolnshire which were grazing in bias had involved the ploughing up of old pastures. Not until after about 1814 did farmers on the Heath marls, limestone and gravel soils really start to raise productivity by folding sheep and growing turnips. Landlords' expenditure had tended to concentrate on enclosure, drainage and canal building in South Lincolnshire, which increased the cultivated area but did little directly for productivity. By about 1825 only increased output was left as a means to survive in an age of lower prices. Underdraining assisted by loans from national sources, fertilizers, claying and the cultivation of root crops eventually reduced costs per bushel. A Driby farmer who clayed at this time at £2 an acre found that output was raised by 50 per cent; an improvement which lasted from five to ten years. In addition, the fears of the effects of Free Trade made occupiers more cost and productivity conscious than ever before. Low prices appear to have acted as a stimulus to high farming.

Lower prices forced upon estate managers more prudent practices.[34] Pipe draining under the government loans of the 1840s produced real progress. From the ridge and furrow system of the first years of the century, methods had advanced through tile draining to the pipe drains of the 1840s and 1850s. Sheep rot in the damp seasons of the 1820s had encouraged it in some areas. From 1812 on the Jarvis estates at Doddington systematic clay draining had gone on. Sir John Thorold had encouraged it by his tenants in West Kesteven from 1832, while Lord Willoughby in the 1820s and 1830s urged it on his occupiers of low-lying land.[35] Tile draining was expensive in labour as the laying was done by hand. On the Lias clays of West Kesteven and at Spalding, tile factories were opened; on large estates like Lord Willoughby's clay beds were opened up and the tiles made close to the fields where they were to be sunk. Older, cheaper methods died hard. Stones and thorns in a covered ditch or even v-shaped drains cut in the land and then covered by sods were, it was claimed, in the 1830s, still competitive in price against tiles though how effective they were is less certain. One Heckington farmer drained an acre by tiles for £3.2s.6d., with thorns for £1.17s.6d. and by sods for 18s. and 6d. an acre.[36] Real cost reductions and increases in effectiveness came with the introduction

[34] Grigg, op. cit., pp. 127–8; Beastall, op. cit., pp. 114–43.

[35] Grigg, op. cit., p. 137; L.A.O. Jarvis 8; 2 ANC 7 7/17/6, 7/7/55, 7/19/57, 7/27/30.

[36] Grigg, op. cit., p. 143.

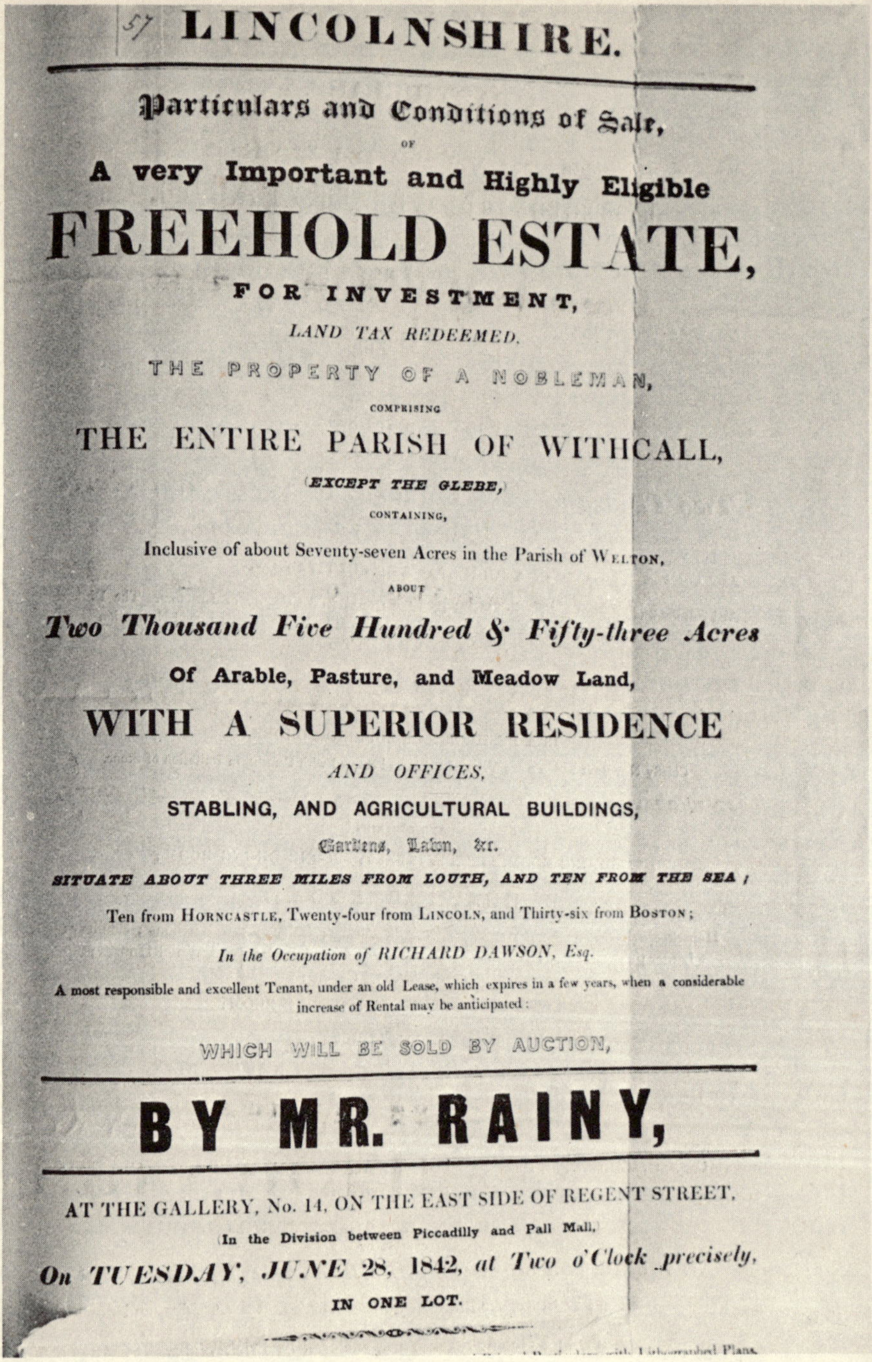

LINCOLNSHIRE.

Particulars and Conditions of Sale,

OF

A very Important and Highly Eligible

FREEHOLD ESTATE,

FOR INVESTMENT,

LAND TAX REDEEMED,

THE PROPERTY OF A NOBLEMAN,

COMPRISING

THE ENTIRE PARISH OF WITHCALL,

(*EXCEPT THE GLEBE,*)

CONTAINING,

Inclusive of about Seventy-seven Acres in the Parish of WELTON,

ABOUT

Two Thousand Five Hundred & Fifty-three Acres

Of Arable, Pasture, and Meadow Land,

WITH A SUPERIOR RESIDENCE

AND OFFICES,

STABLING, AND AGRICULTURAL BUILDINGS,

Gardens, Lawn, &c.

SITUATE ABOUT THREE MILES FROM LOUTH, AND TEN FROM THE SEA;

Ten from HORNCASTLE, Twenty-four from LINCOLN, and Thirty-six from BOSTON;

In the Occupation of RICHARD DAWSON, Esq.

A most responsible and excellent Tenant, under an old Lease, which expires in a few years, when a considerable increase of Rental may be anticipated:

WHICH WILL BE SOLD BY AUCTION,

BY MR. RAINY,

AT THE GALLERY, No. 14, ON THE EAST SIDE OF REGENT STREET,

(In the Division between Piccadilly and Pall Mall,)

On TUESDAY, JUNE 28, 1842, at Two o'Clock precisely,

IN ONE LOT.

Figure 8a. Sale bill for estate at Withcall, 1842. L.A.O.

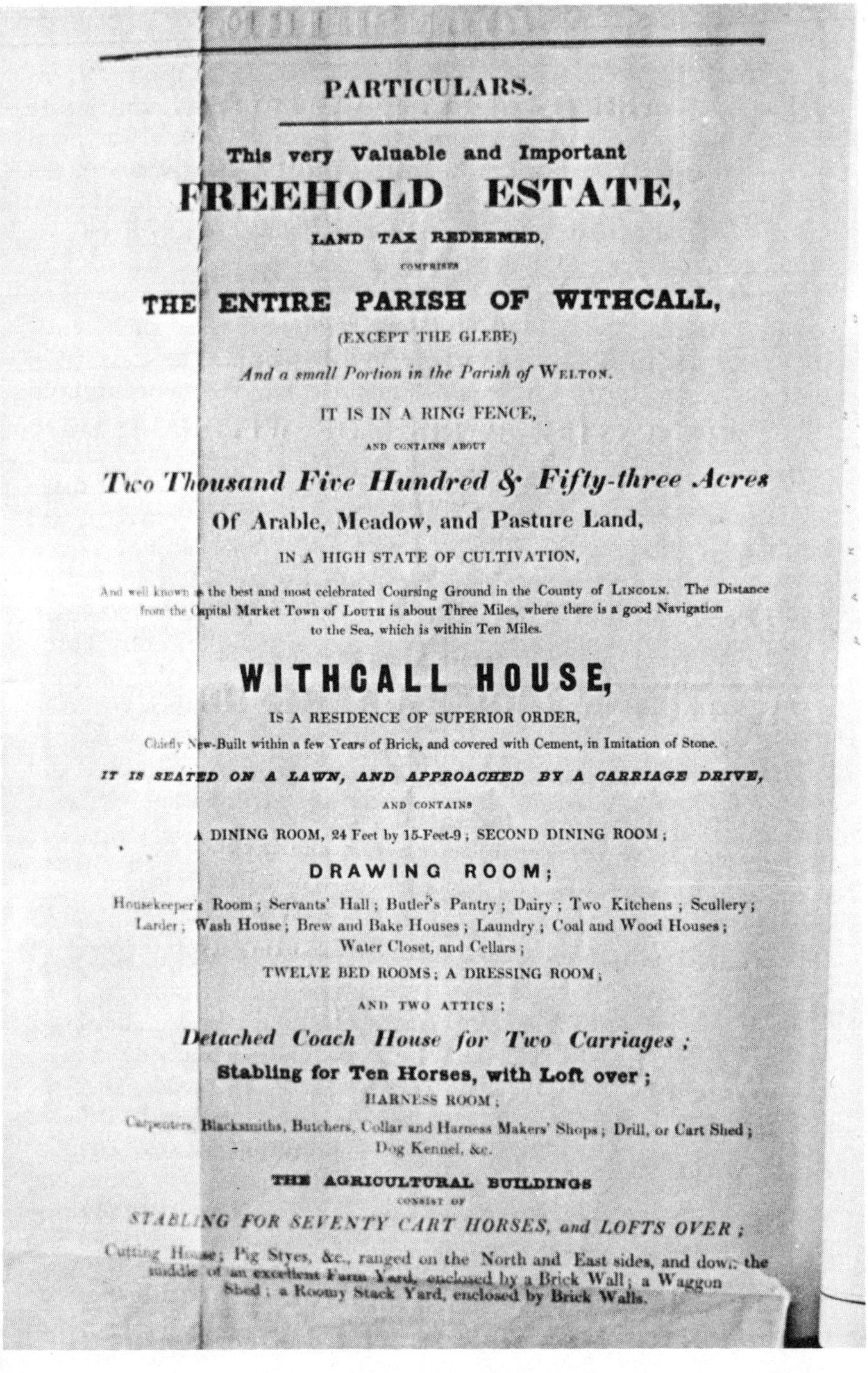

PARTICULARS.

This very Valuable and Important

FREEHOLD ESTATE,

LAND TAX REDEEMED,

COMPRISES

THE ENTIRE PARISH OF WITHCALL,

(EXCEPT THE GLEBE)

And a small Portion in the Parish of WELTON.

IT IS IN A RING FENCE,

AND CONTAINS ABOUT

Two Thousand Five Hundred & Fifty-three Acres

Of Arable, Meadow, and Pasture Land,

IN A HIGH STATE OF CULTIVATION,

And well known as the best and most celebrated Coursing Ground in the County of LINCOLN. The Distance from the Capital Market Town of LOUTH is about Three Miles, where there is a good Navigation to the Sea, which is within Ten Miles.

WITHCALL HOUSE,

IS A RESIDENCE OF SUPERIOR ORDER,

Chiefly New-Built within a few Years of Brick, and covered with Cement, in Imitation of Stone.

IT IS SEATED ON A LAWN, AND APPROACHED BY A CARRIAGE DRIVE,

AND CONTAINS

A DINING ROOM, 24 Feet by 15-Feet-9; SECOND DINING ROOM;

DRAWING ROOM;

Housekeeper's Room; Servants' Hall; Butler's Pantry; Dairy; Two Kitchens; Scullery; Larder; Wash House; Brew and Bake Houses; Laundry; Coal and Wood Houses; Water Closet, and Cellars;

TWELVE BED ROOMS; A DRESSING ROOM;

AND TWO ATTICS;

Detached Coach House for Two Carriages;

Stabling for Ten Horses, with Loft over;

HARNESS ROOM;

Carpenters, Blacksmiths, Butchers, Collar and Harness Makers' Shops; Drill, or Cart Shed; Dog Kennel, &c.

THE AGRICULTURAL BUILDINGS

CONSIST OF

STABLING FOR SEVENTY CART HORSES, and LOFTS OVER;

Cutting House; Pig Styes, &c., ranged on the North and East sides, and down the middle of an excellent Farm Yard, enclosed by a Brick Wall; a Waggon Shed; a Roomy Stack Yard, enclosed by Brick Walls.

Figure 8b. First page of particulars of sale of Withcall estate, 1842. L.A.O.

of Scraggs' pipe-maker. By 1850 most of West Kesteven had been under-drained. (See Figure 5)

Farms on the Wolds had included great acreages of rabbit warrens and sheep walks; when these came under the plough and, more importantly, were used more intensively as arable, their occupiers were able to make fortunes even in a period of relatively low prices for produce. Some farmers built new farmsteads on the Wolds; many of them were prepared, and had the capital to afford, two or three occupations either as owner-occupiers or as tenants. The Yarborough estate with 40,000 acres of north Wold land seems to have set an example by which other landowners fixed their rents. Generally the Yarborough farms were low rented. The steward in 1841 wondered how one of the tenants had the conscience to hold land for 25s. an acre when it would have been cheap at 34s. or 35s. an acre. Rent increases were often held back until tenants' expenditure in enclosure had been remunerated.[37] Large farms or two or three medium-sized ones could be had for reasonable rents. Great Limber, for example, was divided into four farms of about 1,000 acres each. In the 1840s there were probably between 50 and 60 farms on the Lindsey uplands that were over 1,000 acres in extent. The largest consisted of the 2,500 acres of Lord Willoughby's only upland property at Withcall.

The minimum acreage needed for real profit was thought to be 300 acres. Beyond this and up to 1,000 acres, there were few savings in labour, implements and horse power; only after 2,000 acres did real economics of scale obtain. Farms of 400 acres and above were numerous on the Wolds. On the Yarborough estate, leaving aside the small farms of less than 49 acres, some of which were attached to such activities as milling, gardening and innkeeping, the average size of farms was 412 acres. Farms of 300 to 500 acres accounted for 19·8 per cent of the total acreage; those from 500 acres to 800 acres for 34·3 per cent while the largest holdings, 12 in number, of over 800 acres accounted for 29 per cent of the total acreage. Yet large farms were to be found on small estates or on the detached portions of estates whose centres lay at a distance from the Wolds, as in the case of Withcall. A small estate of 1,936 acres on the Wolds had two farms of 1,054 acres and 744 acres.[38] Thomas Moses' farm at Stenigot, held from the Alingtons of Swinthorpe, was about 600 acres in a parish of 1,321 acres in 1840. William Danby in the same parish farmed 650 acres.[39] William Loft of Trusthorpe farmed 500

[37] Perkins, op. cit., p. 133, BPP, 1836, Q. 5951–7.

[38] L.A.O. Hill 36/1.

[39] L.A.O. Hill 36/1, Stenigot Tithe Award B183 and Tithe Map.

9. 'PATRIOT' THE VALUED SHORT-HORNED BULL *bred by George Cotes and owned by James Conington, Thomas Marris and John Richardson. Thomas Weaver was the painter and William Ward, engraver to the Prince of Wales, dedicated this portrait in 1810 to Charles Lord Yarborough, President of the Lindsey Agricultural Society.*

a) Mr Healey's sheep: an example of improvement by crossing. The animal is being hand-fed on pared turnips. The painting is perhaps more accurate in its observation of the farm-worker's dress than of the size of the sheep. The farm servant has his smock rolled up, perhaps to carry a few turnips or for the artist to show that in cold weather it was worn over a thigh-length coat with breeches and leggings, as an all-purpose protective garment. In the heat of harvesting it afforded protection from the sun and maximum ease of movement as then few clothes were worn beneath it. See page 166.

10. THE NEW BREEDS.

b) The prize heifer 'Flower', aged one year and four months, bred by Thomas Moses of Stenigot. She was sold in 1846 for 57 guineas. The farmstead in the background is Thomas Moses', and the high land beyond it is some of the acreage on which he worked so hard, 1829–49, to win the rewards of improved farming from unpromising wold land. See pages 205–211.

11. A COTTAGE *of one storey with bedrooms in the roof space; built of brick c1750, this is an example of improved housing.*

12. HAYMAKING: *tying a load with waggoner's hitch at Pinchbeck in the 1890s. A Lincolnshire waggon is in use. Photograph: F. Parkinson.*

a) Early farmhouse at Kirmond-le-Mire: photograph of 1862. the house, built in 1695, is still standing. It reflects the heritage of Lincolnshire farming at the opening of the period.

13. FARM HOUSES, OLD AND NEW.

b) Manor Farm, Stainton-le-Vale. Built in 1849, it represents the advances in farm buildings during the middle years of the nineteenth century and later.

14. WATERLOO FARM *on Fulbeck Low Fields near Leadenham is an example of a farmhouse with a name reflecting contemporary events. It is one of a number built about the time of Napoleon's defeat in 1815.*

15. NINETEENTH CENTURY FARM BUILDINGS: *This range at Scopwick on the edge of the Heath represents some of the confidence of mid-Victorian 'high farming'. With their window heads, capitals and columns in contrasting brick, they have a style and dignity not found in some later examples.* See pages 214–216.

16. SWALLOW VALE FARM *is a handsome example of estate farm building after enclosure. Swallow was enclosed in 1806 and in the 1820s farm houses in yellow brick were built in the 'new' country at Swallow Vale, Swallow Mount, Swallow Wold and Swallow Grange.* See page 183.

17. TENANT FARMER: *Charles Rowell Fieldsend, his wife, son and two daughters outside their farmhouse at Kirmond-le-Mire in 1862. The Fieldsends had branches at Stainton-le-Vale, Hainton, Sixhills, Gayton-le-Wold and Biscathorpe. Fanny Fieldsend began a diary in her sixteenth year when her parents were farming at Orford; it draws a vivid picture of Wolds' life, 1881–92, in the period after the agricultural revolution when depression once again clouded farming prospects.*

a) Farm workers near Alford c1865 posing with implements representing the farming year against a background of well-built, neatly cut haystacks in a winter landscape. The large wooden fork on the left was used for turning sheaves, the rake comes next followed by a stable scraper for removing horse dung. The saw is a reminder of the repair work needed on a large farm with equipment and fences made of wood, while the hay fork and the scythe represent hay and corn harvests. The smartly dressed figure in the centre seems to stand for general tidiness and efficient supervision of the men judging by his 'bass' broom; his youth suggests he was the farmer's son. Photograph: Starbuck of Alford.

c) The Grainthorpe beadle with a poacher c1860.

b) Scything near Cowbit in the late nineteenth century. The sharpening stone is carried in a belt on the small of the back so as not to interfere with a smooth arm action. Photograph: F. Parkinson.
See pages 185–186.

8. LINCOLNSHIRE COUNTRYMEN.

a) Substantial cottages were built on many estates after the 1840s. These at Saxby All Saints are plain examples in tile and brick with a minimum of decoration on the gables. The iron fencing was in a style adopted on many estates; elegant in appearance, it was cheap to maintain and effective in excluding straying stock. See pages 217–218.

19. ESTATE COTTAGES.

b) This gatehouse cottage on the Earl of Yarborough's property at Brocklesby was probably built to house an estate worker rather than an agricultural labourer such as would be employed by a tenant farmer. The elaborate gable boarding and chimney stack were designed to reflect the grandeur of the Hall itself.

acres of land in the Marsh and 500 acres on the Wolds. The latter he took in 1847 as a tenant-at-will, with only a verbal convenant to revive the holding after its neglect under a 14 years lease.[40]

Lord Monson's estate on the Cliff illustrated in 1842 a tendency towards larger farms in a region where on the whole farm sizes were more modest than on the Wolds. His 5,724 acres had only four farms of over 500 acres each but they accounted for 40 per cent of the land on the estate devoted to farming. As much as 80 per cent of the total acreage, 5,500 acres given to tenants, lay in farms of over 300 acres. Here, as on the Wolds, allowance must be made for farmers who held more than one holding. Frances Iles owned one of 320 acres but he also rented two on the Wolds of 330 acres and 957 acres as well as 60 acres in the Marsh. John Dudding of Saxby owned 500 acres of land yet he rented 1,000 acres as well. Richard Dawson, in many ways the outstanding tenant of the period with his occupation of Withcall parish of 2,500 acres, also held 700 acres outside the parish. William Walker held Skellow Farm at Messingham in 1840 of 183 acres together with 230 acres called Messingham Farm and 147 acres attached to a cottage. As in the Church, plŭralism incurred the displeasure of some observers. A landowner complained that there were 'hundreds' of Lincolnshire farmers who held two or more farms each and he wondered what acreage would satisfy a farmer if five or six hundred would not.[41] The fairly low rents of Wolds and Cliff farms must have encouraged farmers with capital and skill to invest in farm valuations rather than in landowning. Landowners, once a tenant right custom had become established, feared the unlet farm being taken 'in hand' so they and their agents were at pains to accommodate sitting tenants whose tenancies-at-will, resting sometimes on verbal agreements only, looked flimsy security but whose positions were in fact strong, given the shortage of tenants after 1815.

Rents tended to be low on the estates of large landowners and this helped farmers at a time when cost cutting was essential to profitability. The rents charged by smaller landowners were relatively low as a consequence of the standard set by the titled proprietors who by reducing the costs of their households and by borrowing on the security of their land would keep indebtedness at bay without unpopular recourse to rent increases. As prices fell after 1815 the real value of their rents increased. By the late 1840s some owners were raising their rents but even so their tenants—

[40] BPP, 1848, VII, Select Committee on Agricultural Customs, Q. 7771, 7698.

[41] Perkins, op. cit., p. 137; *LRSM*, 19 March 1830, 24 December 1830, 12 April 1839, 20 March 1840.

especially those with more than 300 acres—still enjoyed a generous profit margin. Landlords liked to be lenient to their tenants, to enjoy a reputation for fairness and to be free from disputes over rent, arrears and terms of tenancy so that they could follow a style of life in which fox-hunting, shooting, fishing and political activity were undisturbed by the demands either of direct farming or rigorous estate management. Perhaps the growth of a manufacturing interest and a public press, critical of the traditional assumptions of country life caused landowners and tenants to draw together. Tenants who could take risks, experiment with new rotations and improve the soil by boning and liming were not easily found and once they were, a low rent was thought advisable to encourage their enterprise.

Although on the Yarborough estate by 1833 the gross return from tenanted land was £44,829 a year or 17s. on average per acre, the Wold land, now in a much improved state was let out for only 10s. to 12s. an acre. A valuer in that year placed £72,237 per annum on the agricultural land and rents were raised including the Wold land to 20s. or 21s. an acre or even 27s. Even so, this was a modest rent, yet to the landlord by the mid-1830s the gross income had risen three-fold in a period of 40 years, the last 15 of which had seen a rise in the real value of such a return.[42] Landlords may have been slow to assess the real value of their land, much of which on the Wolds they had long regarded as poor, unremunerative acreages for which tenants needed great encouragement if they were to occupy it to any advantage. A concern with prompt payment of rent rather than its increase motivated the sixth Earl of Scarbrough, for example, in the 1820s when, owing to family debts, he was in need of a substantial income. His agent for the Cliff farms was pressed to keep down the arrears, to seek tenants with capital and skill and to ward off requests for rent reductions or returns rather than to increase rents. Not until 1845 were the farms revalued and eventually rerented at a higher level. As farms in Lincolnshire were not let by auction, tenants were expected to continue in their occupations and to make a reasonable profit. Farming in the second quarter of the century on Wold land undoubtedly demanded both capital and skill. For many small farmers the skill was there but the capital was not, for they had been unable to accumulate it from the base of an occupation of less than 300 acres in the difficult conditions after 1813. Emigration to the colonies and the U.S.A. was an attraction for some of them. A study of their numbers, origins and destinations is needed but it appears that their departure to avoid becoming part of the mass of landless labourers left the more substantial

[42] Perkins, op. cit., p. 141.

tenants who were already risking their capital and skill on the farming of their soils in a more advantageous position than ever. Their landlords now had fewer applicants to choose from and contemplated with growing distaste the prospect of having to pay large tenant-right claims to outgoers only to take the occupation in hand.

'On the uplands of Lindsey, at least, it would appear that farming placed a sizeable surplus of capital in the hands of the tenant farmers.'[43] What did they do with it? More research is needed to establish who were the most successful farmers and what provision they made for their families by way of settlements and investments. Some invested capital in better livestock, built up prize herds and helped to give Lincolnshire its late nineteenth-century pre-eminence as a world producer of fine sheep. One tenant, Samuel Slater, in 1838 purchased all the 1,795 acres of North Carlton from Lord Monson's Cliff estate having enjoyed it for only £1 an acre in rent. The circumstances seem though to have been exceptional. Lord Monson's decision to sell was unusual in that he was making good losses incurred by his predecessor who had bought three 'rotten' boroughs in Kent just before the 1832 Reform Act. Not many estates came on to the Lindsey land market and these were usually bought by established landowners or 'incomers' who wanted an investment. Samuel Slater had, however, the means to raise the necessary £80,000 in the sale of his prize flock of New Leicester sheep.

Few Lindsey farmers appear to have been attracted to landowning. Some lived in style, however, particularly on the Yarborough estates, where their farm houses, surrounded by lawns and woods, were like the homes of substantial gentry. Hunting and shooting in the company of their landlords and his friends cannot have been cheap yet their houses were provided by their landlords at low rents and upkeep and running costs were set against farming costs. Feed for their hunters was obtainable from their own farms at wholesale prices. The breeding of hunters could go hand in hand with the profitable breeding of horses for teamwork on light soils and the nearness of famous horse markets and Horncastle fair meant that rarely was it difficult to sell unwanted horses for a good profit. Their style of life then does not seem to have absorbed all of their surplus capital neither does investment in local business enterprise. Two farmers were involved in the setting up of a Lincoln oil and cake mill in 1840 and three directors of the Grimsby linseed cake manufacturers were Wolds farmers. They were, however,

[43] Perkins, op. cit., p. 138.

exceptions who went into these enterprises to make sure of reasonably priced cake for stock rather than to seek an investment. Richard Dawson of Withcall was considered to have left a fortune at his death. George Nelson who had farmed 865 acres under the Earl of Yarborough in the early 1840s retired to Hull giving out that he had made £80,000 as a tenant. Jonathan Dent, a Quaker farmer of Winterton on the Cliff and something of a miser, made by his death in 1834 a fortune of £500,000.

It seems that government securities, mortgages and relatively secure assets absorbed the capital made by the farmers whose success in the unpromising second quarter of the nineteenth century was so bound up with the agricultural revolution. Perhaps too they kept their capital for setting up their sons in large holdings and saw in that aspiration a socially acceptable alternative to landowning. Some may have believed that cash, when out at interest, was a better security than land affording a mobility and a resource which landowning could not match when farming sank into depression. Farmers tended to be loyal to a way of life rather than to a particular farm and ample liquid assets which had not been sunk in buying land gave the means of keeping up that way of life by facilitating a move to another holding if the need arose. Perhaps there were all too few opportunities for farmers to buy land, before the great sales of 1918–20. By then many tenants probably had insufficient capital to buy land other than the acres they occupied; sometimes not even then after the years of cheap cereal imports which followed 1875. On the whole, preference shares and government securities were more attractive securities than land; returns were better, risks were lower and in emergencies they were more realizable assets.

10

Harvest tools, Engineering, Agricultural Service Industries and Railways

In a revolution in the harvesting of cereal crops between the early 1790s and the late 1860s, the scythe replaced the sickle or reap-hook as the standard corn-harvesting tool. Scythes had been used on the Wolds in the eighteenth century to mow hay for the sheep and its introduction to the harvesting of cereals was relatively quick and easy. In the Fens, however, the sickle continued to be used much longer. The heavy if uneven hay crops were suited to the sickle and Fenlanders, skilled in handling it, continued to use it when corn became more important in their economy than hay. Reaping reeds for thatching was also an age-old tradition which meant a reluctance to adopt the scythe for mowing. The scythe was not easy to use effectively; that is, to achieve the perfect interaction of the mower and the scythe and to keep the blade in good condition. On the clays of the county too where cereals were a traditional crop the art of reaping lingered on and the sickle gave way only slowly to the scythe.

Where, as in Scotland and the border counties, wheat was put through threshing machines of Scottish design it was essential for efficient threshing to have it gathered into neat, tidy sheaves. Farther south, in the East Riding and Lincolnshire, machines of a more advanced design were used which prevented the escape from threshing of any ear of corn so it did not matter how the wheat was fed in. As mown wheat tended not to fall as neatly for sheaf making as reaped wheat, the newer machines were a distinct advantage. Thus in districts where newer threshing machines were in general use mowing by scythe was acceptable whereas in more northern regions reaped wheat threshed better. Use of the new machines and scythes tended to spread together. There were social implications in changing from sickles to scythes. Ownership of the more expensive scythe passed from the labourer to the farmer. A change took place too in the roles of men and women in the harvesting process. Both had used the sickle. In some districts reaping was thought to be a woman's job and children followed her to bind the sheaves. One man could supervise the work of six or seven female reapers. Use of the scythe was seen as a male occupation and it was for the women to follow and to bind the sheaves. Older workers found the scythe difficult to master and as it meant a fall in productivity and earnings they resented its introduction. Younger labourers, encouraged by farmers who wanted to accelerate the harvesting, took to it more readily and enjoyed higher earnings thanks to their newly developed skill.[1]

More effective use of the land made new calls upon the makers of agricultural tools and implements and upon a range of professional and trading services. The development of Lincolnshire's agricultural machinery industry accompanied the rapid and widespread changes of the second quarter of the nineteenth century. By the 1830s the number of towns and large villages with agricultural machinery makers was impressive as indeed was the variety of other agricultural services represented in them. The producers and distributors of bone and rape dust, lime and quano importers and retailers were recorded in the Lincolnshire trade directories by the 1820s. Some merchants like William Mackrill and Sons of Barton-on-Humber combined business as a coal merchant with the selling of linseed cake for animal stock and the supply of bone and rape dust to farmers. Barton had in addition, two corn merchants, five coal merchants and two more merchants in bone dust and lime. Brigg near by had six coal and corn merchants, and by 1825, two more and a civil engineer for the Commissioners of the Ancholme Drainage. By the late 1820s most towns had fire insurance agents like George Bedford agent to the Norwich Union Fire Office at Donington. Burton upon Stather had seven corn millers and merchants and Caistor, by the 1835 list was completed, had James Green Dixon in business in the Market Place in seeds, coal and oilcake. Burton upon Stather, Caistor and Epworth each had its machine makers. Kirton in Lindsey in 1828–9 had a good list of gentry, clergy, professional people, innkeepers, shopkeepers, carriers and a lime burner but only one machine maker but by 1857 there were two agricultural implement makers in this relatively small community.

Gainsborough had long been an important centre for trade in

[1] Perkins, 'Harvest Technology and Labour Supply in Lincolnshire and the East Riding of Yorkshire 1750–1850', *Tools and Tillage*, III, 1, 1976.

agricultural goods and services but by the end of the 1850s its list of traders reflected the growing demands of a developing hinterland for this ancient river port. By 1835 there were four auctioneers, ten fire insurance offices, two bone merchants, nine millers, four seed crushers and oil merchants and by 1859, three iron and brass founders and four guano merchants. Gainsborough had a bye-law against the use of oilcake for fuel as early as 1667 but in the early years of the eighteenth century, George Langton was buying oilcake, and farmers at Riseholme near Lincoln and Temple Bruer on Lincoln Heath were to buy it in large quantities from Gainsborough for feeding. Court Leet records show a rapeseed crushing mill in the town in 1657 but it was the great demand of the nineteenth century that caused the setting up of mills at Skirbeck, Boston and Brigg. James Deultry leased a mill for linseed crushing between 1709 and 1744 in Gainsborough and Luke Martin had one there from 1744–54. Charles Moorhouse had a mill which was destroyed by fire in 1787 so Gainsborough's lead in this important trade was a long one. By the second quarter of the nineteenth century mills were opened in many more places. William Etherington and Co. appeared at Owston Ferry in 1826 while at Sleaford William Sabine was by then in business. At Spalding, Henry Hawkes junior had a hydraulic press mill at work by 1838 and from 1832 Coates, Somerby and Company were bone and seed crushing in Grimsby. Louth was to have an important firm in this business of Nell, Nell and Graves from 1861. Although some of the cole or rapeseed was still coming from the diminishing but fine crops of the East Fen, most was being imported so that the crushing industry became located in or near the sea and river ports, by 1830.[2]

Horncastle combined a coal dealer with a bone dealer in 1828. Here the Farbon family were corn millers as well as corn dealers. Armstrong and Company of Far Street were by 1835 seed, bone and linseed cake dealers. There was in ironfounder in the town in 1828 but by 1857 there were two agricultural implement makers. Louth had four auctioneers, ten corn millers, seven corn merchants, seven coal merchants and five lime burners, and Horncastle listed a similar range of services. Some of the corn merchants were also bone crushers. In 1835 there were four agricultural machine makers in Louth. Spalding had the services of oilcake merchants, bone and corn merchants, lime burners and, befitting its nearness to great drainage activity, like Brigg, a civil engineer and land surveyor, Thomas Pear. Boston had seventeen corn merchants in 1828 and by

[2] Harold W. Brace, *History of Seed Crushing in Great Britain*, London, 1960, pp. 20–9, 101–9, 151–5.

the 1830s there were land surveyors, engineers, and sail makers. There were four auctioneers in Spalding in 1828, one of whom, George Naylor, combined his work with that of town crier. Pigot and Company gave agricultural implement makers a separate entry for the first time in their list for Lincoln in 1835 between 'Academies and Public Schools' and 'Architects' thus according them a prominence and esteem which was, perhaps, not merely alphabetical.

Lincoln in 1828 had two bone crushers, Coupland and Seely in the High Street and William Rudyard in Newland where he was also a coal and a corn merchant. He used the Albion Steam mill. There were sixteen coal merchants in the city and thirteen corn merchants with four limeburners and four linseed cake merchants, Hooker Hill and Company of Brayford, John Keyworth and Son, High Street, Norton and Whitton, Waterside and William Wrigglesworth, High Street and St. Benedict. Grantham showed its position as a local business centre with eight auctioneers in 1828 but its lead as an engineering town for agricultural needs was evident. There were two iron and brass founders, Thomas Barton in the Market Place and Seaman and Hornsby in Spittlegate. Machine makers were James Coultas of Union Street and Seaman and Hornsby. By 1857 there were five iron and brass founders and seven agricultural implement makers yet Grantham's position in a region of great estates was indicated at the same time by the five listed game dealers against Lincoln's three. In 1828 Grimsby was already showing something of its future role in the county's economy with its eleven coal dealers (wholesale and retail) its five oilcake dealers and its two Vice Counsuls, John Peter Brandstrom in Lower Burgess Street for Russia and Blanchard Thorpe of Loft Street for Sweden and Norway.

That farmers by the 1850s were seeing the need to hire farm machinery is indicated by the 33 machine owners advertising hirings in the 1855 Kelly's Directory for Lincolnshire, a publication which contained advertisements from London merchants such as William Inglis Carne who offered all kinds of artificial manures including Peruvian Guano and Nitrate of Soda. John Goucher of Worksop advertised threshing machines to farmers in the 1857 Slater's Directory for Lincolnshire. He took care to incorporate a testimonial from Clayton, Shuttleworth and Company of Lincoln in the advertisement. Richard and Chandler advertised a toothed roller chaff cutter from their Salford works. In the 1850s agricultural machinery makers were listed in towns and villages which in the 1820s and 1830s had none. Alford had W. Thompson and J. Graves specializing in ploughs at Aby while another of the Graves family had a similar concern at Bolingbroke near Spilsby. W. Hunter advertised at Binbrook and W. Kirton at Holbeach. Market Deeping, Market Rasen, Stamford and Ulceby had implement makers at work by then. Another indication of the spreading influence of the machine makers and repairers were the numbers of firms or farmers listed as agents for parent concerns in the larger towns while the greater Lincolnshire firms like Clayton, Shuttleworth and Company of Stamp End Iron Works in Lincoln had London Offices. At Long Sutton where there were no agricultural machinery makers listed before 1840, there were by then, William Warner of Jordan's Gate and George Carter Bennett who were agents for Ransomes the implement makers. The Royal Agricultural Society's exhibition of implements in 1854 at Lincoln gave an opportunity for Lincolnshire manufacturers to exhibit their achievements and to use success there in subsequent advertising. Charles Revill claimed in 1855 that his improved parallel-motioned winnowing machines beat all others shown at Lincoln and sold for eight to ten guineas each. They could dress 20 to 23 quarters of wheat an hour. Improved blowers, hand and steam chaff cutters, combined cake and bean mills and all kinds of weighing machines were on offer. He was a 'Manufacturer of all other kinds of Machinery, too numerous to mention.'[3]

Anthony Hammond reported on the implements to be seen at Lincoln in 1854 where machinery worth £28,878 was on show from 130 exhibitors submitting 1,897 articles. In 1852 at Lewes there had been 1,722 articles from 103 exhibitors, worth £19,121. He observed 'So much has this desire (for agricultural implements) increased, that a new class of manufacturers has sprung up—a class second to none in intelligence, perseverence, and skill—whose inventive powers are severely taxed to keep pace with the requirements of their customers.'[4] Garrett, Hornsby and Smith neared perfection in an exhibition where the need for cheap, light drills was clear. Reapers were improving in that they were designed to keep the horses out of the standing corn but some still required too much horsepower or defied accurate steering. Garretts were showing a McCormick's reaper. Hoes and scarifiers were satisfactory but the cultivators needed too much horsepower and two good turnip singling machines drew a comment that was perhaps applicable to a number of machines in this time of confidence. '... Such implements are not made for bad farmers, and are not wanted by small ones'. A great novelty was Cotgreave's plough which claimed to

[3] Kelly's, *Post Office Directory of Lincolnshire*, p. 22.
[4] *JRA Soc.*, Vol. 12, 1852, p. 363.

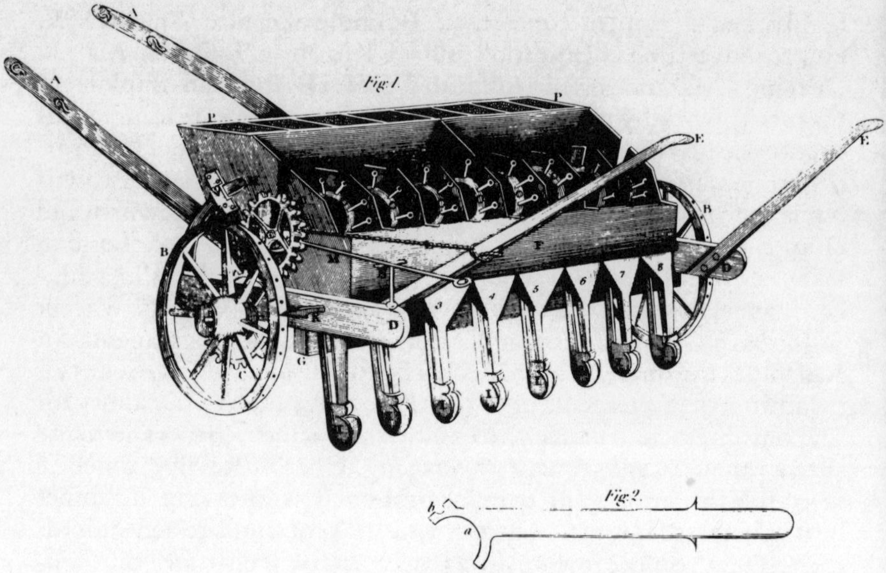

a) Seed drill from William Amos' second edition of *The theory and practice of drill husbandry*, Boston 1802. Amos was steward to John Cartwright of Brothertoft.

Hornsby's Patent Seed Drill, with Steerage.

b) Hornsby's seed drill with steerage 1851, from *JRAS* vol. 12.

Figure 9. Seed drills

MAQUINA DE LAVRAR DE PATENTE, COM O APPARATO D'CULTIVAÇÃO A VAPOR DOS SÑRS. ROBEY E COMPANHIA.

Figure 10. Robey's steam ploughing set as advertised in an export catalogue. There was a demonstration of steam ploughing by the Tetney and Louth Agricultural Society in August 1857 which featured in the *Illustrated London News*.

perform the three operations of ploughing, lifting and subsoiling at once leaving the land as though it had been forked over. It was recommended for claying in the Fens because it could reach the clay which sinks beneath the reach of a plough. Some general purpose ploughs were of wood but for heavy land iron ones were to carry the day. In the early eighteenth century, John Mortimer, in *The Whole Art of Husbandry* had thought the ploughs used in Lincolnshire well-suited to the marsh and fenlands which were free from stones. The coulter was the sharp-edged Dutch wheel which revolved and cut through grass and roots, whilst a very sharp broad share cut the furrow.[5] In the 1730s the Rotherham plough devised by Joseph Foljambe in Yorkshire was being used widely in Lincolnshire. With signs of a Dutch influence, it was light and effective.

The application of steam to the work of the farm has attracted much attention though more needs to be known about steam power in cutting operations and in heating foodstuffs for stock. The most spectacular uses were for threshing machines and traction engines. Lincolnshire was to throw up many firms in threshing machine making from the 1840s onwards in towns all over the county. The first two built were William Howden's marine and portable engines

[5] Michael Partridge, *Farm Tools*, London, 1973, p. 39.

of 1826 and 1839 respectively. Links with steam pumping and the engineering traditions of land drainage gave Lincolnshire a start in the development of the manufacture of steam engines for agricultural use. Richard Hornsby started business in Grantham in 1815. From iron and brass founding, the firm moved on to making paper in 1838 and by 1849 making agricultural implements. William Howden of the Phoenix Works, Boston, had been the apprentice at Blackfriars of the great drainage engineer John Rennie. He started business at Grand Sluice in Boston. By 1826 the firm was in iron and brass founding, specializing in marine engines for use on the Witham. In 1827 for example, they gave a trial run up the river to a 24 feet boat powered by a 2½ horsepower engine. In 1841 Howden exhibited an unusual portable engine at the Lincolnshire show at Wrangle.

William Marshall, who had been the agent at St. Petersburg for William Fairburn and Sons millwrights and steam engineers of Manchester, in 1842 bought up William Garland's business of ironmongers and implement manufacturers in Grantham. Marshall and Sons at the Britannia Works then produced land and garden rollers and ships' winches and became a pioneer in Lincolnshire's engineering industry with its strong links with the sea and agriculture. Ruston and Hornsby were established as Proctor and Burton, millwrights and engineers, and in 1863 B. D. Taplin, a medical practitioner, became a partner in the Patent Crank Works in Lincoln. The Boston and Skirbeck ironworks, however, had more conventional origins. William Wedd Tuxford, a craftsman in wood and metal, tried to ree or dry wheat in 1830 after a number of wet seasons. His family were flour dealers and bakers in Boston. He built an eight-sail windmill near Skirbeck Church in 1826, making his own castings at the foot of the mill. In 1842 he applied steam power to his drying machine. C. L. Hett of the Ancholme Foundry, Brigg, built up an important hydraulic business and used his knowledge of steam draining in the building of engines for agricultural work.[6] Lincoln led the county in the late 1840s with six firms engaged in the making of steam engines. Boston, Gainsborough and Grantham followed with four each but there were 30 in Lincolnshire as a whole and small towns like Brigg, Horncastle and Market Rasen had one or two firms each, as did Kirton Lindsey, Welby, Stamford and Spalding.

At the Lincoln meeting of the Royal Agricultural Society in 1854 portable and fixed steam engines were much in evidence. The

[6] Ronald H. Clark, *Steam-Engine Builders of Lincolnshire*, Norwich, 1960, pp. 60–1, 59–60, 10.

Figure 11a. Hornsby's Manchester No. 3 mower of 1869: a combined mower and reaper, it was a prize winner at the Royal Agricultural Show held in Manchester. The horses in this advertisement were intended to give an impression of speed, efficiency and low costs.

Figure 11b. The Hornsby self-raking reaper. Made in Grantham, it was advertised as new and light and was in use in the 1870s. It appeared in a colour-printed catalogue sold by A. Thompson of Keelby and printed in Nottingham by R. Allen and Sons Ltd, 'colour printers', one of the earliest examples of this process.

famous Lincolnshire firms were exhibiting manure distributors, drain tile machines and corn dressers as well as engines whose particulars were keenly compared.[7]

Portable engines

	Horse power	*Price per horse power*	*Minutes to steam*	*Coal per horsepower per hour*
Hornsby & Company	8	£31.17.6d.	40	41 lb. 55
Clayton & Shuttleworth	6	£36.13.4d.	39	51 lb. 19
Tuxford	4	£47.10.0d.	33	61 lb. 42

Fixed engines

Ransome and Sims	8	£24.7.6d.		6 lb. 15
Clayton & Shuttleworth	6	£29.3.4d.		8 lb. 94
Tuxford	6	£29.3.4d.		9 lb. 13

Steam engines, it was believed by their makers, smartened the intelligent agricultural labourer by assisting the industrious while keeping the lazy man to his work. Regularity and punctuality were enforced by it.[8] Thus the virtues of the railway age were being introduced to the villages by the application of steam.

Through its export of threshing machines Lincolnshire was to lay claim to an international reputation for modern farming. From 1845 to 1914 threshing machines were exported in great numbers. Hornsby's first export, No. 51 went to Vienna in 1852. No. 979, a 9 horsepower engine, was sold to the Emperor of Austria in January 1858 and later that year, a second 9 horsepower model went to Count Karyoli near Budapest. The firm appointed local agents in the Austro-Hungarian empire and in 1883, 64 engines were sent to Hungary alone. A Clayton and Shuttleworth portable engine worked for 48 years until 1900 in Hungary. Built for Josef White of Torok-Becsere, it now rests in the Agricultural Museum, Vajdahunyad Castle, Budapest with its firebox nameplate reading 'No. 310 1852 Manufactured by Clayton and Shuttleworth Engineers and Ironfounders Stamp End Works, Lincoln.' In 1850 the firm sold 140 portable engines, 491 in 1855 and from 1856 to 1882, 19,000 models. From 1849 to 1882 their sales of threshing sets reached 17,000. Farmers with over 300 acres probably made the best use of these heavy sets but in Kesteven and the fenlands, the neighbourliness of the small farmers meant that sharing of equipment gave many access to machinery for little outlay.[9]

By the 1850s more effective drills were on the market. Hornsbys

[7] *JRA Soc.*, Vol. 12, 1852, p. 363. [8] Ibid., p. 374.

[9] J. R. Marshall, *Lincolnshire Life*, January 1968, p. 56; Grigg, op. cit., p. 150.

Figure 12. A combined threshing and dressing machine by Clayton and Shuttleworth of Lincoln in 1851. The firm was a leader with this, since for 7d. a quarter it threshed and winnowed wheat.

with their substantial construction were thought to have the edge over Garretts for drilling turnips on the flat and on the furrow.[10] Thomas Chambers, the son of a tenant farmer, won a prize for a manure distributor at the Lincoln meeting of the Agricultural Society. Light and uncomplicated, it could spread crushed bones as finely as three bushels to the acre. The importance of machines for top-dressing was by then widely acknowledged, especially on the light and chalk lands, so that on the Lincolnshire Wolds and in Norfolk there was a constant search by more progressive farmers for machines to spread manure evenly and thinly from three to five bushels per acre. Drain tile machines were also in demand. Firms like Burgess and Key, Scragg, Whitehead and Armitage produced machines from £17 to £20 to make pipes of 2¾ inches external

[10] *JRA Soc.*, Vol. 13, 1853, p. 376.

diameter. Corn dressing machines to finish corn for market using steam power were a speciality of Clayton and Shuttleworth's while grinding mills to prepare meal for feeding to stock were urged upon farmers by the Lincolnshire manufacturers. Thomas Bartholomew of Langton invented a corn dressing machine which Joseph Dixon of Lincoln manufactured. Charles Revill of Lincoln invented and produced a similar machine to dress corn to a high standard for market.[11]

The mere application of steam to the old threshing boxes would by the 1850s no longer do. The farmer was demanding that his corn should be finished, sacked and weighed for market in a continuous process.[12] Clayton and Shuttleworth produced these improvements which applied steam to the processes of straw shaking, riddling and winnowing. Their 8 horsepower fixed threshing machine sold for £150 while Garrett and Co. with a similar machine of 7 horsepower asked £164.7s.0d.[13] The interest in applying steam to a number of farm processes was intense. Chaff cutting, linseed and oat cutting, cake crushing and turnip cutting were to be done by steam power while Crosskill's bone mill of 10½ horsepower costing £45 reduced unboiled bones to a near powder ready for spreading evenly. Some steam engines like William Tuxford's 'Progress' for which Sir Henry Thorold paid £420 in 1872 were used to haul coal, thresh corn, power a single-engine roundabout ploughing tackle, cut chaff and give steam at night to pig food. Some farmers used them for pumping water from artesian wells. Steam finally replaced man and horse power on the Andrew Meikle threshers which dated from 1786 and were in use in many parts of the county by the 1820s. By the 1850s powerful, portable engines with iron boilers were coming into use. Steel replaced iron in the boilers in the 1870s with a consequent reduction in the number of explosions, even so, a cracked boiler plate caused an explosion at Benniworth in 1876, killing one man and injuring two.[14]

The application of steam to ploughing was less successful though spectacular. Lord Willoughby had a demonstration at Edenham and exhibited a set in 1851. In 1857 there was a steam ploughing demonstration at Brackenborough near Louth where Charles Burrell and Sons showed the possibilities of the process. A bad feature was the compacting of loose soil on the wheels of the heavy steam engine so after a few years cable ploughing came into vogue. Its great draw-

[11] Op. cit., lxxx III, Appendix.
[12] Michael Partridge, *Farm Tools*, London, 1973, pp. 178–9.
[13] Michael Partridge, op. cit., p. 37.
[14] Harold Bonnett, *Farming with Steam*, Newton Abbot, 1974, pp. 8, 32.

back was the danger of cable-snapping when heavy ground was being ploughed. Spectators were not always quick enough in throwing themselves to the ground when the over-strained cable began to 'sing'. In 1857 the two cylinder Burrell engine ploughed 23 acres at 73 minutes to the acre at a cost of 32s. a day in coal and labour.[15] There were fewer than ten steam ploughing sets in the county in 1867 but this was more than in any other at the time.[16]

The spreading of manure on Wold farms and the harvesting of heavy root and cereal crops could not be done without adequate farm carts. The large spindle-sided waggon dominated the Lindsey and Kesteven farming scene. In Holland where farms were smaller the 'Lincolnshire waggon' was not so prominent. It was widely used in the nineteenth century in Rutland, Leicestershire, Nottinghamshire, Derbyshire and in Holderness. Its shape changed little though a wider waggon with a lower centre of gravity would have been useful in the steep fields of the Lincolnshire Wolds. A Horncastle farmer complained that two waggons capsized 12 times in a day's harvesting. Despite these drawbacks the waggons remained high and narrow with a deep spindle-sided body and a tall highly-decorated frontboard. The wheels were narrow-tyred and were linked by wooden axles on all the vehicles built in the nineteenth century. The delicate iron and scroll work on the side supports helped to make the Lincolnshire the most elegant of all English waggons. The name and the address of the owner, the date of building, the name of the builder and the date of the last painting were all to be found against a background of prussian blue on waggons in use in central or east Lincolnshire or brick-red on vehicles in the western parishes. From a length of 13 feet and a width of 5 feet about 1800 the waggons were increased to 24 feet in length and 8 feet in width by the mid-century. Harvest frames were fitted which combined the functions of sideboards and ladders. The large, capacious and heavy bodies rested upon a rather weak under-carriage which owed much to the old road vehicles of European origin used in England since the sixteenth century.

The need for a small cart for manure spreading which could be expanded into a larger waggon for harvesting was met by the Hermaphrodite or 'morphrodite', 'morphey' or 'morph' in eastern England. One of the earliest examples to survive in Lincolnshire comes from Leadenham. Built in 1829 for General Reeve of the

[15] Colin Tyler and John Haining, *Ploughing by Steam*, Watford, 1970, p. 216.

[16] G. E. Russell, 'Steam Cultivation in England', *Engineering*, 30 July 1943; David Grigg, *The Agricultural Revolution in South Lincolnshire*, Cambridge, 1966, pp. 150–1. L.A.O. 2 ANC 7/19/45.

Grenadier Guards, who fought in the Peninsula War and at Waterloo, the waggon was a spindle-sided box-waggon in prussian blue. The two-wheeled Scotch cart was popular in Lincolnshire in the early part of the nineteenth century, having entered the county from the south. Arthur Young notes its importation to Essex from Scotland by sea.[17] The morphey functioned as a two-wheeled Scotch cart or Tumbril for ten months of the year; during harvest it became a four-wheeled waggon by the addition of a forecarriage. The vehicles were light and could be turned in a small space. They could hold as great a load of hay or corn as a Lincolnshire waggon. They were used in East Anglia, Lincolnshire, Nottinghamshire, parts of Derbyshire, the Vale of Belvoir and Holderness.[18]

Progress in farming had a major impact upon business in the towns. Judged by some of its buildings, Louth in the mid-nineteenth century must have been the Manchester of eastern Lincolnshire except that corn, not cotton, was king. Employment in the towns must have been affected by the building and the business activity generated by the prosperity of the surrounding farm land. Louth, with its Parish Church, its Mansion House and its warehouses at the head of the Louth Navigation canal, had architectural evidence of its importance long before the age of high farming but the 1850s saw the building of some formidable tributes to its renewed vigour as a regional centre. William Scorer the occupier of Home farm, Burwell was one of the farmers to subscribe to the building of the Corn Exchange.[19] Three storeys high and in an Italianate style, the Exchange, built in 1853 by Pearson Bellamy was a monument to high farming. His Town Hall of 1854 with its massive balcony, Ionic columns, decorated ceilings and opulent galleries was another sign of confidence in the town's future. The Tudor-Gothic railway station of 1854 completed a demonstration of faith in the future of corn, steam and civic pride. In 1866 Louth saw the building of another reminder of its success when the Market Hall with its giant iron girders was completed. (Frontispiece)

Other regional centres had similar developments. Horncastle had already some imposing canal architecture in its warehouses of 1802 but in 1865 it added an Italianate courthouse. Bellamy and Hardy built a town hall in Grimsby in 1863 while Grantham's Corn Exchange of 1852 had the grandeur appropriate to the regional capital of an arable region. The Town Hall, 1867–9, with its mixture

[17] Arthur Young, *Gen. View*, Essex, 1813, Vol. L, p. 161.

[18] J. Geraint Jenkins, *The English Farm Wagon, Origins and Structure*, Newton Abbot, 1972, pp. 39, 114, 115, 119.

[19] L.A.O. Scorer Farm, 1/3.

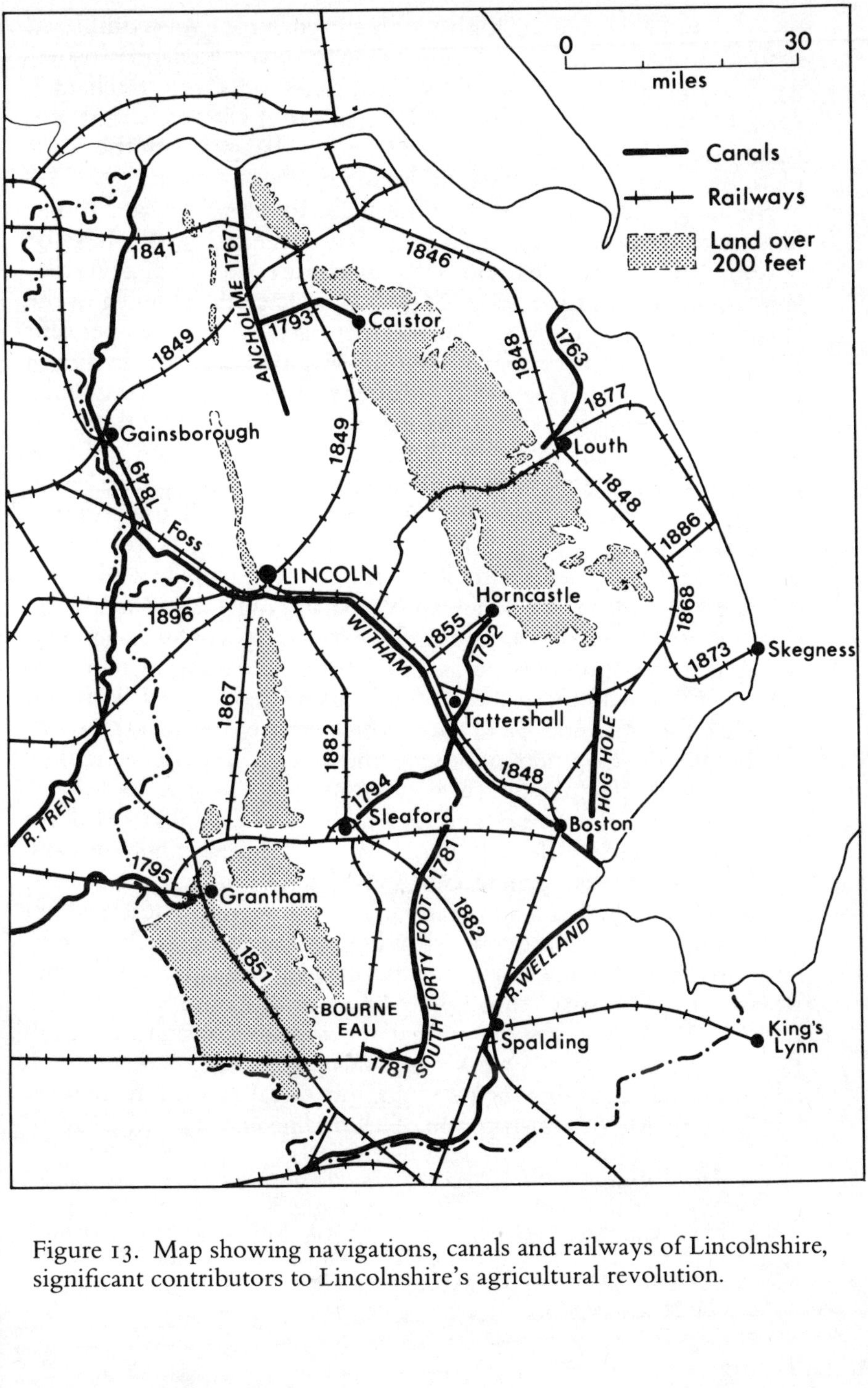

Figure 13. Map showing navigations, canals and railways of Lincolnshire, significant contributors to Lincolnshire's agricultural revolution.

of stone and brick and its high-pitched French roof was completed before confidence in high farming began to waver. Fenland prosperity was reflected in Spalding's Jacobean-style Corn Exchange, 1854–6, and in the imposing bank premises of 1862. Sleaford too, joined in the building of handsome corn exchanges with the completion of its own gothic example in 1857.[20]

Buildings of this style were monuments to the railway age and its links with farming. Yet, though railways came to Lincolnshire for reasons which had little to do with agriculture, they had, nevertheless, an impact on the rural economy. Land agents believed in the 1860s that a farm's letting value was increased from 5 to 20 per cent depending on its nearness to a station. Another estimate earlier in the decade put a 7 per cent increase on the letting value of land when a railway station was within five miles. Landowners like Earl Fitzwilliam, who showed an interest in the routing of the London–York line through Lincolnshire in the 1840s, were in no doubt that railway promotion was largely a speculative venture undertaken by people who had little sympathy for agriculture or the way of life that went with it.[21] Unlike the turnpike and canal developments, local influence among shareholders was weak and routes were devised to capture traffic between towns and manufacturing districts and the ports and not to assist farming or to add to the amenities of an agricultural region. By 1852, however, Lincolnshire had four main railway routes which were to be the framework for the later development of branch lines and local services and they were already affecting the rural economy.

Although local opinion favoured a line from Lincoln to Hull for corn, wool, and cattle, by 1848 the Manchester, Sheffield and Lincolnshire line had penetrated Lindsey to put the industrial areas of south Lancashire and Yorkshire in touch with the southern shore of the Humber and with the growing port at Grimsby.[22] A local enterprise in the same year built the East Lincolnshire's line from Boston to Grimsby through Alford and Louth. The main London–York line was to tunnel its way expensively through Kesteven where great engineering difficulties were encountered near Grantham. As this took so long, the Great Northern Railway hurried on with the construction of a loop line in 1849 which linked

[20] Nikolaus Pevsner and John Harris, *The Buildings of England, Lincolnshire*, London, 1964, pp. 256, 268, 303–4, 479, 545–6, 637, 650.

[21] F. M. L. Thompson, *English Landed Society in the Nineteenth Century*, London, 1963, p. 256, 257; BPP, 1863, VII, SC of HL on Charging Entailed Estates for Railways, Report, iii, Evidence, Q. 33.

[22] L.A.O. Stubbs deposit.

Peterborough, Boston and Lincoln and was planned to join the main or 'Towns Line' between Bawtry and Doncaster. In the short-term railway building had an influence on the local demand for timber, gravel, bricks and sand. Railway building demanded horse power and when completed a line needed horses for its delivery vans. Railway company agents must have influenced trading at horse fairs at Caistor and Horncastle. Migrant labour seems to have left little opportunity for local labour to be recruited as navvies but when it was finished, a line did provide a few jobs for platelayers, carpenters, shunters, porters, drivers and signalmen, guards and firemen to which farm workers might aspire. The rural population benefited through cheaper and more regular coal supplies and the increased numbers of hot dinners made possible by the railway was a real addition to the villagers' standard of comfort. In 1855 coal was being moved in great quantities on the Earl of Ancaster's private railway from the main line at Little Bytham to Grimsthorpe for use in the greenhouses, stables and laundry. Flour from Grimsthorpe was despatched to Glasgow by rail via Little Bytham and Edinburgh while livestock, wool and grain could reach Manchester and London with a new speed and regularity. Fertilizers could be moved more easily by rail as could root crops, potatoes and market garden produce. Traffic in these and similar agricultural products was a reason for the extension of Lincolnshire's railways especially in the Marsh when in 1871–7 lines were built to Skegness and Sutton-in-the-Marsh. The holiday traffic potential of these routes was exploited later. Although it should not be exaggerated, the railways' passenger services did a little towards improving the quality of life in some of the remoter villages. Visiting speakers could reach village meetings, rural families could make occasional trips to market towns and church and chapel Sunday schools could arrange treats and visits to the seaside. In April 1867 the G.N.R. ran three stopping trains and two expresses each way a day on its newly opened line between Lincoln and Grantham. The villages through which they passed were put in closer touch with the world beyond the Heath than they had ever known before.[23]

[23] Alan Rogers, *A History of Lincolnshire*, Henley-on-Thames, 1970, pp. 80–2.

11

Two Upland Farmers

William Scorer's farm accounts indicate some of the costs and returns from a Wolds farm in the mid-nineteenth century. One of three large farmers in the parish of Burwell, he occupied the Home farm, three miles from Louth on the Spilsby road, under Henry Lister of Burwell Park. The village

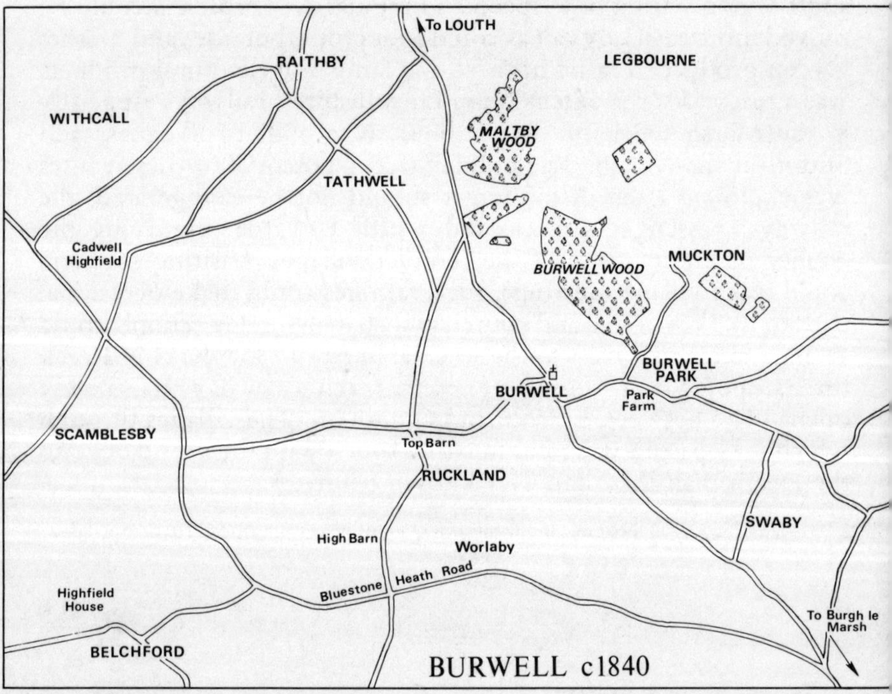

Figure 14. Map showing location of Burwell, based on Greenwood's map of Lincolnshire.

nestled in a sheltered fold of the hills with Maltby, Haugham and Burwell woods lying on its edge to check the north-east wind. Burwell Park of 200 acres had a herd of deer and about 600 large oaks. The house had been rebuilt in 1760. William Scorer took his holding in 1841 without a lease. He paid £650 a year for about 600 acres. In 1854–5 he estimated his annual profit—his costs included all his living expenses—at £639.17s. 2½d. His previous year's profit had been £693, a marked increase on the years 1849–52 when his profits had been £166, £135 and £216. His loss of £68 for 1853–4 had to be seen in the light of a note 'Add to the profit on farming a sum of £250 spent in the alteration of my house.' He paid his bills by cheques drawn on the Lindsey bank; he subscribed 10s. 2d. a year to the North Lincolnshire Agricultural Society and contributed to the building of Louth Corn Exchange.

From 1842 to 1848 he had average wheat yields of 32 bushels an acre which he calculated produced a return of £8.17s. 9¼d. an acre for the seven year period. In 1849 he received £1,026 for his wheat, £248 for barley and £88 for beans. His acreage under wheat that year was higher than usual at 110 acres and his yield of 40 bushels an acre was good but prices were down to 38s. and 6d. a quarter. Thereafter his returns from wheat varied from £715 in 1850, when he had 123 acres but with lower yields of 28 bushels and prices at 37s. and 3d. a quarter, to a good year like 1854 when with wheat at 67s. and 8d. a quarter he had an astonishing 48 bushels to the acre on 83 acres. He sold wheat for £1,674.18s. and 6d. that year. His farm stock stood at £2,034 for 18 horses, 646 sheep, 83 beasts, 10 pigs, 7 store pigs and three gelts in pig. His returns from sheep rose during his tenancy to become an important source of income.

	£ from sheep
1857	686. 4. 8d.
1859	629.13. 7d.
1860	512.10. 2d.
1861	591. 7. 1½d.
1862	655.19. 5d.
1863	1,171.19. 0½d.
1864	1,365. 4. 5d.

His income from beasts rose from £159.10s. in 1856 to £486 in 1865.

Returns from wheat in the 1850s and early 1860s were steady. He kept about 95 acres under wheat each year from 1855 to 1865.

	Acreage in wheat	Quarters sold	Income
1855–6	118	459	1,668
1856–7	96	418	1,308
1857–8	120	497	1,161
1858–9	90	515	1,230
1859–60	100	351	881
1860–1	113	341	777
1861–2	106	433	1,301
1862–3	110	410	933
1863–4	104	524	1,060
1864–5	100	529	1,012

Yields per acre were just below 35 bushes.

Labour costs for a seven year period ending in 1847 were £451 a year. There was an increase after 1853.

Wages 1849–50	£433.12. ½d.
1850–1	396. 0. 0d.
1851–2	435. 0. 8d.
1852–3	437.12. 7½d.
1853–4	499.10. 3½d.
1854–5	515. 2. 6d.

By 1853 the waggoner received £25 a year, 30 stones of pork, what potatoes he required and a cottage and garden rent free. The foreman had been paid £17 a year but his successor in 1854 received £21. A plough boy had £7 a year and Anthony Abbot of Goulceby had £13 a year in 1854 as an under-waggoner and 10s. extra if he stayed the year. Both he and the plough boy ran away. House and kitchen maids were paid £5 or £6.10s. a year and they were expected to help in the fields at harvest for which they were paid extra. The skills of the shepherd were recognized in his wage of about £35 a year and payments in kind.

William Scorer calculated his profit on farming as £805, 1855–6, £390, 1856–7, £279.17s. 8d. 1857–8. In his outgoings he included all his household and living costs including payments for furniture, rat catching, watch repairs, gardening, chimney sweeping, market costs at Caistor, Boston and Louth, coals, Great Northern Railway charges and mouse poison.[1]

[1] L.A.O. Scorer Farm, 1/3, 1/4, 1/5, 1/6, 1/9; William White, *History Gazeteer and Directory of Lincolnshire*, Sheffield, 1856, 1862.

William Scorer's Household, Home Farm, Burwell, 1851.[2]

William Scorer, aged 36, born at St. Margaret's parish, Lincoln.
Susan Scorer, his wife, aged 29, born at Tydd St. Mary's, Lincolnshire
William Scorer his son aged 7, born at Burwell.
James ,, ,, ,, ,, 5, ,, ,, ,,
Charles ,, ,, ,, ,, 4, ,, ,, ,,
Robert ,, ,, ,, ,, 2, ,, ,, ,,
Frederick ,, ,, ,, ,, 8 months born at Burwell.
Noah Grant unmarried farm servant aged 30, born at Driby, Lincs.
Frederick Coggles unmarried farm servant aged 20, born at Legbourne, Lincs.
William Thacker ,, ,, ,, ,, 20, ,, ,, Langton, Lincs.

John Bingley ,, ,, ,, ,, 16, ,, ,, Calceby, Lincs. Lincs.
Ann Croft ,, servant (kitchen maid), aged 28 born at Grainthorpe, Lincs.
Ann White ,, ,, (house maid) aged 19 born at Gayton le Marsh, Lincs.
Ann Goodhand ,, (nurse maid) aged 15, born at Tathwell, Lincs.

Though our most tangible and lasting memorial to the agricultural revolution lies almost as much in the changed use of the uplands as for the fenlands, documentary evidence of the former process is rare. The general picture is painted by the witnesses before parliamentary commissions of enquiry into agriculture but the field by field improvement of the second quarter of the century eludes us until more work is done on the surviving cropping books and farm accounts. At Stenigot, however, between Louth and Horncastle in a secluded valley whose waters join the river Bain lay the farm of Thomas Moses. His field records, 1829–49, survive.[3] He farmed under the Alington family at Swinhope, without lease or written covenant on an annual tenancy which ran from Lady Day with the stipulation that he managed the occupation 'in a Tenant-like manner according to the custom of the county'. The only other landowner in the parish was Samuel Rowe and the only tenant farmer of any importance was William Danby. In 1829 Thomas Moses took on 548 acres of arable, meadow and pasture for a rent of £657 a year and in 1833 he added to them on the same terms of occupation the 62 acres of James True for a rent of £62 a year. He was allowed to burn lime on the farm and to sell off any surplus. At the beginning of his tenancy underdraining tiles were valued at 26s. and 27s. a thousand with a larger variety at 35s. to 40s. a thousand.

[2] PRO, HO, 107 2111/217.
[3] L.A.O. Hill 36/1.

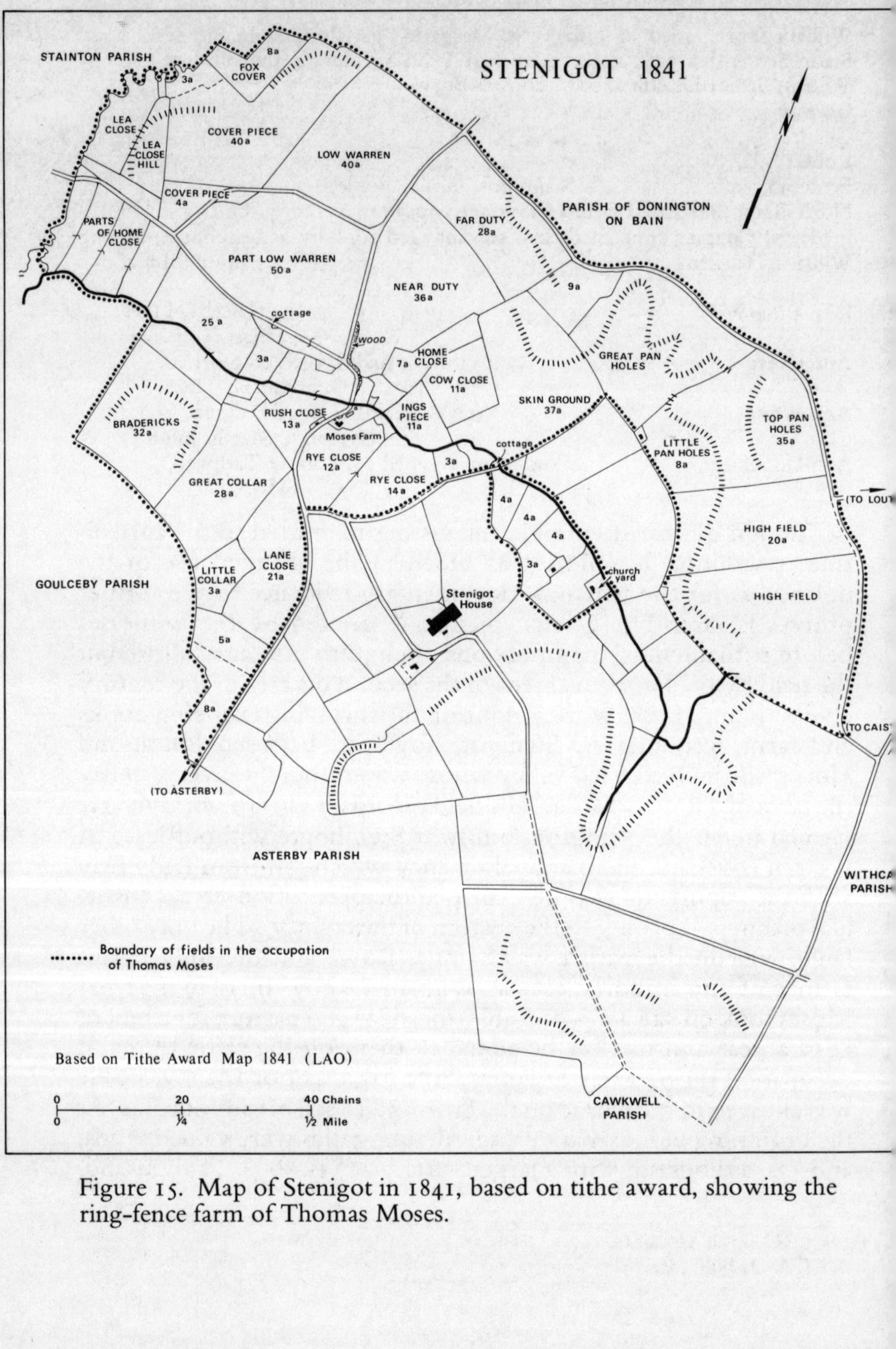

Figure 15. Map of Stenigot in 1841, based on tithe award, showing the ring-fence farm of Thomas Moses.

Cake for feeding to livestock cost from £9 to £10.10s. per ton and soot for spreading cost 4d. to 6d. a strike.[4]

Thomas Moses' land lay to the north, west and south-west of the parish. He held some wold land, some damp closes in the middle of the village near the stream, and by 1841, six gardens and four cottages, the churchyard, the parsonage house and a stock yard at the corner of a field on the edge of the wold land. Some of his fields were as large as 36 acres (Near Duty Ground) or more. Painstaking improvement and careful management were recorded in his field book to register his 'Tenant-like manner' of farming to safeguard the compensation for improvements he would expect on quitting. Of the fences he wrote 'The Fences and ditches were in a very bad and neglected state wherefore their present appearance will be proof of what has been done.' He also recorded crop yields and quality, and his building and underdraining. His building operations were regular and modest on his main farmstead and some of his costs were shared with his landlord.

1830	Three-part calf shade in the main farmstead	£3
	Enlarging and planting garden	£4
1831	New beast shade in the Great Crew-Yard	
	General repairs	£5
	Half the cost of a new waggon shed in brick and tile	£20
1832–3	New shade for waggon horses and waggon shed	
	Shed of part-stone and part-clay with tiles	£9
	Willows planted; new road to brickyard, new pump, garden enlarged, new trees and shrubs planted	£4
1834	Coal house converted to a back kitchen	£7
1835	New gear house in brick and tile	£5
1836	Waggon shed enlarged for two more carts, timber walls and tiled roof	£6
	Garden walled in, crew-yards enlarged	£3
	New stable and pigeon cote	£15
	New stone pig shade with tiled roof and brick pig troughs with lids	£10
1838	Old cart sheds converted to piggeries	
	New shade for foals built on to the pig house on the paddock	
	Minor repairs and limewashing of the farm house for the past 10 years	£50

[4] A measure of corn varying from ½ to 1, 2 and 4 bushels. In Yorkshire it was two bushels. *The Agriculturist's Calculator*, Table XIII, p. 337.

1839	Timber, labour and lime towards a blacksmith's shop and a brewhouse in brick and tile	£12.5.6d.
	New back kitchen—part cost shared with landlord	£13
1840	New plough and harrow shade	£3.10.
1841	Two new crew-yards made near the piggery	£3.10.

Buildings on other parts of his farm were not neglected and as with his improvements at his main farmstead he was concerned with providing more accommodation for waggons and for livestock so that the task of conserving and spreading the manure from the crew yards was to some extent decentralized. Between 1832 and 1836 two cottages were repaired and a shepherd's house was given a new brick gable end and a chimney stack. After one year of his tenancy Thomas Moses made a beast shade in one of his fields, Low Warren, with oak posts and 'barn thatching' for £5.10s. In the same year he repaired the barn and yard in another of his fields, the Panholes, and in 1834 the barn end there was given a new brick floor 'for threshed corn to lay upon'. In 1837 and 1838 the Low Warren beast shade was enlarged and a new small crew-yard was set up in another field, Near Pringle. The total of the tenant's expenditure was only £24 in ten years on these items but they illustrate the process which seems to have been general on the Wolds, of placing crew-yards where they best suited the needs of the arable for regular manure spreading and so reducing carriage costs and time.

It is the fields of the occupation that give the most telling account of his investments. Draining, boning, the spreading of soot, town manure, ashes and 'cake manure', the claying and marling of some poor surfaces and the liming of others were undertaken with energy and expense between 1829 and 1849. The results in crops were carefully noted for each field and the comments of neighbours and his landlord were included when they expressed approval or astonishment. It was 1838 or 1837 before Thomas Moses was able to report good crops; by then his wheat yields were above the county average at about 40 bushels per acre. After spending years of effort to improve the Near Duty Ground of 36 acres by careful cropping, manuring and the spreading of ashes he recorded in 1837 wheat 'a very good crop indeed'. Boning, claying, the spreading of cake manure and compost further improved the field whose turnips in 1847 caused the landlord to observe that half the acreage had 'the best crop he had ever seen on any land in his life'. Wheat in 1849 reached a triumphant yield of just under 40 bushels per acre.

A small but good example of the occupier's persistence in tackling an unpromising acreage was his attention to part of Low Warren or Hob's Hole Bottom; four acres of rushes, ling, gorse and bog near the stream at the centre of the village beside the road to Stainton. As waste it was given no value in 1829 but in 1830 underdraining of a part began with the laying of 2,000 tiles at 27s. the thousand. One hundred roods were tackled at 6d. a rood or a total cost to the tenant of £5.4s. A further sum of £4.8s. was spent on paring and burning and £1 on stubbing trees. White oats were grown in 1831 and potatoes on ten loads of manure per acre in 1832. Turnips and more underdraining followed in 1833 together with lime and eight loads of good manure per acre. Spring 'tars' in 1834 were followed by black oats in 1835 and potatoes in 1836. Liming in 1837 was considered expensive at 5 chauldrons per acre at 8s. a chauldron because of a rise in coal prices which affected lime-burning costs. The field was then sown with Talavera wheat and laid down with seeds. From 1829 to 1837 it was calculated £32.5s. had been spent on the four acres. In 1838 rams were grazed on the land after the seeds and rye grass of 1837–8 had been mown and then the eddish was eaten by sheep. Rye in 1839 was followed by turnips in 1840 and 12 loads of cake manure per acre and 40 strikes of good ashes. The turnip crop was good. The seeds of 1841 were followed by a wheat crop in 1842, the soil having had six chauldrons of lime per acre and ten loads of manure. The crop was a good one and the land was then laid down to clover grazed by lambs in 1834. Oats in 1844 were good considering the dry season. Turnips in 1845 and ten loads of manure per acre and 60 strikes of 'good compost' helped to produce a fine crop. The barley undersown with seeds cropped light in 1846 but the field was grazed with sheep in 1847, 1848 and 1849, the last years of the occupation.

Thomas Moses may be forgiven the occasional note of self-congratulation, but the expressed satisfaction is tempered when appropriate with qualifications owing to weather conditions, mildew or light cropping. Clearly Thomas Moses had his critics; when they were proved wrong his satisfaction with a crop was all the greater. With some of the higher land on the edges of his holding his problem was not one of drainage but of thin subsoil and here his results seem to have been spectacular. With 'Near Braderick's', nearly 16 acres of sandy, light arable, the best he was prepared to say was that the 1838 oats were fair and in 1849 the barley was 'very good for the land'. Yet with other fields he seems to have confounded his critics. His earliest encouragement must have come with his turnips in the 35 acres of 'Top Panholes'. After manuring and applying 18 strikes of bones per acre he reported 'A most excellent crop, after being called the poorest piece in the lordship for years.' This high field gave satisfaction thereafter for the seeds in 1836, the turnips in 1843 and the oats in 1847 were good, the oats being called '... a very nice crop for High Land'. Satisfaction came too when this field, which varied in character within itself, gave a uniformly good crop as with the turnips of 1848 which, when the poor parts of the field had been especially well-manured, emerged as 'A very great crop all over the field.' Next year's barley was 'capital' at 56 bushels an acre. The 'Great Panholes', another high field of nearly 40 acres, had in 1829 produced an inferior wheat crop varying in yield across the acreage. It was treated with bones, ash, lime and crew-yard manure. Stock was grazed on it in 1832 and 1833, some five feet deep underdraining was done and nine acres of the highest ground were marled in 1838 but it was 1839 before oats and wheat in sections gave satisfaction. More marling, manuring and boning in 1840 helped to produce excellent turnips, followed the next year by good oats in two-thirds of the field and barley in the remainder. 1843 saw the underdraining of the lower part of the field and the marling of the upper part and by 1845 consistency of crops seemed assured with turnips 'Very good crop the whole of the field' and the spending of £18 on bones. Barley in 1846 gave nearly 64 bushels per acre. Of the 1847 turnip crop in the 29 acres of Low Warren, Thomas Moses wrote 'The turnips were decidedly the best on the side manured and ashed and it is much the poorest side of the field and always has been.'

With the 40 or so acres of 'The Cover Piece', high on the western side of the parish near the fox cover wood, Thomas Moses recorded no satisfactory crops until after 1838 when in another example of his attempts to gain a more uniform fertility he wrote 'In August and September I had part of the weakest land clayed over', about 15 acres were treated by a John Crow for £32.2s. and 8d. A further claying took place in 1840 for a similar sum. The 28 acres known as the 'Far Duty Ground' were brought round by means of underdraining in the lower parts, liming, boning and ashing to a degree of consistency which was unknown. By 1846, 'To the great surprise of many judges not been (sic) turnip land and never known to have such a crop before by the oldest man in the parish ... A very splendid crop the whole field.' In 1848 he drilled in wheat, after excellent crops in 1847 of oats and barley, the latter abundant at over 56 bushels per acre, and linseed in another part of the field. He commented 'Talked of by some to be very bad farming and sown with seeds and on account of unfavourable season for that sort of land the seeds missed. The wheat did not for after all remarks I had an average of 3 quarters 7 stones of best wheat per acre.'

Thomas Moses' tenancy ended in 1849 but the effect of his efforts and those of occupiers like him on the Wolds landscape was considerable. Through their building, draining, re-arrangement of fields and improvements to their houses and gardens they created a man-made landscape where less and less land was wasted. Stenigot was to undergo much more physical change in the second half of the nineteenth century. By 1884 when a map of the estate was drawn by George Booth Walker, the Wainfleet surveyor, the Louth and Lincoln railway curved through the parish from Donington station to a cutting and tunnel on the edge of Withcall near the Bluestone Heath road. More striking than this was the creation of extensive plantations which kept roughly to the 120 feet contour line in the north and east of the parish to form a dramatic background and windbreak to an enlarged Stenigot House. Further planting had gone on beside the river Bain so that the prospect from the parish to the south-west was now wooded and park-like while to the north and east protection was given by the conifers clinging to the high ground.

12

The Physical and Social Remains of the Agricultural Revolution

As 'new style' farming gave the means for new styles of living and new landscapes, the old unfenced tracks gave place to fenced or hedged roads, old broad divisions of land gave place to smaller but still sizeable cultivated fields. Outlying barns developed into new farmsteads with new farm houses surrounded by trees for a windbreak and dignified with drives and lawns. Wold Newton showed something of this orderly process from 1772 to 1832. Its roads were by 1832 hedged; in 1772 they had been unfenced tracks. The road north from Wyham to East Ravendale had formerly by-passed the village by crossing West Field. Divided in 1772 into two areas of 89 and 69 acres, this field was by 1832 lying in three divisions and traffic through the village was confined to the road east of the parish church with its right-angled bend at the northern end of the settlement. On the border with Beesby, Furz Hill and Fox Cover were divided and cultivated and Coney Hills south of the village near the Wyham–Louth road now lay in two fields and the old unfenced track of the 1770s had been removed.[1]

The farm known as Hainton Walk Farm[2] stands as a memorial to the process of dividing, sub-dividing and cultivating an area of unpromising walk land. It represents too the culmination of the process by the building of new accommodation for the occupier in 1850. Much of its total acreage lay on Oxter Hill which in 1789 had been a walk of some 135 acres in the occupation of Farr Brumpton. By 1814 much of it was still pasture but by 1836 it appears to have become arable land divided into four acreages of 22 acres, 31, 42 and

[1] L.A.O. Yarb. 4/19/1.

[2] L.A.O. 3 Hen. 3/32, 41.

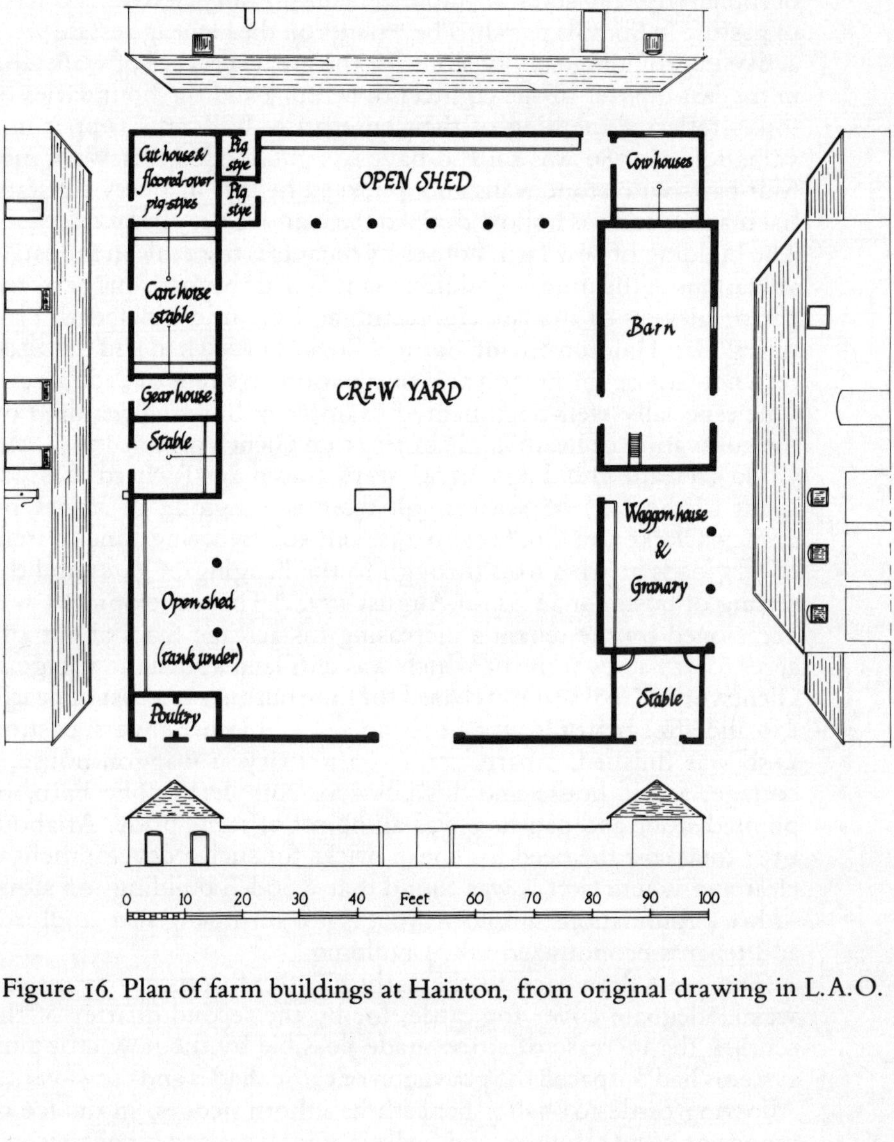

Figure 16. Plan of farm buildings at Hainton, from original drawing in L.A.O.

28 acres. By 1842 these were all arable and in 1850 plans were drawn up to give new farm buildings to Charles Fieldsend the occupier. Executed in red brick with a water tower, a barn and a crew-yard, they represent a good example of mid-nineteenth-century farm building designed to give appropriate accommodation for an occupier with 280 acres of arable in Hainton and just over 100 acres of pasture in Sixhills parish. The tenants on the Heneage estate were active in providing subdivisions for the great acreages of walk land in the last quarter of the eighteenth century and the boundaries of today reflect something of their enterprise. William Cropper in a valuation of 1789 was said to have '... subdivided this Walk into four parts with stone walls and quicksett hedges in a very substantial manner and has hollow drained the land at a very great expense'. The building of new farm houses by tenants is traceable in the estate valuations of the time in building plans and in comparisons between parish surveys of the late eighteenth and the mid-nineteenth centuries. One Hainton tenant, Samuel Sugar in 1789 had laid out £100 on a new house for his 300 acre occupation on a rent of £200 a year. One especially well-documented example of building required by the cultivation of heath land comes from Glentworth in 1774. 'Mr. Codd's Heath Buildings 1774' were traced by Richard Bassett, agent to the Earl of Scarbrough from the digging of stones by Francis Clarke and Co. for £16.13s. and 5d. involving a major item of 757 loads at 5d. a load through to the hanging of gates and the setting of posts for £4.8s. in August 1774.[3] This development was occasioned by the tenant's increasing his acreage from about 475 acres to 527 acres some of which was cliff land above the village at Glentworth. Coal was purchased for lime burning at a cost of nearly £30 and after mason's work costing £81 and joiner's work costing £150 was finished, a barn, stables, a granary, a waggon house, a cottage, a calf house and a well were completed. The barn, of pointed stone and pantiles, was an object of some pride. At about £325 total cost the need for cheap bricks for such a development is clear and where later it was found that wooden buildings on stone or brick foundations would serve it is not surprising that landlords and tenants economized when building.

The great drawback to the early nineteenth century farmstead was inadequate cover for cattle, for by the second quarter of the century the increase of stock made possible by the new cropping systems had outpaced the provision of cattle shades and crew-yards. Allowing cattle to shelter beneath hawthorn hedges, in the lee of woods or beside stone or sod walls in winter was no longer accept-

[3] Lumley MSS, EMBA/10.

able.[4] Expensive oil cake feeding made farmers understand that warmth and shade were equivalents to food and better shelter meant economies in cost. The manure which was essential for improvement of the thin subsoils of the uplands deteriorated if it were exposed to rain before it was spread. Valuable residues were washed away so, here again, roofing and protection helped to reduce costs. Ancient crew-yards began to expand so that they soon covered more ground than the rest of the farmstead. Low and dark, with raised edges in brick or stone, they became the centres of most large holdings. They continue in the Lincolnshire countryside as monuments to the later stages of the agricultural revolution. By the 1860s roofing was considered essential though in areas of low rainfall partly open yards were built and a realization that sunshine was good for young stock resulted in open, south-facing accommodation for calves.

The provision of better buildings on a farm was considered to improve the status of an occupier. Building was carried out with an eye to attracting successive tenants with capital and skill and to add to the prestige of the landlord. It accompanied a change in land use, for example, valuers recommending a ploughing up of old grassland advised improved buildings to work the increased arable that would result.[5] Careful siting of new buildings and the re-use of old materials together with carting by the tenant could all combine to keep down costs. When Thomas Chambers of Reasby had new stables and a carthouse built in 1853 as a result of his being advised to increase the arable acreage on his 280 acre farm, old stone from a former outbuilding was to be worked in with the brick of the new and the stable was to have a stone, rather than an earth floor. When a Mr Wells, tenant of a farm at Wharton, was to be provided with two new crew-yards at the fairly low cost of £152 for bricklayer's and joiner's work in December 1852, the plan depended upon 'folding' walls, that is, making the new accommodation lean to existing buildings to save the erection of new walls and to give the complex a warm, confined appearance, itself often a sign of this period of building. The walls were only 9 inches thick but 9 feet high, the cow house was 55 feet long and the beast shed 111 feet long.[6] Use of local timber kept down costs in the case of a Blyton tenant who was provided with a new house, 27 feet in length with two front rooms and two back rooms on the ground floor, in 1854. The house appears to have been built for less than £100 for a holding of 184

[4] Nigel Harvey, *A History of Farm Buildings in England and Wales*. Aylesbury, 1970, pp. 118–54.

[5] Lumley MSS., Downes Survey. [6] Lumley MSS., EMBP/2.

acres valued at £186 a year. The old house had little to contribute to the new so it was pulled down but the tenant seems to have earned a new home by his improvements to the land. He had tile-drained it and spread sand and town manure upon his moory soil on Morton Carr to give 'abundant crops'. When the Grimsby to Gainsborough railway was built, £160 an acre was paid to the landlord so the holding could claim to have produced a good return.[7]

Foreign timber was used, however, for the farm buildings of larger holdings and estate agents at this time were conscious of the need to locate and exploit beds of clay in an age of house, cottage and outhouse building. An Architect's specification for stables, a gear house, a cake house and a calf house for a Stainton-by-Langwith farm in 1849 stipulated '... good red pine or Memel or Petersburgh timber' to complement a farm house which had been described as 'an ornament to the estate'. The buildings were to have 1 foot 6 inch brick piers, rounded to prevent damage to stock and to carts and the barn door was to be 'large enough for a waggon to draw in with a load of wheat'.[8] The buildings, put up between August 1849 and August 1850, cost £1,318. For another holding in the same parish, Christopher Chapman tendered for £565 for new buildings and £492 for a house on a holding of 192 acres valued at £241 a year. In 1845 it had been recommended that as the quantity of grassland 'is greater than is required and to some of it being very ant hilly and unproductive in its present state it would be well to allow those parts to be broken up. This would enable the tenant to grow more straw and consequently to make more manure for the other lands ...' A barn was needed as the building of the railway would involve the demolition of the existing one. (Plate 13b)

The activities of country builders specializing in farm buildings require more detailed study, but a glimpse of them is afforded by Christopher Chapman of Market Rasen who tendered for contracts on the Scarbrough properties in West Lindsey. He and his kind must have been in demand in the 1840s and early 1850s. In 1849 Chapman wanted an advance of £200 on which he promised to pay interest until the agent collected the Skegness rents when he was engaged on a contract worth £1,057. He claimed that he had built a farm house for Mr Cracroft of Hackthorn in 1848 at West Keal near Spilsby and that he was to build another for Lord Brownlow at Snelland, both along the lines suggested for Lord Scarbrough's Stainton-by-Langwith house. In 1836–8 he had built a large house at Reasby then in the occupation of Mr Brocklesby and described by Lord Scarbrough's Essex valuer in 1845 as an 'excellent and genteel

[7] Lumley MSS., EMBP/3. [8] Lumley MSS., EMBP/1.

mansion'. It was the home for the occupier of 264 acres valued at £319 a year in white brick but with its chimney pieces done in 'Lincoln stone'. Its doors were panelled to befit the style of the holding. The tenant in this case had assisted the builder by doing all the leading for the demolition of the old house and the finishing of the new building.

In the 1850s box systems for stock feeding found increasing favour as the provision of food was seen to be expensive and therefore rationing and the elimination of bullying became cost-savers. Spouting was used more and more and so gutterless buildings were found only on the backward farms of indifferent occupiers. Glazed windows were considered essential in buildings on advanced farms and by the 1860s Dutch barns to cover ricks were being accepted. While little interest appears to have been shown in better housing for pigs and poultry, cheaper materials began to make more substantial temporary shelters easier and cheaper. Patented in 1838, creosote for treating woodwork appeared on farm buildings in the 1840s while asphalt for damp-proof courses and flooring was used in the same period. Galvanized corrugated iron sheeting and concrete were soon to add their unlovely contributions to the mixture of materials that made up the farm building complex, hitherto the domain of local craftsmen or at least rural improvisation in wood, sacking, thatch, tile and brick. By the early 1860s proprietory names in the technical literature of the time suggest that the age of the local craftsman was over.[9]

Specifications for farm cottages by the 1840s suggested a concern for convenience and comfort which was no doubt long overdue. Their appearance, location and style are themselves remains of the agricultural revolution and perhaps of the industrial revolution too. The industrial interest, whose influence in Parliament was strong enough to defeat any plan to rescue the graziers and was to check the arable interest in 1846 with the repeal of the Corn Laws, moved through the English countryside making judgments on their political opponents based on what they saw from their railway carriage windows. Concern for good housing on well-established estates was of course older than the railway age but the appearance of the countryside from the new routes was a matter of interest to land agents and the design of many railway stations and other features of railway architecture in bridges, viaducts and tunnel entrances was influenced by the taste of landowners. In 1847 it was realized at Willoughby that a new railway had so severed some of the arable that fields would have to be put down to permanent pasture. The

[9] Nigel Harvey, op. cit., pp. 144–5.

'shape and angle' of the fields made them unsuitable for the plough. The whole appearance of the village from the line would be improved by permanent grass, the removal of unnecessary hedges and the judicious planting of trees.[10] Cottages were designed to give privacy to the occupants by having their doors at each gable end, so preventing gossiping and the possibility of doorstep clustering which tended to give rise to idleness and the disrespectful scrutiny of passers-by. All was not for outward decency, however, for by the 1840s a more realistic concern for good design was evident in better materials and greater comfort and safety within the new cottages. The specifications for seven new ones for Willoughton in 1849 mentioned a kitchen range with hot water on one side and an oven on the other. Floors were to be of deal and the dwellings were to be of brick with well-baked tiles for the roof. There were to be open shelves in the kitchen and no wood was to be used nearer any smoke flue than nine inches. The doors were to have Suffolk handles and in 'the best room' there was to be a cement skirting six inches deep. Lower windows were to be shuttered and there were to be dwarf cupboards on each side of the chimney breast in 'the House'. There were to be 9 inch walls, fireplaces in bedrooms and a stone sink in each house.[11] (Plate 19)

The countryside near Brocklesby is perhaps the most dramatic physical reminder of the great estate's influence upon the landscape in the agricultural revolution.[12] By the 1830s there were five brickyards on the 55,000 acre Yarborough estate each producing bricks and drainage tiles for the exclusive use of the estate farmers and for the landlord's improvement schemes. Farm houses, cottages, schools and estate farm buildings were invariably built of the Kirmington yard's yellow bricks. There was a distinctive style for estate buildings with panelled doors studded with nails for decoration, ornamental chimney stacks, wooden gable posts, barge boarding and rounded brick labels round the doors and windows of farm buildings and moulded stone labels for more formal works. The family's crest or coat of arms was displayed in stone in a variety of buildings. The Dixons too saw fit to attach their family name to the buildings on their 3,000 acre property at Holton-le-Moor. An institutional landlord like the Bethlehem Hospital with 4,000 acres at Wainfleet St. Mary's worked in the Hospital's coat of arms in lead on its buildings in the 1830s. Cottage building was affected by the fear of attracting paupers to estate villages and one of the physical

[10] L.A.O. 3 ANC 7/23/50/40. [11] Lumley MSS., EMPB/1.

[12] See the detailed treatment of this estate by Heather A. Fuller, *Annals of the Association of American Geographers*, Vol. 66, No. 1. March 1976, pp. 14–24.

remains of the revolution is the relatively uniform architecture and low populations of the closed villages and the more varied buildings, layouts and higher populations of the open villages. Until the passing of the 1865 Union Chargeability Act which took responsibility for the poor from parish authorities, cottage building was kept well within strict limits. The second Earl of Yarborough, however, built many cottages between 1847 and 1860. Building at Swallow is an example of the concern at this time to provide decent housing for estate and farm workers. A product of a deliberate policy of improvement, these homes were inspected by the landlord, personally. On the Heneage estate though an excess of cottages at Hainton had been noted in a survey of the 1790s, building was undertaken in the 1830s. William Danby was responsible for the design of some of the cottages at Hainton while at Blankney the Chaplin estate entrusted the laying out of the village to W. A. Nicholson in the 1830s and the building of cottages in a Tudor style. Normanton and Nocton reveal similar evidence of estate development of this type and from this period. In spite of building, the estate villages remained thinly populated. Brocklesby had 207 inhabitants in 1801 and 232 in 1861, while Binbrook increased from 255 to 1,334 in the same period. A comparison between closed villages like Croxton, Searby-cum-Ormby, South Ormsby and North Willingham and open parishes like Caistor, Kirton, Market Rasen and Winterton suggests the same trend; a steady population increase in settlements largely in the hands of one owner and a dramatic increase in the open parishes.[13] Normanby, 1805, Aswarby, 1845–50, Belton, 1828–35, South Stoke, 1840–5 and Revesby frcm the 1850s are further examples of the county's estate villages.

Plantations were physical evidence of the confident changes in land use made by landlords and their substantial tenants. Here again, the twelve and a half million trees planted on the Yarborough estate, a process recorded on Pelham's Pillar at the highest point on the Wolds at Fonaby Top, is the county's most dramatic example. A ten mile arc of woodland was created from Brocklesby in scheme started in 1788 and completed in 1823. A plan for 'Disposing of the Plantation in the Estate of Great Limber and Audleby' dates from 1770 and the Hall itself was remodelled by Lancelot Brown who dressed some of the parkland at both Great Limber and Audleby. He created Newsham Bridge, a neo-Norman and Gothic essay in Lincolnshire limestone. Later in the railway age, Brocklesby with its carefully styled 'estate' station was to be a North Lincolnshire

[13] Fuller, op. cit.

showpiece, its parkland and woods open to visitors and celebrated in the first edition of White's *Historical Gazetteer and Directory of Lincolnshire* in 1856. Lord Yarborough had assisted in the siting of the Manchester, Sheffield and Lincolnshire line and its disturbance to the estate was minimal. With these magnificent woods arranged as a shelter belt and a mausoleum, Brocklesby was to compare with Castle Howard in Yorkshire for scale and grandeur of execution. At Blankney the link between the railway at Metheringham and the Hall was by a sunken, wooded coachway which enabled the railway traveller to reach the station without using a public road and remaining for most of the time out of the sight of one. Though the park at Blankney lies on the other side of the Hall, it was possible by planting and road-cutting to have an almost secret access to one of the most public forms of transport, the railway. Rural sport has left its mark upon the landscape particularly when aristocratic patronage combined with local enthusiasm. At Normanby Park a shady tunnel of yew to give cover for the rearing of pheasant runs for 60 feet with iron gates at each end. Near Gibraltar Point three unusual iron posts mark out shooting rights; one is in a sand-dune but the other two are in mature marsh, formerly open foreshore. They mark grazing and shooting rights in Croft to the north belonging to the Lord of the Manor, Thomas Tyrwhitt-Drake, and have TTD on the posts, while those in Wainfleet St. Mary to the south belonged to 'Ld. B' or Lord Bayning. They were erected in 1850–60 when the land was evolving from sandy, muddy seashore to saltmarsh and sand-dune.

Another indication of the agricultural revolution in the county lies in its farm houses, parsonages and restored parish churches. These reflect in local brick, stone, timber and Victorian stained glass the new confidence of the tenant farmers and of the clergy whose lives too were bound up with the prosperity of agriculture. Although farm houses await their thorough exploration by an architectural historian, indications of riches to be discovered do exist. Chapel Farm at Keelby in late Georgian gothic and Gokewell Priory Farm at Broughton, a Georgian house on the site of a nunnery, together with Woodlands Farm, Gosberton complete with Doric columns dating from 1820 to 1830 are three examples of farm houses touched by grandeur. It is in farm names, however, that links with the breaking in of cliff, warren, heath and wold abound. On the southern Wolds names using the adjective 'high' suggest the process like High Barn Farm, Hagworthingham, and High Barn Farm, West Keal. At Holton Holgate there is High Farm and to the north-west as the land rises on the edge of the Wolds there are three Highfield Farms, one between Grebby and Welton le Marsh, one at Old Bolingbroke and another at East Keal. Near Tetford, Fulletby and Hemingby 'high' combines with 'field' or 'barn' to give more farm names on similar sites. In this region 'high' serves for 'cliff' on the limestone ridge north of Lincoln and for 'top' in north Lindsey denoting a farm situated on the thin, light soils of the uplands.

At their edge, however, near the Fens, farm names retain something of the artificial or man-made landscape which was first secured by wind drainage and then consolidated by steam-driven pumps. The personal names of landowners involved with draining schemes and names associated with other parts of the world where land was being reclaimed, or where modern history was thought to be in the making, were used to name new farms or areas of new fields. Mexico, in the news in 1846 with the American war and again in 1861 with the intervention of Napoleon III, appears on the Bell Water Drain near Midville while Pelham's lands and Carrington lend personal names to an area so blank that resort was had to such inventions as Eastville, Westville, Langriville, and Frithville. New York near Coningsby with nearby Providence House and Bunkers' Hill, the latter a favourite farm name in many parts of the county, suggest the time of the American war in the 1770s, whereas Engine farm, Stickford and Royalty Farm near Hemholme Bridge reflect the continuing battle against flooding. There are few fox coverts to be found in this countryside or indeed any woodland but the occasional Decoy Wood, Pool Decoy and The Deeps such as those on Friskney Fen preserve the links with the old farming economy, links which Cranberry Farm and Cranberry Bottom Farm near Wainfleet St. Mary support.

From Bourne to the South Forty Foot Drain lies a landscape which owes almost everything to the work of successive drainers and the new-style farming which followed them, a drained landscape as regular in its names as in its physical features: Bourne North Fen, Dyke Fen, Morton Fen, Hacconby Fen, Dunsby Fen, Rippingale Fen, Dowsby Fen, and so on down to Heckington in a succession of drains, roads and regular fields with farm names to match. Some like Black Sluice Farm, Newlands Farm and Forty Foot Farm are clearly part of the new landscape; others like Old Decoy Farm, Dowsby and Mallard Farm near Horbling Fen hark back to the old farming economy. Even more expressive of the triumph of man over the Fen is the landscape between Boston and Spalding and south to Crowland with the remains of old sea banks, and unfenced roads running beside dikes and drains. Its farm names encapsulate both old and new; Engine Bank Farm (Whaplode) the new, and Swanpen Farm (near Moulton Chapel), Magpie Holt Farm (Weston Hills) and Windcatch Farm (Low Fulney) the old economy. Woad Farm, Fishtoft and Woad Farm, Tydd St. Mary record the growing of this crop which was locally important in the late eighteenth century. Farther north at Brothertoft, the Hall dating from the 1780s stands as a gaunt reminder of the profits to be made from woad cultivation.[14] At Wyberton on the road from Boston to Frampton and Kirton the remains of a woad processing plant indicate the continuation of this local cultivation of a special crop to satisfy the needs of the dyers.

Never a very extensive crop, the rotation for woad consisted of woad for three or four years followed by two years of oats, one of cole, one of oats and then grasses for seven or even eight years. A holding of about 1,000 acres was needed to grow enough woad to keep the processing plant in economic use. Major Cartwright who settled in the Fens from Nottinghamshire in 1788 had a holding of this size. His mills and homes for 30 workmen formed the settlement of Isatica (from the Latin for woad) and attracted the attention of both Arthur Young and John Cragg. Situated near the north Forty Foot Drain, it was placed conveniently for sending the processed crop to Boston by water. Woad processing continued there late into the nineteenth century and the remains of his red-brick buildings stand as a memorial to this once important trade. At Algarkirk woad cultivation continued in the 1830s and a mill for processing it still exists.

East, West and Wildmore Fens contain much physical evidence of the revolution in land use and drainage. The end of Hobhole Drain, constructed in 1802–6 using barrow and plank methods, and the different designs of the brick bridges along it mark Sir John Rennie's work between 1804 and 1806. Midville Church, by Jeptha Pacey, of brick brought perhaps from the Stickney yard in 1819, is a similar monument; the townships of Midville, Eastville, Westville, Frithville, Langriville, Carrington and Thornton-le-Fen were formed by the 1812 Act from extra-parochial land sold to pay for draining, enclosure and the endowment of churches. At Eastville the old East Lincolnshire railway of 1848 met with construction difficulties in the quaking peatlands at the northern end of East Fen. Even in a relatively treeless region like this some evidence of enclosure remains. Near Stickney which lies on a tongue of boulder

[14] Joan Thirsk, *English Peasant Farming*, London, 1957, pp. 228–9; Nikolaus Pevsner and John Harris, *The Buildings of England, Lincolnshire*, London, 1964, p. 486.

clay extending southwards from the Wolds and dividing East from West Fen stands Medlam where at the junction between the Stickney road and the Seven Mile Straight to Revesby, large old hedges remain as monuments to the Medlam enclosure. Again at Haven Bank on Wildmore Fen, former home of the Wildmore pit ponies, there are old, unchecked hedgerows, eaten away at the bottom and assuming tree-like proportions at the top. On the Heath-edge at Branston and Mere are good examples of enclosure landscapes with as much as 60 feet between the road-side hedges, broad grass verges and regular field patterns.[15] Wide verges are found in South Nottinghamshire and North Leicestershire as well. Cottagers were compensated for a loss of common by roadside grazing. Sometimes the surveyor of the highway let the verges annually to provide an income for road maintenance.

Some of the most tangible physical remains of the revolution that created a new country in the Fens are to be found in the small churches and chapels. New York's red-brick chapel dates from 1828 just after the draining of the surrounding fen. St. Paul's, Carrington, in brick, from 1816 is another ecclesiastical link with the new landscape while Eastville's red-brick church built between 1830 and 1840 retains a missionary appearance in a setting which with its straight roads, small cottage-farmsteads and regular fields, proclaims the triumph of steam draining. The small churches of Frithville and Midville raised above flood levels and dating from 1812 and 1819 respectively proclaim in their design, building materials and location the modest scale of the new colonies. At New Bolingbroke the whole settlement is a 'new' creation, the work of Sir Joseph Banks' steward, John Parkinson, who saw in it easy waterway links with Boston some five miles away on Medlam Drain. The village was a kind of colony pushed out from Revesby to the south, a taking in of fenland from an old agricultural base situated on the rising ground of the southern tip of the Wolds. In 1824 a factory for the weaving of crêpes and bombazines was built as well as a crescent of homes for textile workers; an attempt to encourage manufacture within the county at a time when cereal production was clearly replacing wool in the rural economy. In February 1818 the Revesby accounts had recorded the first annual instalment of the tax upon land in South Holland to 'the Committee men'. An area of over 2,200 acres was assessed at 1s. an acre.[16] From 1802 portable engines were at work on the estate draining the fields south of

[15] David N. Robinson, *Tour of East West and Wildmore Fens*, Louth, 1975, p. 224.

[16] L.A.O. RA 2/A/1/4.

Revesby, at least one of which was adapted to serve as a bone mill to break and crush bones for fertilizer.[17]

Hunting never flourished in the Fens where the broad dikes made the chase hazardous but it has left its mark upon the countryside between the Cliff north of Lincoln and the river Trent to the west and on the Heath south of Lincoln to Stamford. It was a social as well as a sporting phenomenon and it required not only the leadership of landowners but, like shooting which has left similar traces in the landscape, the active participation of the new-style farmers. Near Gainsborough there is Top Fox covert at Lea and Fox covert, Knaith near Gate Burton, Stow and Coates, Broxholme and South Carlton have their fox or long coverts. Similar woods spread across to Swinderby to the south-west and over to Greetwell, Toft Newton and Caenby with kennels at Riseholme. South of Lincoln the pattern is similar with Branston's Fox covert and others at Nocton, Metheringham and Digby with kennels at Blankney. Here the heath farms abound. From Cranwell to Old Somerby there are seven lying off Ermine Street and one or two like Victoria Farm, Caythorpe or Alma Wood, Belton suggest mid-nineteenth-century activity in farm building and planting. From Waterloo House near Fulbeck Low Fields to Wellingore, a small area of heath edge and western lowland, there are numerous fox coverts and farms whose names suggest that they were established as the Heath was put under the plough; Wellingore Heath, Highfields and Highfield House, Wellingore and Welbourn Heath.

The country to the north and north-east of Lincoln, however, is perhaps the richest in names which seem to capture the spread of the cultivated area and the setting up of new farmsteads in the middle of cliff, walk and wold land. Not all the farms were of late eighteenth- or early nineteenth-century origin but they do present an invitation for more local study to establish whether their names denote their being set up or merely rebuilt or modernized. To the east of Ermine Street from Saxby Cliff to Hibaldstow there are no fewer than seven cliff farms and eleven more east of the cliff edge road from Fillingham to Winteringham. Political or historical names seem to have attracted landlords and their tenants. Canada, near Caistor, could commemorate Wolfe in 1759 or Canada's reorganization in 1840 or her dominion status in 1867. Odessa farm near Irby upon Humber probably dates from 1824 when Odessa became the seat of government of New Russia, a free and prosperous port for a vast agricultural region. Zulu farm at Ulceby near Immingham suggests a settlement or a rebuilding in 1879, the date of the war, while

[17] L.A.O. RA 2A/1/2.

Nebraska farm in the low fields west of Kirton Lindsey invites a connection with the setting up in 1867 of the 37th state of the Union with its capital at Lincoln. Near by at Scotter, St. Helena farm, judging by the architecture of its roadside farmhouse just before alteration in 1976, dates from the period when Bonaparte lived on the island after 1815. Timaru Farm, Elsham suggests links with the South Island seaport of New Zealand with its industries based on wool and chilled meat. Twelve Month Farm between Grasby and Caistor Moor catches the change from leases to annual tenancies, a move that varied in time from one estate to another in Lincolnshire but probably in this case dates from the post-Napoleonic War period. Near the seats of titled proprietors there appear London names like Pimlico and Stepney at Brocklesby, or Hanover, after Hanover Square in London developed partly by the first Earl of Scarbrough, at Glentworth. (Plate 14)

The more characteristic names are the numerous 'tops' on the north Wolds or farm names, which include 'wold' or 'walk'. Turnpike Top Worlaby, Worlaby Top Farm and Bonby Top Farm lie on the high side of the parishes while to the west a mere two and a quarter miles away beyond the village centres are new farms of the lowlands: Worlaby Carrs Farm, Rennison's Carr Farm and Clarkson's Carr farm near Worlaby New Ings in the Ancholme valley. There are many farm names which preserve the long struggle against flooding and the attack upon sandy acreages. Ashby and Broughton Decoy farms, Warp farm Morton, Gainsborough and Risby Warren farm are four while the remains of warping drain banks are to be found running from Messingham to Scotterthorpe and Scotton Common to the Trent at Kelfield. Towards Grimsby the 'top' farms are supreme: Grasby Top farm, Clixby Top, Audleby Top, Fonaby Top near Pelham's Pillar with farm settlements bearing similar names at Rothwell, Ravendale, Walesby and Otby. Many of these are identifiable as farms planted in a new agricultural landscape by the accommodation roads which run up to them from the highways which connect the older areas of settlement in the villages. A good example of the new farmsteads is Searby Top; built of chalk with brick surrounds for windows and doors, it stands at the end of its own farm lane. At Horncastle, Stonehill farm stands in its own block of fields created during the parliamentary enclosure movement, an almost text-book example of a new farm with its own accommodation road.

In the villages lying at a distance from the homesteads of the prosperous tenant farmers of the uplands were the churches, rectories, vicarages and village schools over which the farmers as

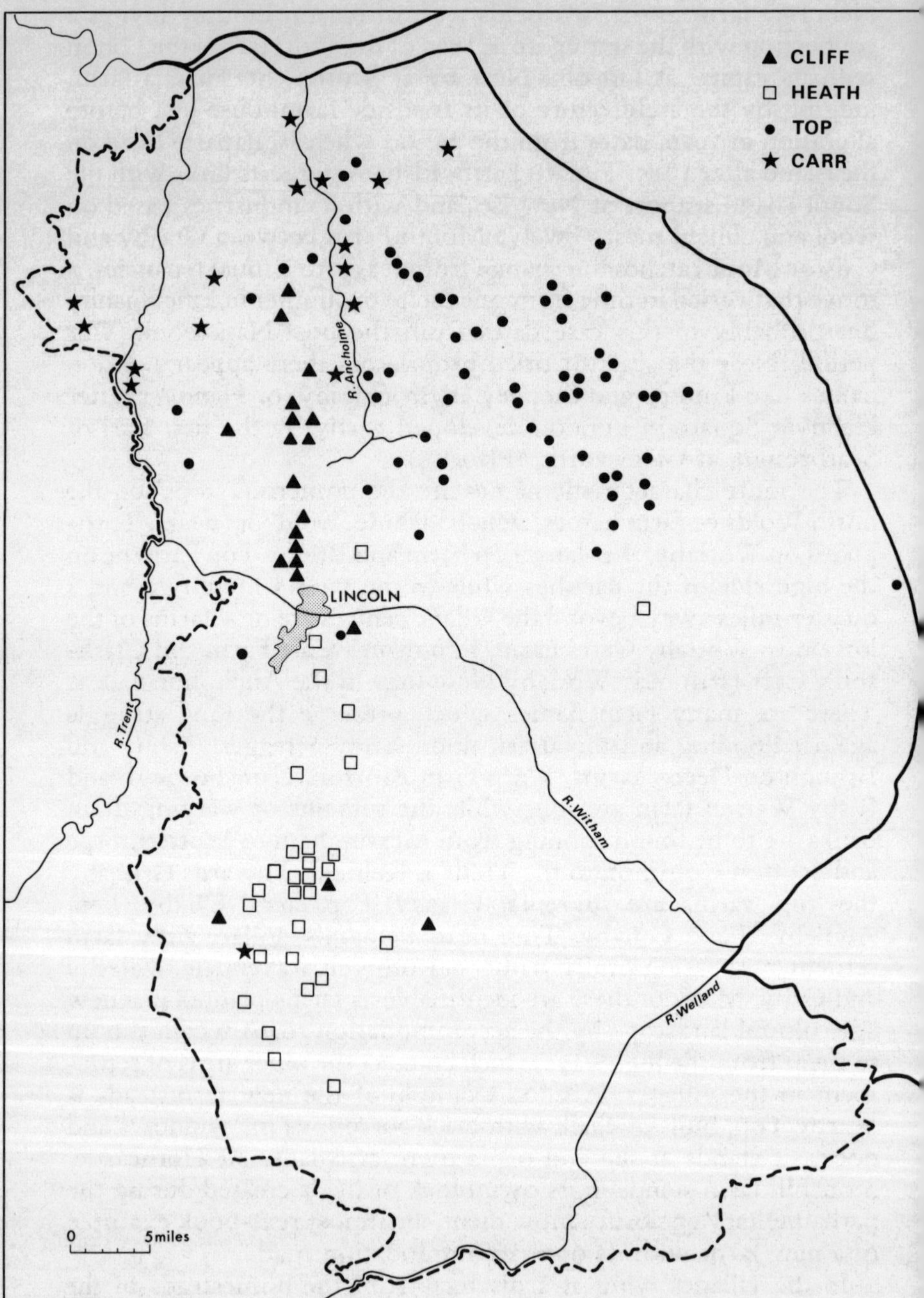

Figure 17a and b. Maps showing distribution of types of farm names in Lincolnshire.

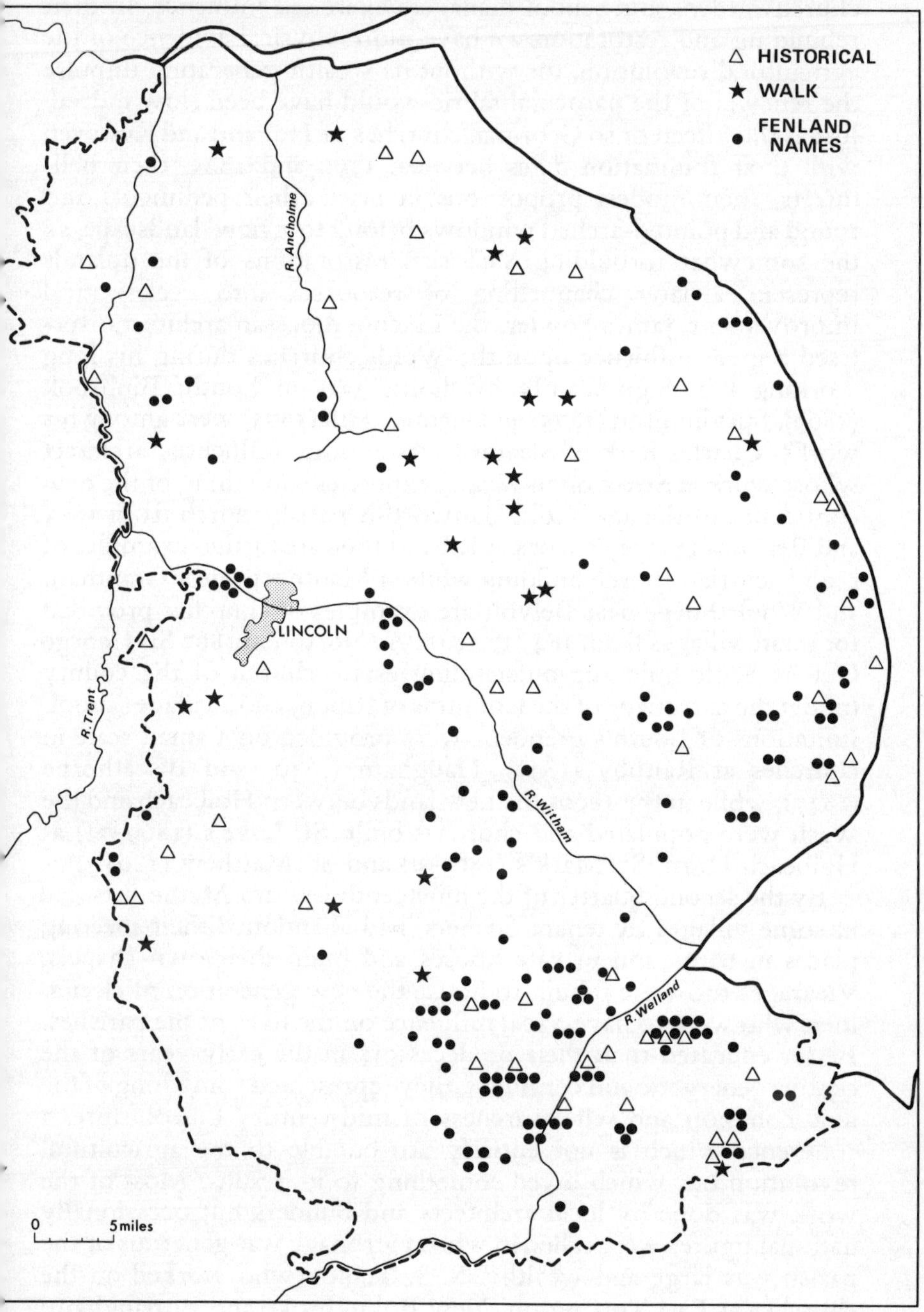

HISTORICAL
WALK
FENLAND NAMES
R. Ancholme
LINCOLN
R. Trent
R. Witham
R. Welland
0
5 miles

churchwardens and school managers exercised influence. In their rebuilding and restoration we have more physical evidence of the agricultural revolution, for without its wealth-generating impulse the renewal of the parochial fabric would have been slow indeed. Just as the fifteen or so Georgian churches of Holland and Kesteven with their foundation dates between 1790 and 1825, their bell-turrets, their modest proportions in brick, their pediments and round and pointed-arched windows belong to a 'new' landscape, so the somewhat forbidding Victorian restorations of the uplands represent a later channelling of resources into ecclesiastical improvement. James Fowler, the Lincoln diocesan architect, exercised a great influence upon the Wolds churches during his long working life. Significantly his home was in Louth: Binbrook (1869), Spridlington (1875) and Gedney Hill (1875) were among his works. Charles Kirk of Sleaford was another influential architect whose work at Stroxton in 1874–5 expresses something of the new confidence of the age. Cold Hanworth's parish church from 1863 and Benjamin Ferrey's work at Riby in 1868 are further examples of high Victorian church building while at Manthorpe near Grantham and Woolsthorpe near Belvoir are examples of churches provided for estate villages from 1847 to 1848. At Nocton in 1862 Sir George Gilbert Scott built the outstanding estate church of the county (under the patronage of the Countess of Ripon) and a village school. Imitations of Louth's grandeur were provided on a small scale in churches at Raithby (1839), Haugham (1840) and Biscathorpe (1847), while in the 1860s the new lands between Holbeach and the Wash were populated and churches built: St. Luke's (1869–71) at Holbeach Hurn, St. Mark's (1863–9) and St. Matthew (1868–9).

By the second quarter of the nineteenth century Methodists, led in some villages by tenant farmers, had abandoned their meeting places in barns and private houses and build their own chapels. Vicarages too were rebuilt to house the new generation of clerics, men who were to have a real influence on the lives of the parishes. Better educated than their predecessors in the early years of the century, energetic and confident, they represented something of the new cohesion and self-awareness of mid-century Lincolnshire, a coherence which is not entirely attributable to the agricultural revolution but which owed something to its results. Most of the work was done by local architects and builders but occasionally national figures were called in when patronage was generous or the parish was large and wealthy. S. S. Teulon who worked on the churches at East Torrington, New Bolingbroke and Burringham, designed Harrington rectory in 1854. Benjamin Ferrey built Fleet rectory in the same year and H. A. Darbyshire gave Navenby its stone and gabled rectory. James Fowler and Charles Kirk rebuilt or improved parsonages but on a more modest scale. Village schools, often gothic in style, accompanied the restored churches and improved vicarages. Great Gonerby in 1841 and Sir George Gilbert Scott's composition at Algarkirk from 1857 are but two examples of this manifestation of rural renewal. About 1850 Stow church was restored and given the character of a small cathedral, not without some opposition. In south Lindsey between 1840 and 1875 major work on 127 churches was undertaken at a cost approaching £130,000.[18] There had been activity in restoration from the late 1830s which reached a peak about 1850 then fell off and then revived from 1857 to 1880.

Increasingly the clergy, some of whom thanks to allotments of land to replace tithes became important landowners in their parishes, took the lead in rebuilding and restoration. Clerical homes were substantial rather than ostentatious but they demonstrated a new social assurance, affluence and a determination to use them as working capital for the parishes. There were more clergy to minister to the people, non-residence declined and incumbents were expected to live in their parishes and to share the social life of the more congenial of their neighbours. Hence the larger dining-rooms in which to entertain, to conduct parish business with churchwardens and overseers of the poor and to hold Bible and confirmation classes. Private boarding scholars were taken in to augment incomes and to keep learning alive. More room was needed for larger families and living-in servants and better outhouses for the horses and carriages of the clergy who now expected like the larger tenant farmers to travel in style and to receive those who were accustomed to doing so. It has been calculated that in south Lindsey the number of clergy increased by 50 per cent between 1850 and 1875 and nearly all were resident in their parishes. Clerical landlords were not indifferent to the needs of their tenants. The Reverend Gleed of Donington, for example, held a leasehold farm from the Bishop of Lincoln. Early in the 1830s he wrote asking for new buildings for Rectory Farm, Quadring near Gosberton. Having taken advice from 'a Gentleman of large Occupation and experience who dictated the plan of the Buildings which are an accommodation to the farm and myself', he stressed that his tenant who had carried all building materials hitherto could not be expected to farm without proper buildings. He needed a beast shed

[18] J. Obelkevich, *Religion and Rural Society in South Lindsey, 1825–1875*, Oxford, 1975, p. 111.

44 feet long, 7 feet high and 12 feet in depth with brick pillars and a roof of faggots thatched with straw. When the improvements were completed the rector was left out of pocket, a fact he placed before his Bishop without comment but in hope.[19]

Recent research in the period 1825–75 suggests that in south Lindsey at least one of the social consequences of the agricultural revolution was a pulling apart of the classes and some weakening of a sense of community. 'In the eighteenth century and the first half of the nineteenth, they (the tenant farmers) became conscious of themselves as a class with common interests and a common culture. Enriched by agricultural "improvement", "new style" farming families adopted a more luxurious, and recognizably middle-class way of life.'[20] Living in by farm servants declined, children were sent to school outside the parish and in the absence of resident landlords, tenants took the lead in hunting and shooting and found social satisfaction in visiting other farmers of similar social standing. Governesses were engaged to teach daughters and sons were sent away as weekly or termly boarders. Louth, Caistor and Horncastle grammar schools received more farmers' sons while village schools like the one at Gayton-le-Marsh with 32 children, 1867–75, numbered only two scholars who were farmers' children. William Ellis, Casitor Grammar School's headmaster advertised his establishment in 1836 by means of a printed testimonial among 'the Lords of the Soil' during the hunting season. He observed that at Caistor he could live well on less than half of his costs at Blackheath; a reason perhaps for Lincolnshire's attractions for clergy as well as schoolmasters.[21]

In the agricultural societies of the early nineteenth century, technical education, social harmony and self-help were three aims. Perhaps 'new style' farmers were saved from an unfeeling pursuit of their own interest by the example of some of the greater, resident Lincolnshire landlords who ran their estates in ways designed to promote social harmony and physical well-being. Cottage building, pensions for old employees, roods of land for gardens and the provision of blankets, calicoes and coal for the poor and distributions of game at Christmas and the beginning of the shooting season were customary on estates like the Heneage estate at Hainton and at Revesby, for example. Rent-day dinners and the celebration of national and family events were a feature of many estates. Such activity must have left some mark on the tenant farmers who were

[19] L.A.O. Misc. Don. 435/1–4.
[20] Obelkevich, op. cit., pp. 26–7 and 53–7.
[21] L.A.O. Dixon 17/5/5, 17/5/5/2.

to become so influential and as they adopted changed patterns of social behaviour they appear to have grown conscious of the need to keep contacts with their labourers. To this end agricultural societies, church services, treats like harvest thanksgiving and sheep shearing and harvest home suppers were given a new significance and function. J. A. Clarke writing in 1852 thought that there were at least 17 agricultural associations, farming clubs and societies for encouraging self-help among farm labourers. He found 178 members of the Royal Agricultural Society. Here were the signs of an emerging community of interest, wider than the old parochial loyalties but still related to village life. Some of the earlier societies were the ploughing associations like the one at Donington and Hainton started in 1808, the Lincolnshire Agricultural Society dating from 1819, the North Lincolnshire Agricultural Society of 1836 and societies at Grantham and Horncastle set up in the 1830s and the Alford Agricultural Labourers' Society started in 1838. This last was designed to promote among farm labourers and servants, good conduct, skill and industry. Tetney's Agricultural Society, 1854–77, tried to touch all classes engaged in farming. Its purpose was '... For the advancement of agriculture generally; for the excitement of enterprise and emulation amongst owners and occupiers of land and for the encouragement of skill, industry and good conduct amongst labourers, farm servants and others connected therewith ...' At Benington in 1857 a society was founded with the object of improving the labourers resident in the district, an aim clearly set out in its title. At Horncastle the agricultural society sought to promote '... Good Conduct, Skill and Industry amongst Labourers and Servants....'

On 24 November 1820 the *Stamford Mercury* thought that the Lincolnshire Agricultural Society would be a great benefit to the county 'by creating a spirit of emulation and improvement in husbandry'. The need to bring classes of society together was expressed by clergy like the Vicar of Grimsby and the Vicar of Tetney who saw in them ways of bringing the sons of farmers and the labourers together in a common pursuit of intelligence and industry in agriculture. By the early 1870s it was evident that Trade Unionism among farm workers was likely to put strains upon rural social harmony. The Vicar of Barton-on-Humber observed in November 1873 that, 'The ploughing competitions ... (tended) ... to counteract the efforts which had been made in this county and throughout England to set class against class.' Ploughing societies were numerous. Barton and North Lincolnshire had one as had Saltfleet and District, founded in 1867. Langrick, Brothertoft and

District started another, while in 1874 Timberland, Martin and Thorpe Tilney Ploughing Society was formed. Sometimes their concern was close to that of the labourers' improvement societies. At Horncastle the Ploughing Society in 1868 offered a prize 'To the wife or widow of a labourer in Husbandry who shall have the best-ordered house and furniture, number of children at home to be taken into consideration....'[22] The Lincolnshire Agricultural Society offered in 1843 a premium or prize of £5 for '... the best Labourer in Husbandry, in the county of Lincoln, who has brought up the largest Family, without Parochial Relief ...' Premiums of £10 were offered at the same time to the owner of the best stallion 'for getting hunters', for the best bull of any age and the best ram of any age.[23]

Membership of the North Lincolnshire Agricultural Society rose from 61 members in the early 1840s to 110 by 1860. On the Cliff and in the central vale east of it, membership remained steady. There were 11 members on the Cliff and 29 on the soils of the central vale at both dates but the most striking increases were on the southern Wolds from 3 to 19 and on the northern Wolds from 9 to 33. The middle and outer Marshes and the edges of the Fens showed small increases. Membership of societies was not the only way attempts could be made to strengthen a sense of community at a time when agricultural changes were altering the old contexts for social life. Harvest thanksgiving services and harvest home suppers played their parts as well. At both the leading farmers and the 'new' clergy many of whom were young or middle-aged men, graduates, unmarried but paternalistic in outlook and Conservative in politics gave an energetic lead in parish life particularly after about 1850. If the process can be seen as a form of labour relations it seems equally appropriate to see in it a making good of decades of neglect at the parochial level and some attempt by the prosperous farmers to do something, albeit paternally for the social life of the villages. That the farmers of South Lindsey were growing richer is borne out by a study of their wills in the 1850s. The more capital a farmer had and land over 300 acres the richer he became but the small farmers of less than 100 acres prospered too. A study of the wills of 92 farmers in South Lindsey from 1851 to 1855 shows that 3 left over £10,000, 15 left between £5,000 and £10,000 and 26 left between £1,000 and £5,000.[24]

Although labour unrest continued in the fifties and sixties, the

[22] *SM*, 6 November 1868.

[23] *SM*, 7 April 1843; Notes provided by Rex C. Russell, 1977.

[24] Obelkevich, op. cit., p. 32, 51; L.A.O. TLE 2, List of subscribers 1838–46.

ugly scenes of violence with rick burning and machine breaking of the 1830s were by 1870 a thing of the past. Early in 1872, however, unionism amongst farm workers sprang to life in all parts of the county. Within months it had reached a degree of organization and intensity that alarmed the farmers. Why were unions formed so rapidly in the small towns and villages of Lincolnshire? Land hunger, fear of unemployment, dissatisfaction with rural housing and a sense of alienation amongst labourers who worked on the large arable farms all played a part.[25] The more distant a farm was from a village, the larger its arable acreage and the higher its proportion of day labourers in its total labour force, the likelier it was to be affected by union activity. Aggrieved farmers emphasized the role of agitators, and journeymen shoemakers in Louth and mechanics from Spilsby were active, but something more than the arguments of disgruntled town craftsmen was at work. The feeling that only a reduction of the labour supply by migration, emigration or strike action would raise wage rates above the inadequate level of 15s. a week for a labourer and his family was a major cause. Thousands were moved to meet in the market-places and inn yards of Lincolnshire, not to burn stacks or to destroy machines but to form unions which were idealistic, responsible and non-violent.[26]

The *Louth and North Lincolnshire Advertiser* pointed out on 13 January 1872, that many were hovering on the verge of pauperism, that they were becoming 'bold' and that they needed help. Another article showed that from Caistor and district the best men were already emigrating and that a strike was imminent by those who remained.[27] Soon there were reports of meetings all over the county. Town criers in places like Spilsby announced meetings of the nine hours movement of labourers and mechanics to win a wage of 3s. a day. In Redbourne, Hibaldstow, Louth and Boston similar demands were made. A Labour League was formed in Lincoln before the end of February 1872 while agitation continued in Withern, Holbeach and Long Sutton. In the yard of the Red Lion at Market Rasen, Saturday evening meetings resulted in the formation of the Market Rasen Labourers' Protection and Emigration Society. The distances walked to work by day labourers was a great complaint. It was claimed that those who walked miles to work should be allowed 20 minutes off their working day for each mile walked

[25] J. P. D. Dunbabin, 'The Incidence and Organisation of Agricultural Trades Unionism in the 1870s', *AHR*, Vol. 16, pt. II, 1968.

[26] Rex C. Russell, *The 'Revolt of the Field' in Lincolnshire*. Barton-on-Humber, 1956, pp. 16, 22, 29.

[27] *LRSM*, 2 February 1872.

after the first. The working day should be no longer than nine hours. By March 1872 there were strikes by farm workers near Spalding and Lincoln but the county's agricultural labour force was splintered into many separate unions with different entry fees, subscriptions and rules of membership.

Lincolnshire found its own labour leader in William Banks of Boston who led the Lincolnshire Amalgamated Labour League. His movement tended to stay aloof from the National Labour Union formed in May 1872. Its leader Joseph Arch first spoke in Lincolnshire in 1873 and unions from Spalding and Market Rasen joined his organization, causing degrees of separation and bitterness. In April 1872, after a meeting at the Spread Eagle in Grantham, presided over by the Hon. A. Herbert, M.P. for Nottingham, the Lincolnshire Labour Emigration and Migration League was formed. Unfortunately national migration only added to Lincolnshire's problems for by comparison with some of the southern counties it lay in a high wage area and labourers were encouraged to move in from less fortunate regions. Around Spalding there was evidence that inadequate wage levels were lowered even farther by this policy.

In 1873 Joseph Arch was welcomed on a speaking tour of Canada in which he called for English labourers to be settled on the land. From then on more attention was given to the emigration of labourers to North America as well as to Australia and New Zealand. From 1871 to 1881, 29,000 people left the county—not all of them agricultural workers, but their going deprived the agricultural unions of good leaders. From 1872 when 21s. a week wage was asked for, farmers were preparing to defend their position. In 1874, by which time the Labour League was publishing the *Examiner*, the leading farmers were organizing. In March, 57 occupiers of about 38,000 acres of Wolds land met in the Temperance Hall, Binbrook and resolved not to employ League members. The attendance list reads like a roll-call of all the pioneers of the agricultural revolution on the Wolds. Other meetings, and strikes and lockouts followed. During March and April 1874 locking out spread to counties farther south. The Bishop of Manchester condemned the lockout and Edward Heneage in calling for its end said that good cottage accommodation in the hands of landlords rather than tenant farmers would ease the situation.

Gradually the atmosphere cooled. By late 1874 Agricultural unions were no longer news. Many turned to the better administration and distribution of local charities, others concentrated on self-help and mutual benefit schemes. Emigration and migration had reduced the labour supply and by 1875, some wage increases, signs that better cottages would be built and the provision of allotments helped to restore a degree of calm. Farmers began to ask landlords to build cottages near their out-lying farms and followed the request with an offer to help.[28] Then interest in local and national elections with the granting of the franchise to county wage earners in 1884 and the continuing divisions between unions ushered in a new era. The conflict of 1874 in Lincolnshire was followed by a drive for emigration. By May 1874 the districts were advised to 'aim at making the Amalgamated Labour League one of the best organized, and best managed benefit clubs in the world'. New ideas, hopes, aims and a fresh confidence had been felt in a development that was akin to a religious experience. In a sense, the farm labourers, like the great tenant farmers with whom for a time they were locked in combat, had become a new class whose creation was a legacy of the agricultural revolution. The *Stamford Mercury* reported in the summer of 1885 'A considerable number of farm labourers left Grimsby station for Glasgow on Monday last to join the steamship *Gulf of Carpentaria* for various parts of Queensland.' There were three brothers from Fosdyke and families from Welton, Stainton-le-Vale, Heckington, Swineshead, Scopwick, Skirbeck, Revesby and Skegness—a melancholy list, but the writer put upon it a hopeful interpretation '. . . ploughmen and domestics of the very stamp that are likely to make the waste places glad and the wilderness blossom'.[29]

[28] Russell, op. cit., p. 57.
[29] *SM*, 12 June 1885: Russell, op. cit., pp. 137–49.

Appendix

Agricultural Terms

baulk or balk	a length of land in an open field. It could be a path by which a tenant reached his land; a parcel of land between strips of cultivated land; a piece of land for grazing; a headland where the plough team was turned.
beast gate	cowgate, land on which to pasture a cow or the right to pasture one cow on the common grazing before enclosure. Cottagers' beast-gates were set aside for them during enclosure in many parts of Lincolnshire.
boon	voluntary help given by neighbours or a service performed by tenants, sometimes freely or for an agreed charge.
breast plough	a long spade pushed at chest-level by farm-workers to cut away topsoil which was then burned and worked back into the soil as ash.
carr	low-lying land which in an unimproved state produced inferior hay. Some carrs were flooded seasonally but gave good pasture in the summer.
cole	kinds of cabbage, rape or sea-kale; cole-seed yields colza oil.
colts	a young male horse from the age of leaving the dam to the age of four or five years.
couch grass	grass with long creeping roots. Ridding the Lincolnshire uplands of couch grass increased the demand for female and child labour in the early nineteenth century.
crew yard	yard where manure accumulated before being spread on the cultivated fields.
drainage	field drainage was attempted in the following ways:

(a) ridge and furrow and gravity in the eighteenth century.
(b) hollow drains partly filled by small wood and straw at a depth of two feet and earthed over.
(c) hollow drains bottomed with stones.
(d) in the nineteenth century pipe drains laid 8 to 10 yards apart.

dressing — reaping, mowing or the spreading of crushed bones or other fertilizers on cultivated land.

eatage — grass on the verges of lanes, for general use between January and March but sold by the parish to buyers for the rest of the year.

eddish — oats or beans sown after ploughing in spring on the stubble of the wheat crop.

fallow — land ploughed and harrowed but left uncropped.
(a) bare fallow; land uncropped and ploughed and harrowed several times.
(b) green fallow; land from which a green or vegetable crop is taken.

fallow crop — beans, peas, turnips which follow the grain crop in a rotation.

farm servant — a farm worker with an annual contract who lived free in the farmhouse.

high farming — an increase in capital investment in farming to offset lower prices which resulted from increased output. The extension of mixed farming with its productive interaction of cereal growing and the keeping of livestock was called high farming in the nineteenth century.

furze — an evergreen shrub with yellow flowers, gorse or whin. It was used to describe land which 'runs to furze'.

gelding — a young horse.

gelt — a castrated animal.

gilt — a sow, a female pig.

gimmer — a young ewe.

glebe — land which belonged to the parish church.

guano — a manure imported from Chile.

heifer — a young cow that has had no calf.

hemp — a fibrous plant sown in spring and harvested

	four months later and used for the manufacture of ropes and strong fabrics.
hind	a farm labourer or servant who in some areas acted as a foreman, steward or bailiff.
ings	meadow land.
kale	a descendant of the wild cabbage used as a winter feed for sheep and cattle.
kidd	a faggot or bundle of twigs, brushwood or gorse.
leys	rotational sown grasses laid down after the corn crop and grown for a number of years before being ploughed up again.
liming	the spreading of lime on acid soil to increase yields and to assist the good effects of manuring. Lime helps the decay of organic matter and breaks up the elements of inorganic matter so making them available for plant food. It loosens heavy clay soil and gives cohesion and firmness to light sandy soil.
marl	calcareous clay which when spread on light sandy soil reduces acidity, encourages water retention and discourages soil erosion. On heavy soil it improves texture, reduces acidity and makes the land easier to work.
messuage	the part of a holding accounted for by the dwelling house and garden.
ming	a sub-division of a large arable field.
mud and stud	houses made of posts, lath and plaster or mud.
paring and burning	the removal of a thin layer of ground which was then burned and worked back as ash as part of a preparation of land for cultivation.
pulses	a collective term for the edible seeds of leguminous plants, peas, beans and lentils.
rape	a forage and green manure crop growing about 3½ feet high with succulent leaves, yellow flowers and narrow pods. Oil for the oil cake fed to livestock was derived from it.
sainfoin	a low-growing leguminous plant with long leaves and pink flowers. It was the first artificial grass to be received into husbandry in the seventeenth century. In Lincolnshire it often appears as 'St. Foin' in estate surveys and crop books.

shearling	a sheep once shorn.
stinted commons	common grazing limited to so many animals per common right owner.
tillage	cultivated land; land under the plough.
todd	a weight of wool; usually 28 pounds.
tup	a ram, a male sheep.
walk	ground made over to sheep for grazing. In Lincolnshire new farms were made on the walks during the agricultural revolution and the land was put under a mixed-farming system.
warping	the controlled flooding of low-lying land near a tidal river like the Trent so that muddy alluvium is deposited when the water is withdrawn.
wether	a castrated ram.

I. H. Adams *Agrarian Landscape terms; a glossary for historical geography*, Institute of British Geographers Special Publication Number 9, London, 1976 has an exhaustive list of agricultural terms and an excellent bibliography for agrarian studies.

Bibliography and list of abbreviations

Adams, I. H.	*Agrarian Landscape Terms: a Glossary for Historical Geography*, London, 1976.
AHR	*Agricultural History Review.*
Albert, W.	*The Turnpike Road System in England, 1663–1840*, Cambridge, 1972.
Barley, M. W.	*Lincolnshire and the Fens*, London, 1972.
Beastall, T. W.	*A North Country Estate*, Chichester, 1975.
Beckwith, I.	*The Making of Modern Gainsborough*, Gainsborough, 1968.
BL	British Library.
Bodl. Lib.	Bodleian Library Oxford.
Bonnett, H.	*Farming with Steam*, Newton Abbott, 1974.
BPP	British Parliamentary Papers.
Brace, H. W.	*History of Seed Crushing in Great Britain*, London, 1960.
Brears, C.	*Lincolnshire in the Seventeenth and Eighteenth Centuries*, London, 1940.
Caird, J.	*English Agriculture in 1850–51*, London, 1852.
Carter, J.	*Observations on the Proposed Improvement of the Nene Outfall in reference to the Drainage of South Holland*, Spalding, 1822.
Chivers, K.	*The Shire Horse, A History of the Breed, the Society and the Men*, London, 1976.
Clarke, J. A.	*On the Farming of Lincolnshire*, London, 1852.

Clark, R. H. — *Steam-Engine Builders of Lincolnshire*, Norwich, 1960.

Collins, G. E. — *Farming and Fox-hunting*, London, n.d..

Darby, H. C. — *The Draining of the Fens*, Cambridge, 1956.

Davies, M. L. (ed.) — *Life as we have known it*, London, 1970.

Defoe, D. — *A Tour through the Whole Island of Great Britain, 1724, 1725 and 1727*, ed. Cole, G. D. H., London, 1927.

D. D. Dashwood — Dashwood MSS in Bodleian Library, Oxford.

Dunston, G. — *The Rivers of Axholme*, London, 1912.

EcHR — *Economic History Review*.

Eden, P. — *Dictionary of Land Surveyors and Local Cartographers of Great Britain and Ireland, 1550–1850*, Folkestone, 1975.

EHR — *English History Review*.

Gen. View — *General View of the Agriculture of the County of Lincoln*, Young, A., London, 1813.

Gillett, E. E., Russell, R. C., and Trevitt, E. K. — *The Enclosure of Scartho, 1795–1798 and Grimsby, 1827–1840*, Grimsby, 1964.

Grigg, D. — *The Agricultural Revolution in South Lincolnshire*, Cambridge, 1966.

Harris, R. — *Traditional Farm Buildings*, Arts Council of Great Britain, London, 1978.

Harvey, N. — *A History of Farm Buildings in England and Wales*, Aylesbury, 1970.

Hatfield, C. W. — *Historical Notices of Doncaster* 2, Doncaster, 1868.

Hawke, G. R. — *Railways and Economic Growth in England and Wales, 1840–1870*, Oxford, 1970.

Hill, J. F. W. — *Georgian Lincoln*, Cambridge, 1966.

Hills, R. L.	*Machines, Mills and Uncountable Costly Necessities*, Cambridge, 1967.
HL	House of Lords..
HMC	Historical Manuscripts Commission Reports..
HO	Home Office..
Hobsbawn, E. J., and Rudé, G.	*Captain Swing*, London, 1969.
Jenkins, G. J.	*The English Farm Wagon, Origins and Structure*, Newton Abbott, 1972.
JRA Soc.	*Journal of the Royal Agricultural Society..*
Kirkby, A. E.	*Humberstone, the Story of a Village*, Lincoln, 1953.
LAAS	*Lincolnshire Architectural and Archaeological Society.*
LAO	Lincolnshire Archives Office.
Lincolnshire Library	MSS in Lincoln Central Library.
LH	*Lincolnshire Historian.*
LHA	*Lincolnshire History and Archaeology.*
LNQ	*Lincolnshire Notes and Queries..*
LRSM	*Lincoln, Rutland and Stamford Mercury.*
May, J.	*Prehistoric Lincolnshire*, Lincoln, 1976.
Mingay, G. E.	*The Agricultural Revolution 1750–1880*, London, 1966.
Mingay, G. E.	*Arthur Young and his Times*, London, 1975.
Obelkevich, J.	*Religion and Rural Society in South Lindsey 1825–75*, Oxford, 1975.
Olney, R. J.	*Lincolnshire Politics, 1832–1885*, Oxford, 1973.
Olney R. J. (ed.)	*Labouring Life on the Lincolnshire Wolds, A Study of Binbrook in the Mid-Nineteenth Century*, Sleaford, 1975.
Partridge, M.	*Farm Tools*, London, 1973.
Perkins, J. A.	*Sheep Farming in Eighteenth and Nineteenth Century Lincolnshire*, Sleaford, 1977.

Pevsner, N. and Harris, J.	*The Buildings of England, Lincolnshire*, London, 1964.
PRO	Public Record Office.
Rennie, J.	*A Plan for Completely Draining South Holland*, London, 1913. *Report and Plan for the Improvement of the Outfall to the Sea and for the Drainage of the North Level and South Holland*, London, 1814.
Rogers, A.	*A History of Lincolnshire*, Henley-on-Thames, 1970.
Rogers, A. (ed.)	*Stability and Change: Some Aspects of North and South Rauceby*, Nottingham, 1969.
Russell, R. C.	*The Enclosures of East Halton, 1801–4, and North Kelsey, 1813–1840*, Barton upon Humber, 1964.
Russell, R. C.	*The Logic of the Open Field Systems*, London, 1974.
Russell, R. C.	*The Enclosures of East Halton, 1801–4, and North Kelsey, 1813–1840*, Barton upon Humber, 1964.
Russell, R. C.	*The Enclosures of Market Rasen, 1779–1781 and of Wrawby cum Brigg, 1800–1805*, Market Rasen, 1969.
Russell, R. C.	*The Enclosures of Scarby, 1763–1765, Nettleton, 1791–1795, Caistor, 1796–1798 and Caistor Moors, 1811–1814*, Nettleton, 1968.
Russell, R. C.	*The Revolt of the Field in Lincolnshire*, Barton upon Humber, 1956.
SC	Select Committee.
Sinclair, A. C.	*A History of Beelsby*, London, 1947.
Sitwell, O.	*The Scarlet Tree*, London, 1951.
SLHA	*Society for Lincolnshire History and Archaeology*.
SM	*Stamford Mercury*.
Stone, T.	*General View of the Agriculture of the County of Lincoln*, London, 1794.

Stonehouse, W. B. — *The History and Topography of the Isle of Axholme*, London, 1839.

Thirsk, J. — *English Peasant Farming*, London, 1957.

Thompson, F. M. L. — *English Landed Society in the Nineteenth Century*, London, 1963.

Tillott, P. M. and Stevenson, G. S. — *North-West Lindsey in 1851*, Sheffield 1970.

Tyler, C. and Haining, J. — *Ploughing by Steam*, Watford, 1970.

Watson, J. A. Scott and Elliott Hobbs, M. — *Great Farmers*, London, 1937.

Wheeler, W. H. — *South Lincolnshire*, Boston, 1896.

White, W. — *History Gazetteer and Directory of Lincolnshire*, Sheffield, 1856, 1862.

Young, A. — *General View of the County of Lincoln*, London, 1813.

Index

Index